Human Resource Management in the Hotel and Catering Industry

For Juliet
and for my mother and father

Human Resource Management in the Hotel and Catering Industry

FOURTH EDITION

Previously called Personnel Management in the Hotel and Catering Industry

M. J. Boella, BA, MHCIMA, MIPM

Hutchinson
London   Melbourne   Sydney   Auckland   Johannesburg

Hutchinson Education

An imprint of Century Hutchinson Limited

62–65 Chandos Place, London WC2N 4NW

Century Hutchinson Australia Pty Ltd
PO Box 496, 16–22 Church Street, Hawthorn,
Victoria 3122, Australia

Century Hutchinson New Zealand Limited
PO Box 40–086, Glenfield, Auckland 10, New Zealand

Century Hutchinson South Africa (Pty) Ltd
PO Box 337, Bergvlei 2012, South Africa

First published by Barrie & Jenkins 1974
Second edition published by Hutchinson 1980
Reprinted with amendments 1981
Third edition 1983
Reprinted 1983
Fourth edition 1987

Set in Linotron 202 Plantin Roman by
D. P. Media Limited, Hitchin, Hertfordshire

Printed and bound in Great Britain by
Anchor Brendon Ltd, Tiptree, Essex

British Library Cataloguing in Publication Data

Boella, M. J.
  Human resource management in the hotel and catering
  industry. — 4th ed.
  1. Hotels, taverns, etc. — Personnel
  management   2. Food service — Personnel
  management
  I. Title   II. Boella, M. J. Personnel management in
  the hotel and catering industry
  647'.94'0683   TX911.3.P4

  ISBN 0-09-173071-6

Contents

List of figures

Foreword

The ultimate test of hospitality management occurs at the point of contact between service staff and the customer. But this also depends on the quality and consistency of work performed by production staff. The co-ordination of efforts made by these working groups will determine the degree of satisfaction experienced by the customer, whether it is in a hotel, restaurant or institutional operation.

It seems self-evident to me that the standards achieved must depend on the system of recruitment, selection and training in any particular enterprise. Sophisticated techniques of marketing, planning, food and beverage control or computer application may be used in a business, and these are important, but the extent to which employees can successfully cope with their job will determine the level of 'service', so often stated as being our basic endeavour. Human resource management is concerned with how people cope with their jobs; in retrospect it seems puzzling that it took until 1974 for the first edition, the first on the subject, to be published. It gives me great pleasure to introduce the fourth edition of this book. That it has reached this stage is a testimonial to the contribution which earlier editions have made to our industry. Michael Boella has incorporated new material, in the light of his experience, which the contemporary hospitality manager now needs to know. At the same time, emphasis has been maintained on the responsibility of line managers for the human resources under their command.

Human Resource Management is not, therefore, a text for personnel managers, although such specialists will find the contents of interest and benefit; it is essentially concerned with presenting the information required by a line manager to complement his or her technical knowledge. *Human Resource Management in the Hotel and Catering Industry* has its origins in the series of short courses for managers which I organized in the early 1960s. I had great difficulty in collecting suitable case material from the industry and was heavily dependent on a small number of enlightened personnel managers. The lack of a suitable text was strongly felt and made Michael Boella, one of the students, vow to remedy this when he had gained experience in his newly chosen career. After nine years of dealing with just about every facet of personnel and training work with Forte's and Bass Charrington, he finally undertook the task. But the book was only completed after he had gained a wider experience, as a consultant dealing with problems of several large organizations, as well as many smaller ones. Subsequent experience as Principal Lecturer and Course Director for hotel and catering courses at Brighton Polytechnic has provided an opportunity of sharing his knowledge with a new generation of managers as well as to extend his consultancy work in more specialized areas.

Effective staff, committed to company objectives, confident of their skills and deriving satisfaction from their work will not result from reading this or any other text. Nor will it happen overnight; a good standard of human resource management can only be evolved over a lengthy period of co-operative effort between line managers and specialists. In order to achieve this a shared understanding of the processes involved is requisite, and *Human Resource Management* provides this in relation to recruitment, selection and maintenance of staff, together with the associated techniques. As such, it can be useful to the practising manager as well as being a starting point for the potential manager. But this book will also be a valuable source to that jack-of-all-trades of our industry, the predominating small-unit operator.

Philip Nailon, BSc., MPhil., FHICMA
Professor of Hotel and Catering Management
Department of Management Studies
for Tourism and Hotel Industries
University of Surrey

Preface to the first edition

The idea of writing this book first came to me about ten years ago when, as a very inexperienced personnel officer with one of the country's largest hotel and catering organizations, I was unable to find a concise book which dealt with both the 'nuts and bolts' and the more important concepts of personnel management and which could be applied readily to the hotel and catering industry.

Since that time, although many more books of a general nature on personnel management have been written, still nothing covering the subject with particular application to the hotel and catering industry has appeared. This is in spite of the fact that over a million people find full or part-time employment in the industry's various sectors, and in spite of the fact that the Commission on Industrial Relations (no doubt prompted by the industry's doubtful labour relations reputation) has subjected the industry to no fewer than three separate reports.

Within these past ten years the industry has seen tremendous changes, the most important probably being the emergence of several major companies in the United Kingdom which now rank amongst the world's largest hotel and catering undertakings. At an industry level, considerable efforts from some sections to improve the industry's expertise have resulted in the establishment of the Hotel and Catering Industry Training Board, and a National Economic Development Committee for the industry. In addition the British Hotel, Restaurants and Caterers Association (BHRCA) and the Hotel, Catering and Institutional Management Association (HCIMA) both came into existence as a result of the merging of several smaller bodies, with the result that the industry is now beginning to present a more united front in trade, professional and educational matters.

Considerable progress has been made within the educational field, too, with over 10,000 students now following various courses, including university degree courses, leading to careers in the industry.

In spite of these developments and the efforts of some employers' and managers' associations such as the Hotel and Catering Personnel Managers Association (HCPMA) the industry is currently faced with an ever increasing staff problem.

In writing this book, therefore, I hope to make some contribution to improving the industry's standards of personnel management by indicating what I believe to be some of the more common shortcomings, with suggestions for improvements which may result in more people coming into the industry in return for rewarding and satisfying jobs and careers. As a consequence, I believe that the industry will be able to play an even more important part in the economy of the nation.

I have two main readers in mind — the busy practising manager, and also the future manager — the hotel and catering student. In particular I hope that certain chapters, such as those dealing with job descriptions, recruitment, advertising, staff selection and remuneration, will be of value to all those managers and executives responsible for managing hotels, restaurants, public houses, and the many sectors of industrial and institutional catering. I hope also that the book will prove of value to those many managers who, without any training or preparation, find themselves suddenly appointed staff or personnel officer (in one of its many different guises). I hope that it will also prove useful to all those students following courses (such as the OND, HND, HCIMA membership, City and Guilds and university degree courses) which lead on to supervisory and management positions.

Some of the more formal techniques I describe here are applicable to larger organizations, to which the majority of graduates will gravitate early on in their careers. I hope, however, that the proprietors and managers of smaller undertakings will not feel that the underlying principles do not apply equally to them — because the only differences should be of degree and detail. The principles of sound personnel management apply equally to all organizations whether small or large.

In writing a book of this nature, which draws upon my experience and knowledge gained during the past twenty years, there must be many people who have contributed in some way to the contents to whom I am grateful. In particular I would like to thank those who I believe contributed significantly. These are my ex-colleagues at Price Waterhouse Associates and my fellow directors of HCS (Management Consultants) Ltd, who over the last two years have had to act as my personal 'sounding board'. Then I must thank Miles Quest, Editor of *Catering Times*, for giving me the encouragement to write this book and for permission to reproduce from articles written by me for his paper. I would also like to thank Alfie Forte of Forte's Autogrills Ltd, Derek Gladwell and his staff at Sheffield Polytechnic, and John Fuller, HCIMA President, for reading my first draft and for their invaluable suggestions, also Des Floody, depot personnel manager of J. Sainsbury & Co. and Peter Coulson, Ll.B, for checking the chapter on law, also the libraries of the British Institute of Management, the British Association for Commercial and Industrial Education, the Institute of Personnel Management, the Hotel, Catering and Institutional Management Association, and the Industrial Society, for their considerable assistance in providing me with a steady stream of books and articles.

Finally, I wish to thank my wife Juliet because without her continuous encouragement, comments and assistance, which included the typing of two drafts, this book would certainly not have been written.

Michael J. Boella
30 July 1973

Preface to the second edition

Five years have passed since publication of the first edition of this book. In those five years there have been such far-reaching changes within our society, and to a lesser extent within the hotel and catering industry, that a completely revised edition has become essential. Of these changes, two more than any others have affected the nature of managing people within our industry.

First, there are the many legal changes which, following in the wake of the Industrial Relations Act, have done more to increase individual job security than just about anything else. The attitudes to staff, held by many in the past, have been considerably tempered by legislation covering dismissals, discrimination in employment, health and safety, and consultation. At the time of writing, we are also faced with far-reaching changes in the relationship between management and labour — industrial democracy.

The second major influence is the steady, even relentless, growth of the trade union movement within the industry. When the first edition of this book was written, the number of hotels where union presence was felt was limited to a handful. Today, however, union membership has undoubtedly increased to significant levels. Whether this is by inevitability of circumstances, or whether it is the deliberate result of trade union recruitment policy is debatable. It is argued by some writers that trade union development is inevitable given certain conditions. It can be argued that those conditions are now emerging in the hotel and catering industry and consequently trade union growth is inevitable. How individual employers are reacting to this development varies considerably. Some have taken the initiative in encouraging union organization, whilst others argue that there is no evidence that staff want a union presence.

Other changes, too, have taken place. High unemployment and reduction in foreign worker quotas have probably altered the dependence on foreign labour. Also, the Industrial Training Board has done a considerable amount to improve the standards of training within the industry by introducing its levy exemption scheme. At an educational level, questions about the value of certain City and Guild courses are being raised owing to the increasing use of pre-prepared foods, and there has been considerable debate, too, over the value of high level courses such as degree and HND courses.

From the point of view of this revised edition, I have been most fortunate. In the last five years, I have run in the region of seventy-five courses for about a thousand delegates, including area managers, unit managers, assistant managers, heads of departments, staff trainers and trainee managers. Their experience, with both current and previous employers, reaches into just about every branch of the hotel and catering industry and it is such experience which enables me to offer this second edition, which I trust will be relevant to the industry's needs and which will make a contribution to further the industry's personnel relationships.

My thanks are due to all those who have contributed to this second edition, in particular to those who have attended, participated in and contributed to the many courses we have shared in the last three years. Also to Liz Cullen for her help on this revision.

Michael J. Boella
20 October 1979

Preface to the third edition

Within a few months of publication of the second edition of this book it became apparent that because of the volume of sales a reprint was going to be needed very soon. At the same time it became clear that whilst the book dealt with most techniques of personnel management, there existed some important omissions. Nowhere did the book actually deal with organization structure, labour costs or productivity. The first omission, organization structure, has been put right by the inclusion of Chapter 18, which comprises what I hope to be a representative selection of organization charts from most sectors of the industry. The second omission has been dealt with by the addition of Chapter 19, which includes a table of reasonably representative examples of what labour costs are likely to be in viable establishments in various sectors of the hotel and catering industry.

I have also taken the opportunity to update information and to add new material where appropriate. Unfortunately I have been unable to cover all the topics some correspondents would have liked. For example, Synne Campbell of Sheffield Polytechnic would have liked to have seen included 'a chapter on the differing problems to be coped with by women'. The omission is because I believe the subject is more appropriate to a specific work on the subject.

I have also considered carefully the further reading list. The problem is that of selecting from a vast quantity of published material, both old and new. This book is designed specifically as an introductory text devoting at most one chapter to a whole area of personnel management; areas which may have complete books devoted to themselves. Because of this *embarras de richesses* I have decided to direct readers to two organizations in particular, who publish books which take readers naturally beyond the basic introductory levels without going into too detailed or academic treatment of the subject. These are the Institute of Personnel Management and the British Institute of Management, and most of the recommended texts are published by these two institutes. Readers wishing to go beyond these levels should seek advice from competent management libraries.

For the assistance provided with this third edition, I should like to thank my students who worked on the organization charts; Katie Dunkason, Chris Laycock, Veryan Hussey and Chiew Sun. I should also like to thank those employers who provided these students with their industrial release experience and also those employers who provided organization charts and other help.

Finally, my thanks to Bob Godfrey for some of the data in Chapter 1, Sue Hanna for her help on the typescript, and Rosemary Smith for help with library material.

Michael J. Boella
1 April 1982

Preface to the fourth edition

Since the first edition of this book was written nearly fifteen years ago, substantial and far-reaching changes have taken place in our society which were hardly imaginable then. For most people the most significant change has been the rise of unemployment from under one million to over three million. This has been largely the result of the decline of our manufacturing and related industries. In the three-year period between 1981 and 1984, for example, the workforce in manufacturing declined by nearly three-quarters of a million. At the same time, employment in services generally grew by 430,000. The problem of course is that service sector jobs tend to be part-time, whereas the lost manufacturing jobs tended to be full-time. In addition, service sector jobs attract a large number of women workers whereas the majority of manufacturing jobs lost were occupied by men. The shift in balance between the service industries and manufacturing is best evidenced by the fact that, in 1979, for every manufacturing job, there was one service job, whereas today there are now two service jobs for every job in manufacturing.

The vital importance of the service sector to the economy can be well illustrated. In value terms, the contribution made by tourism, as one sub-sector of the service sector, has grown since 1974 from £900 million to nearly £5.5 billion in 1985, and is predicted to create 50,000 new jobs a year for many years to come. In order to improve further on these figures industry is looking forward to some radical changes, such as the further relaxation of licensing legislation, in order to make us more competitive internationally as a tourist destination.

Employment in the hotel and catering industry is now estimated to be around two million. A major point, however, is the nature of employment in the industry. For many, jobs are part-time and offer little continuity or security and, as the Education and Training Committee for the Hotel and Catering Industry discovered, the vast majority of workers and management have little formal training. At a time when our economy is becoming increasingly reliant upon our tourist industry, the need to provide high standards which are internationally competitive is a crucial issue for the industry to confront. It was a welcome move, therefore, when the industry's three main bodies, the HCIMA, the HCTB and the BHRCA, announced that they were to form a body aimed at determining how to attract and retain high-calibre people. This is no simple task, however, because of the industry's heavy reliance on the 'secondary labour market'.

One could have expected the trade unions confronted by a fall in union membership from over twelve million a few years ago to ten million now to have done more recruiting in the service sector. However, union membership does not appear to have grown significantly and remains around twelve per cent (in services generally), compared with over forty per cent in manufacturing. There is obviously a great deal for them to do if they are to play any significant role in services in the future.

In terms of technology, the major feature probably has been the increasing adoption of computers in the industry. My thanks are due to Marian Whitaker, of Brighton Polytechnic, for permitting me to reproduce a summary of her research findings on the impact of computers on employment in the industry. From this research, it appears that in many respects they have had less impact than at first anticipated, the major areas affected being those concerned with administration, such as wages, rather than the customer contact areas, and certainly they have not contributed to job losses.

Probably the most exciting developments have been within the industry's 'product range'. This is in response to wide-ranging social changes, which include the increased number of foreign visitors and also the increased expectations of the British consumer. This is best seen in the emergence of a wide range of 'fast food' and take-away operations responding to the new 'grazing' pattern of consumption of many consumers. In parallel, we see the demand growing for high-quality operations where personal service is a key ingredient in the 'product'. Never before has the customer had such a wide range of choice and, likewise, never has the prospective worker in the hotel and catering industry had such a wide choice of sectors and employers.

Another major change has been the government's decision to open up public sector catering to competition. This has resulted in some dramatic changes in some sectors and the importation of commercial practices, not always considered appropriate by some, to the public sector.

Within personnel management in the industry it is encouraging to note a steady improvement. Particularly welcome is the trend to employ professionally trained personnel specialists rather than delegating personnel matters to junior line managers. There is still a long way to go, however, and the good practices of the better employers are considered by some to be very much out-weighed by the poor practices of a majority in shaping the industry's reputation as an employer.

In talking with colleagues in colleges and in industry, I have learned that earlier editions of this book have contributed in some small way, at least, to improving the standards of managing staff. It is my hope that this edition, with the additional material, can continue to help the industry's managers in the management of their human resource.

Some readers, who are familiar with earlier editions of this work, may wonder at the change of title. This has been made after serious discussion with colleagues and my publisher, and it was concluded that the new title more accurately reflects the contents of the book. After all, much of what is advocated in this book should be normal practice for all managers and supervisors, not just the personnel specialist.

In this new edition I have taken the opportunity to include the latest material available and I would like to thank the Hotel and Catering Training Board for permission to use some of their data. I would also like to thank Pam Carter and Joy Simmonds of Brighton Polytechnic Learning Resources Department for their help in finding and providing material essential to this fourth edition.

M. J. Boella
May 1987

'Customer satisfaction begins not with the customer, but in the relations between those who manage and those who are managed, so one must start right at the top and ensure that company policy about personnel management is clear and unmistakable.'

LORD ROBENS, Sir Julian Salmon Lecture, 28 October 1976

'In a service industry the most important ingredient in the product is people. The quality of our people determines the quality of the service we give to customers and thus our success in the market place. Not surprisingly almost every discussion we have in the company starts or finishes with personnel matters. We recognise that we can only continue to exist by attracting, training and motivating good people. Doing that successfully means having a caring and efficient personnel function to assist line managers in what is one of their primary responsibilities.'

ROCCO FORTE, *Personnel Management*, August 1982

chapter 1

A background to the industry's workforce

Since the end of the Second World War the United Kingdom has seen many important developments and changes in society, the major one probably being the considerable improvement in the standard of living of the vast majority of working people. These improvements have come about as a result of many different factors including greater national productivity, the improved welfare state, more enlightened management and pressure from trade unions.

The contributions made by the hotel and catering industry to this general rise in standard of living are considerable and varied, providing essential and leisure services, employment and wealth creation. Tourism, of which the hotel and catering industry is a principal element, is now claimed to be the country's fastest growing industry and also one of the leading earners of foreign currency. The fact that millions of people eat meals at or near their places of work or study, rather than at home, would not be possible without restaurants, cafés, public houses, fast food and take-away establishments, and 'in-house' catering facilities. Furthermore the improved standard of living enjoyed by most people has resulted in many more ordinary people being able to 'enjoy a meal out' for pleasure rather than necessity, and in spite of some reports hospital patients and school children, by and large, enjoy a better standard of food than ever before, thanks to a more efficient and professional body of catering officers.

Yet in spite of these improvements to the standard of living for the majority of the country's population, and the technical improvements within the hotel and catering industry itself, the conditions of employment of large numbers of the industry's staff have not even kept pace with those enjoyed by working people elsewhere. Admittedly at the top of the scale craftsmen, such as chefs who are in short supply, can command very high incomes, but at the other end of the scale kitchen porters, for example, may be lucky to earn a third of what they would earn for broadly similar work in many offices, factories and warehouses.

The reasons for the slow rate of improvement in the industry's conditions of employment are considerable including an understandable reluctance on the part of many proprietors and managers to be among the first to charge higher prices for their services, particularly when Britain is reported to be already among the most expensive of tourist destinations. Another reason, however, is probably that the trade union movement exerts little influence in most sectors of the industry and the wages councils have certainly not been a substitute. A third reason is that the industry's workforce consists largely of people drawn from the 'secondary' labour market, i.e. those people who use the industry on a short-term basis (such as students, housewives, school leavers) and who are prepared to accept low pay as they may not be the primary 'bread winner'. Because of low pay, low union presence and the high proportion of staff drawn from the secondary labour market the industry has its own less obvious but very costly labour problems, including such things as a high labour turnover rate and 'institutionalized pilfering' and low standards in many establishments.

It is, of course, to be expected that some aspects of working in the hotel and catering industry are unattractive. There are the intrinsic problems which are unavoidable such as having to work evenings, weekends and bank holidays. Other problems, however, can certainly be reduced or eliminated by determined management action. These problems include unnecessary 'split shift' working, staff reliance on tips, ignorance of methods of calculating pay and distributing service charges, and management's reluctance to 'involve' staff in matters that affect their working lives. A number of reports have highlighted these difficulties which, together with management attitudes, undoubtedly cause much of the industry's labour difficulties. Even today for example many employers and managers expect their ordinary employees to be dedicated to their jobs, to have a 'vocational' attitude to their work, to sacrifice leisure time for pay that is not high by most standards. This attitude is not confined to the commercial and more entrepreneurial sectors of the industry but is found as a discordant element in many organizations. These same employers and managers fail to recognize that their own motivation to work is usually completely different from that of their staff, and that many work people throughout the community are becoming less work-orientated for various reasons. Employers in industry must reconcile themselves rapidly to the fact that the majority of potential staff are less likely to be vocationally committed unless ways and means are found to harness what some researchers claim is a natural motivation to work. And employers in the hotel and catering industry must recognize that. Instead, staff, if they are to stay, expect competitive conditions of employment and leisure, and unless these are offered the industry's staffing problems will persist.

Even in the midst of high unemployment and a significant drop in labour turnover, many employers claim that they are unable to attract and retain competent and committed staff and they must ask themselves 'why?' It is interesting to note that the major sector in the industry, where there are the least, and in many cases no staff problems, is the institutional and industrial catering sector where leisure time and other conditions are generally more attractive than in many other sectors.

The hotel and catering industry and the British economy

The hotel and catering industry (see Figure 1.1) employs in excess of two million people, and in 1985 Britain was reported to be earning £20 billion in the hotel and catering industry (HCTB — Catering for Employment Seminar 1986). To do this owners, local authorities, management and employees within the industry provided for the needs of millions, including holidaymakers, business travellers, schoolchildren, students and hospital patients. The industry is now a vital part of our economy and is slowly but increasingly being recognized as such. In recognition of this importance, Mrs Sally Oppenheimer, Minister responsible for tourism in 1981 said, '. . . tourism must be accorded to its full status as an industry of absolutely major importance' (*British Travel News*, 1981). Five years later Lord Young, Employment Minister, said '. . . tourism is already one of our largest employers . . . I therefore, want tourism to have a high profile' (reported in *Tourism in Action* 1986).

Future trends affecting the hotel, catering and leisure industries

As Mrs Oppenheimer said Britain is 'moving into a different world — a world in which service industries are growing and tourism itself will become increasingly important as leisure time increases' (ibid). Leisure is bound to increase as a result of several different technological and social forces such as increased productivity arising from the 'microchip' revolution, earlier retirement and more paid holidays.

The European Travel Commission forecast that by 1990 there will be a norm of eight weeks' annual holiday in most Western European countries.* This is likely to result in a substantial increase in second and third holidays and also in extended weekend breaks.

Increased leisure has also resulted in a significant increase in the demand for action-centred recreation. Suppliers of leisure services are responding by increasing the range of leisure facilities offered. The tremendous boom in the provision of various sports facilities and cultural centres is an example of growth in the supply of leisure facilities which are basically meeting new demands. At the same time, some of the more traditional products are again in demand. For the first time in many years a number of luxury liners have been, or are in the process of being built.

The growth of tourism

The European Travel Commission also predicts a doubling in European tourism by 1990, with the creation of 6–8 million new jobs in Europe. Of these, the British Tourist Authority (BTA) predict there will be around 50,000 new jobs per year in Britain. The BTA predicts an increase of around 15 million overseas visitors in 1985 to around 20 million in 1990.

This anticipated expansion in demand for tourist facilities is likely to be felt across the full range of the leisure and hospitality industries. Hotels, tour

*European Travel Commission, *Tourism Prospects to 1990*.

operators, airlines, shipping lines, tourist site operators, promoters of events and various public sector organizations are all likely to be affected.

The growth in demand for conferences, exhibitions and short courses

A major feature of technologically advanced societies is the need for business men, professionals, administrators and others to meet in order to obtain and exchange information through attendance at exhibitions, conferences, seminars and short courses. The growth in this demand has been partially satisfied by the traditional hotel sector. Increasingly, however, the provision of specifically developed facilities such as exhibition and conference centres is necessary to satisfy the continued growth in this market. In the course of the planning of the majority of these developments the opportunity is also taken to provide for leisure, entertainment and hotel facilities.

The changing hotel and catering industry

Within the hotel and catering industry itself there are important developments which have long-term implications for the industry.

First, as hotel and catering groups become larger, and also as individual establishments become larger and more complex, there has been an expansion in the junior and middle management cadres. As an example one company which only increased its total room numbers marginally, found it necessary to increase its specialist managers in the areas of marketing, sales, training and personnel by some 300 per cent between 1976 and 1980.

Also during recent years hotel and catering organizations have become more market oriented. This has led to increased market segmentation. These developments have led to many of the larger companies establishing specialist subsidiary companies, which are concerned with a range of highly specialized products. This has involved, in some cases, considerable changes in products and managements, or the negotiation of franchise-type agreement with international branded names such as Wendy's, Huckleberry's and Dayvilles.

This last development is associated with the rapid growth of fast food outlets in Britain and elsewhere in Europe. The nature of such operations, dependent as they are on the maintenance of rigorous operational and quality standards, is altering the face of British popular catering and is putting many of the traditional operators in jeopardy.

Even some of the new entrants with considerable resources, it was reported, found fast food a difficult market. In spite of this, popular catering is still a relatively easy field to enter but nowadays success demands considerable expertise and promotional effort, which are increasingly becoming beyond the resources of the independent. The franchise side of the industry is growing therefore along with franchising generally.

Growth of the industry, however, has not been regularly distributed across the various sectors of the industry. Industrial catering, for example, has declined considerably losing over 100,000 employees between 1974 and 1982. Restaurants and cafés have also suffered a decline. On the other hand the fast food sector is now providing more opportunities for employment and rapid promotion. In particular it is providing openings for young people, with a significant proportion of the workforce aged under 21.

While the industry has established its importance from an economic point of view, it could be hoped that those employed in the industry would be reaping rewards that echo this increased importance. In many cases this may well be so with key people such as chefs and waiters at leading restaurants and good managers earning high rewards. However, there is still a great deal to criticize within the industry and this book would not be serving the industry if the findings of relevant research were not highlighted. An important contribution was made by the Hotels and Catering EDC report, *Manpower Policy in the Hotel and Restaurant Industry*. Although this report dates from 1975, it is likely that an industry which employs two million people has considerable inertia and consequently much of what was said then is just as relevant today. However, it would be unfair to leave the impression that changes are not being made. Several of the larger employers (and some smaller ones as well) have been involved in pioneering work in the industry, in introducing better conditions, more job security and more opportunity for participation and promotion.

Having said this, a variety of reports from organizations such as the Low Pay Unit, The New Earning Survey and the Labour Research Unit put the industry's workers amongst the lowest paid in the country. The Labour Research Unit's 'Bargaining Report' in 1984 reported that hotel and catering workers were among those receiving the lowest basic pay in the country, working longer than average hours and receiving less than average holiday entitlement. The report placed the Licensed Residential Wages Council minimum pay agreement at 389 out of 392 agreements listed, the Unlicensed Residential at 342. This question of low pay is discussed later in the book, because it is not as simple a matter as outside observers appear to think. The value of tips, food, accommodation, laundry and savings on fuel and fares all have to be taken into account so that anyone 'living in' has been largely protected against the worst of recent inflation. Also it must be borne in mind that a very large proportion of the industry's workforce is drawn from a 'secondary labour market'. Because of this many work people may not have high value skills to offer, or alternatively their motives to work may put a premium on the convenience of their work (location, hours) for which they will sacrifice higher incomes.

Undoubtedly, low pay in the industry exists, but it is not something that can be put right overnight. Britain's hotels and restaurants are already reported to be amongst the most expensive in the world, so increases to tariffs are not the answer. Instead, a thorough reappraisal of the services offered and the consequent manning levels and staff training may lead to greater productivity. In this field, strides have been made; capital investment is underway to replace the most menial tasks, and considerable efforts are being made to improve the standard of training.

Most improvements and efforts seem to be made at the tip of the iceberg, mainly amongst the larger companies. The remaining 80–90 per cent of the

Figure 1.1   *Structure of the industry*

Accommodation	Hotels and motels	21,000	
	Bed and breakfast, farm houses	18,600	
	Holiday camps, camping and holiday caravan sites	1,600	
	Licensed private hotels and guest houses	4,500	
Meals	Unlicensed restaurants	14,590	
	Licensed restaurants	12,750	
	Department store catering	4,000	
Public houses and clubs	Public houses	76,250	
	Clubs	35,000	
Tourism and travel	Historic buildings, etc. (with catering)	700	
	Railway stations	370	
	Motorway services	42	
	Airports	66	
	Trains	420 per day	
	Ferries	40	
	Cruise ships	12	
Industrial	Factories and offices (with catering)	22,000	(35% are run by contract caterers)
Public services	Education	35,700	
	Hospitals, homes, etc.	11,500	
	Total:	259,140	

Source: HCTB. *Statistical review of the Hotel and Catering Industry, 1984*

industry is made up of smaller employers who each employ a few staff only and who for a variety of reasons are not able or prepared to evaluate their own business methods as rigorously as is required in today's aggressive business climate. One consequence is the growth of the larger companies, at the expense of smaller companies, which is a phenomenon not confined to the hotel and catering industry, but is a general phenomenon of industrialized societies.

The industry's workforce

In 1985 the Hotel and Catering Industry Training Board (HCITB) published its report *Hotel and Catering Manpower in Britain 1984*. The principal findings are illustrated in Figures 1.2 to 1.6 (reproduced by courtesy of HCTB).

Figure 1.2 Estimate of the numbers employed in hotel and catering occupations, 1984

	Nos.	Proportion of full-time employees
MAIN ACTIVITY SECTORS		
Hotels, guesthouses and other tourist accommodation	375	59%
Restaurants, cafés and snackbars	304	58%
Public houses and bars	373	32%
Nightclubs and licensed clubs	155	20%
Canteens and messes (contract catering)	117	52%
Others (self-employed)	9	—
All main activity sectors	1,332	45%
SUBSIDIARY ACTIVITY SECTORS		
Tourism and travel catering:		
Recreational and cultural services	211	N/a
Travel	24	N/a
Public services catering:		
Education	294	N/a
Medical and other health services	190	N/a
Public administration and national defence	48	N/a
Retail distribution	33	N/a
Personal and domestic services	73	N/a
Industrial and office catering (i.e. all other industries and services)	126	N/a
All subsidiary activity sectors	998	38%
All hotel and catering	**2,330**	**42%**

Notes
A 'main activity' sector is one where the main business of the enterprise is catering or the provision of accommodation.
A 'subsidiary activity' sector is one where the main business of the enterprise is something other than catering or the provision of accommodation. This distinction is reflected in statistics published in the *Employment Gazette* which only identifies hotel and catering employees for the main activity sectors.

Figure 1.3 Numbers employed in hotel and catering by sex and full or part-time working, 1984

	Men		Women		Total	
	Nos.	%	Nos.	%	Nos.	%
MAIN ACTIVITY SECTORS[1]						
Full-time	301	60	301	36	602	45
Part-time	200	40	530	64	730	55
Total	501	100	831	100	1,332	100
SUBSIDIARY ACTIVITY SECTORS[1]						
Full-time	80	93	297	33	377	38
Part-time	6	7	615	67	621	62
Total	86	100	912	100	998	100
ALL INDUSTRY						
Full-time	381	65	598	34	979	42
Part-time	206	35	1,145	66	1,351	58
Total	**587**	**100**	**1,743**	**100**	**2,330**	**100**

Note
1   See note to Figure 2

Figure 1.4 *Changes in the size of the hotel and catering workforce between 1981 and 1984*

	Nos. of employees 1981	Nos. of employees 1984	Growth/decline Nos.	Growth/decline %
MAIN ACTIVITY SECTORS				
Hotels, guesthouses and other tourist accommodation	324	375	+51	+16%
Restaurants, cafés and snackbars	307	304	−3	−1%
Public houses and bars	351	373	+22	+6%
Nightclubs and licensed clubs	150	155	+5	+3%
Canteens and messes (contract catering)	114	117	+3	+3%
Others (self-employed)	9	9	—	—
All main activity sectors	1,255	1,333	+78	+6%
SUBSIDIARY ACTIVITY SECTORS				
Recreation and cultural services	200	211	+11	+6%
Travel	27	24	−3	−11%
Education	294	294	—	—
Medical and other health services	190	190	—	—
Public administration and national defence	49	48	−1	−2%
Retail distribution	32	33	+1	+3%
Personal and domestic services	72	73	+1	+1%
Industrial and office catering (i.e. all other industries and services)	133	126	−7	−5%
All subsidiary activity sectors	996	998	+2	*
All hotel and catering	**2,251**	**2,330**	**+79**	**+4%**

* rounds down to zero

Figure 1.5 *Main activity sectors: breakdown of occupations by sex and full or part-time working, September 1984*

	Men	Women	Full-time	Part-time	Total
Self-employed working proprietors	77.7	52.7	130.4	—	130.4
Employed managers	146.6	60.9	199.0	8.5	207.5
Supervisors	20.9	29.2	40.2	9.9	50.1
Chefs/cooks	72.0	62.7	56.2	78.5	134.7
Waiters/ waitresses	32.1	75.8	31.8	76.1	107.9
Barmen/barmaids	30.7	123.7	24.0	130.4	154.4
Hotel porters	8.8	0.7	3.7	5.8	9.5
Kitchen porters/hands	21.9	122.4	23.9	120.4	144.3
Counter hands/assistants	4.0	71.7	14.4	60.7	75.1
Domestic staff	2.3	78.8	9.3	71.8	81.1
Butchers/bakers	0.8	0.4	0.4	0.8	1.2
Receptionists	2.0	25.4	14.7	12.7	27.4
Self-employed non-managerial staff	6.1	3.3	9.4	—	9.4
Others (in non-catering occupations)	75.4	123.7	45.5	153.6	199.1
Total	**500.8**	**831.4**	**602.0**	**730.4**	**1,332.2**

Notes

This table is primarily based on the figures for employees in employment for September 1984 in the *Employment Gazette*, divided between occupations in the same proportions as in the Census of Population 1981.

Figures for self-employed are taken from the Census of Population 1981. A figure of 180,000 has also been added to the *Employment Gazette* figures to allow for employees of self-employed working proprietors. This is equal to twice the estimated number of establishments run by a self-employed working proprietor. The figures in other tables have been calculated in a similar manner.

Figure 1.6 *Subsidiary activity sectors: breakdown of occupations by sex and full or part-time working, September 1984*

	Men	Women	Full-time	Part-time	Total
Employed managers	10.7	15.9	23.6	2.9	26.5
Supervisors	10.3	26.1	29.9	6.5	36.5
Chefs/cooks	18.8	81.1	63.5	36.4	99.9
Waiters/waitresses	3.9	9.9	7.7	6.1	13.6
Barmen/barmaids	3.8	15.5	5.7	13.6	19.4
Counter hands/assistants	5.0	196.0	69.8	131.2	200.9
Kitchen porters/hands	7.4	52.2	18.7	40.9	59.7
Domestic staff and school helpers	5.9	407.7	85.9	327.7	413.6
Hospital ward orderlies	10.0	88.5	52.8	45.7	98.5
Travel stewards and attendants	8.8	17.6	17.7	8.7	26.4
Butchers/bakers	1.5	0.4	2.0	—	2.0
Others			Not available		
Total	**86.1**	**912.8**	**377.3**	**620.7**	**998.2**

The main points to be drawn from *Hotel and Catering Manpower in Britain 1984* are:

1 The hotel and catering industry employs in excess of 2.3 million. This represents nearly 11% of the total working population. (These figures include the self-employed.)
2 1.3 million are employed in establishments where catering and hotel services are the main activity. One million are employed in sectors, such as offices, banks, hospitals, etc., where catering is subsidiary to the main activity.
3 Just under 1 million are full-time workers; 1.7 million are women, i.e. nearly 75% of the workforce.
4 The workforce of the industry has grown by 4% since 1981.
5 Hotels and guest houses have shown the greatest growth, 16%. Restaurants, cafés and industrial catering showed a slight decline. Recreation and cultural services catering showed a growth of 6%.

(In order to follow some of the changes that have occurred since 1978 reference can be made to Chapter 1 of the third edition of this book or the HCITB report *Manpower in the Hotel and Catering Industry*, 1978.)

One important fact to bear in mind is that whilst the industry is described as the hotel and catering industry, it does in fact consist of a number of separate sectors. To what extent each sector is a discrete labour market, still has to be determined. Without a doubt, however, there is movement between sectors and chefs are probably a prime example of this.

Labour turnover and employment

The industry has, for many years, had a reputation for a very high level of labour turnover. In 1984 the HCITB published its report *Manpower Flows in the Hotel and Catering Industry.* The report predicted that there would be in the region of 1.4 million vacancies per annum, 3 per cent arising from growth, 2 per cent from retirements, the remaining 95 per cent from staff turnover. It found the following gross turnover rates: managers 19 per cent; supervisors 94 per cent; craftspeople 55 per cent; operatives 65 per cent. Cafés and public houses had the highest rates of losses to the industry, caused largely by young people using the industry as an interlude between school or college and full-time career.

While some reports categorize the industry's problems very much in statistical terms, it is possible to illustrate some of the problems in more human terms. These range right through the employment process from the initial selection to the termination of employment. All of these aspects will be discussed at more length later, but it is important to see some of the industry's practices in terms that are related to the employee — the individual — who is subject to an employer's employment practices. These examples are intended to paint some of the background in human rather than in statistical terms.

Initial selection

At one end of the scale, there are employers who use only expert techniques including group selection procedures and psychological tests. In addition, many companies and the HCTB are now training their managers in most of the skills of management, such as interviewing techniques. At the other end of the scale, however, are many employers who do not even acknowledge receipt of application forms. One manager applied to over fifty employers and received less than twenty acknowledgements. Another employer uses box numbers for the express purpose of avoiding the need to acknowledge applications. On the other hand many employers are frustrated by the casual approach to employment of employees — with many just not turning up for a prearranged interview.

Induction and training

This is an area that has shown considerable improvements in the last few years because of HCTB pressure. However, there are still serious problems which are completely ignored by many managers; for example, some managers or supervisors do not have the empathy to recognize that skills such as laying a table formally, making a bed correctly, using telephones, which are second nature to themselves, may be worrying to some, such as a middle-aged housewife who has come out to work for the first time.

A related problem is the large number of small and medium-sized employers, and large company managers, who continue to insist upon 'experience' rather than being prepared to recruit and train staff, in spite of the fact that about 80 per cent of the industry's workforce does not need other than ordinary 'life and social' skills.

In a more general sense, there is still the argument that because of tight staff budgets, there is no time to train, so to acquire training skills is not worthwhile. Some managers are persuaded, however, that even with understaffing or reduced staffing, training does take place somehow and that training skills become *more* not *less* necessary as staff levels are reduced.

Pay

While there are many instances of very high rates of pay in the industry, its image overall is not good.

The reliance, in some sectors, on tipping still exists to a greater extent than some consider desirable. The practice of paying employees the basic or near basic wage and also putting notices on tariffs that service charges are included, has had the effect of diverting guests' tips into company revenue. In many cases this practice has had an adverse effect on net earnings. First, all of the service charge may not be distributed to the staff, and second, income from such a source is taxed, which it was not previously. In spite of this it is to be hoped that the practice of 'all inclusive pricing' (including service charge and VAT) will become common practice in Britain, as it is in some other European countries. However, this practice will have to be linked to a fair system of distribution and the establishment of realistic minimum rates.

In these circumstances, where low pay and distrust of the employer's wages practices exist, it is to be expected that pilfering on a significant scale takes place. A report based upon an Open University case study *Room for Reform* claims that pilfering appears to be an institutionalized part of wage bargaining in hotels. Management often recognizes it as a way to boost inadequate pay. 'Fiddles' range from straightforward short-measuring and short-changing of customers to supplying one's own household with cleaning materials, toilet paper, light bulbs, crockery, cutlery and even towels and other linen. Some 'fiddles' are quite sophisticated and at quite high levels. It has been known for managers to redecorate their own homes at their employer's expense, or for a manager to deduct 'the cost of grass cutting' from the hotel's petty cash and to arrange for a farmer to pay the manager for some acres of hay taken from the same land. In a recent spot survey only 6 per cent of industrial release students questioned had *not* witnessed pilfering.

Such practices, however, must be seen in proper perspective bearing in mind that some other industries, trades and professions provide vastly more lucrative opportunities than those provided in the hotel and catering industry.

Labour costs and capital investment

The considerable increase in many of the overhead costs (such as rent, interest and fuel) of running hotels has put considerably increased pressure on other variable costs, such as labour. One of the effects has been to reduce services (such as portering facilities and room service), in many cases substituting self-service facilities for providing beverages and meals in rooms. This, linked with more reliance in some sectors on pre-prepared foods and labour-saving equipment, has reduced the industry's labour-intensive nature. One example is the low labour cost achieved (around 14 per cent) by fast food, take-away establishments. Another consequence of this, however, is the reduced contact between customers and staff.

At the same time as these economies have been exercised, pressure to increase revenue has been applied. As a result of the need to maximize on occupancy rates, 'overbooking' is now an accepted part of many hotels' normal routines. Once again, this has to be seen in perspective. If tour operators and individual guests do not take up their bookings, the hotel companies cannot be expected to carry the loss of rooms not taken up. If in fact 'overbooking' were to be outlawed, room rates would have to go up to compensate for reduced occupancy levels. In spite of these 'economic points', the guest who discovers that he is 'booked out' to another hotel is hardly ever happy about the situation. Consequently, hotel staff working in busy city hotels where overbooking is normal policy work under considerable pressure and stress, and they may see every arrival, not as someone to be welcomed, but as one person nearer to the point where irate guests will have to be informed that they are 'booked out'. It is no surprise, therefore, that most large city hotel reception staff are young and that some leave, 'burnt-out', after two or three years.

Work peaks

Another problem which causes considerable stress is the peaking of work, and this is not confined to meal times in restaurants and canteens. Receptionists and housekeeping staff all have their peaks too. In one small survey conducted by a Post Office supervisor, she found that a hotel receptionist had to deal with twice the Post Office rate of telephone calls per hour between 6 p.m. and 7 p.m., while also registering arrivals and dealing with other queries. The country hotel manager also has his problems because staff may live over a very wide area. In one case, the manager of a small hotel had to drive 60 miles a day to collect and deliver staff.

In spite of all these problems, many establishments in the industry are good places to work in, with fierce loyalty being shown to individual managers and to colleagues. There is the spirit that the 'show must go on', and many staff will struggle into work with illnesses that would deter many people in other work situations. This fact is missed completely by some union recruiting officers who, without a proper understanding of the industry, have set out to try to recruit members by 'management bashing'. The result was large-scale walk-outs from union meetings by hotel staff.

Personnel management in the hotel and catering industry

Until the early 1960s personnel management as a specialist function in the hotel and catering industry was almost non-existent. Where it did exist, it was devoted to small elements of personnel management, such as recruitment and training. It was not until the introduction of employment legislation, such as the Contracts of Employment Act 1964, and the establishment of the Industrial Training Board, that personnel managers began to appear in the industry in any numbers. Today all of the larger companies now employ personnel specialists and personnel management is seen as an essential part of the organization. There is still, however, too little regard paid to it by many employers where personnel managers are frequently junior managers 'learning the ropes' at the staff's expense. In other cases, and increasingly so, the value of professional personnel managers is being recognized and they are increasingly joining management teams at senior level.

The development of personnel management in the industry is examined in much greater detail in a paper published in the *International Journal of Hospitality Management* in 1986 (see Appendix 1).

Participation

One conclusion about the future for management is that much greater participation by all levels of the workforce in decisions that affect them is desired.

Within society at large, critically important changes are taking place, the major one being that individual expectations are considerably higher. No longer are basics enough — people now want more leisure and more money to enjoy their leisure. They also want a greater say in the way their lives are arranged. In some respects the industry is adapting to these needs. For example, how many hotel managers twenty years ago would have expected to work 'office hours' and to have a high proportion of weekends off? This is not uncommon practice today in many of the larger companies.

With regard to staff participation, or having a say about the way an enterprise is managed, there is probably much further to go, but even in this area, the first steps have been taken — larger establishments now have their staff consultative committees. The extent to which staff really do become involved, and the nature of the involvement (i.e. dealing with more than the quality of the staff food or the next staff outing), is vital, however. The reception given to the Bullock Report in 1977 illustrates just how emotive an area industrial democracy is, but it is only by facing up to such issues that management can have an influence over its future industrial relations. The industry's future managers are going to have to take a creative, forward-looking role rather than a passive and defensive one which, unfortunately, has been the case for too long.

Further reading

Hotel and Catering Training Board Publications
  Manpower in the Hotel and Catering Industry, London: 1978
  Manpower Changes in the Hotel and Catering Industry, London: 1983
  Manpower Flows in the Hotel and Catering Industry, London: 1984

Hotel and Catering Manpower in Britain 1984, London: 1984

Statistical Review of the Hotel and Catering Industry, London: 1984

Magurn, J. P., *A Manual of Staff Management in the Hotel and Catering Industry*, London: Heinemann, 1977

Mars, G., and Mitchell, P., *Manpower Problems in the Hotel and Catering Industry*, Farnborough: Saxon House, 1979

Medlik, S., *Profile of the Hotel and Catering Industry*, London: Heinemann, 1979

chapter 2

Human resource policies

Policies provide a framework within which organizations operate. Some companies within the hotel and catering industry, such as McDonalds, have a policy to operate within a narrow market sector. Other companies, such as Trusthouse Forte, have a policy to operate within many market sectors. These policies provide management with the framework within which they make their decisions; for example, where to expand; what to divest, etc.

Human resource or personnel policies normally are a subpolicy of the overall policy for the organization. One definition states that personnel policy 'should provide a framework that sets patterns of behaviour for the organization and the individuals within it. People want to know how the organization is going to behave towards them and what it expects from them' (Pratt and Bennett 1985).

Policies should embrace a number of different but interrelated issues. The first may be to do with deciding to be a 'leader' or 'follower' on the terms and conditions offered. The second may be concerned with human resource policies such as career prospects and to what extent an employer sets out to offer long-term secure careers to a significant proportion of the workforce. The third may deal with employee involvement and management style. To what extent do senior management really want to involve staff in decisions? Interestingly one general feature of the top US companies identified by *In Search of Excellence* has been a statement of company credo, and in particular, the emphasis this has put on policy towards employees (Sheila Rothwell, 1984).

An organization's human resource policy is commonly known as its personnel policy. In considering personnel policies we must look first at a definition of personnel management. Personnel management, as a distinct specialization of management, is relatively new and consequently its specialist role and definition varies much more than is the case with older established specializations such as management accounting. In addition, because it leans heavily on the social sciences, its definitions and duties are more fluid. Hence there are many definitions of the role of personnel management, but probably a suitable one is that adopted by the Institute of Personnel Management (1963).

Personnel management is a responsibility of all those who manage people, as well as being a description of the work of those who are employed as specialists. It is that part of management which is concerned with people at work and with their relationships within an enterprise. It applies not only to industry and commerce but to all fields of employment.

Personnel management aims to achieve both efficiency and justice, neither of which can be pursued successfully without the other. It seeks to bring together and develop into an effective organization the men and women who make up an enterprise, enabling each to make his own best contribution to its success both as an individual and as a member of a working group. It seeks to provide fair terms and conditions of employment, and satisfying work for those employed.

From this definition, it will be seen that personnel management is *part* of the normal activity of every supervisor and manager. It states that the aim of personnel management is to achieve efficiency, so it is concerned with the welfare of the enterprise as well as the individual within that enterprise. In practice, because of economic forces, the scales frequently tip towards the side of the enterprise rather than towards that of the individual, hence the spate of employment protection legislation of the 1970s.

It should be clear from this definition, that personnel management is the responsibility of everyone managing people. However, because of the steadily growing size of organizations and the body of knowledge within the personnel management field, it has also become a specialist branch of management itself. The Institute of Personnel Management's (IPM) Code of Practice in Personnel Management (Appendix 2) describes how the IPM interprets this branch of management.

Personnel management as a specialist function

However, to some, personnel management is seen as no more than the welfare branch of the company — concerned with looking after individual employees when in need. To others, it is the 'in-house staff agency', whilst in other cases the personnel management function is integrated completely into the whole company activity. It is concerned with assisting in the harnessing of the employees' energies, in order that the enterprise operates efficiently, and it is also concerned with ensuring that the enterprise meets fully its social responsibilities to every employee.

This is no easy role, and frequently the personnel manager is seen, particularly in the private sector, as no more than a 'cost centre', or the company's 'social conscience', by those managers who have to 'make the profits'. This should not be the case, because it must be recognized that for every organization there are two major functions. One is to achieve the 'group goals' such as increased sales or profits or, in the public sector, to provide services. The other is 'group maintenance', that is, the role of creating and maintaining the group so that it can achieve its goals. Personnel management is concerned primarily with this latter role and in carrying it out should assist line managers to achieve their objectives in the most effective manner by ensuring conditions of employment that attract, retain and motivate the appropriate labour force. Personnel managers assist management to find the best possible candidates and provide training for the successful applicants. Effective personnel management requires imagination in obtaining a fair share of the available labour. Consequently, good personnel policies can make considerable contributions to the success of an undertaking, and although their efforts

Figure 2.1 *The personnel function*

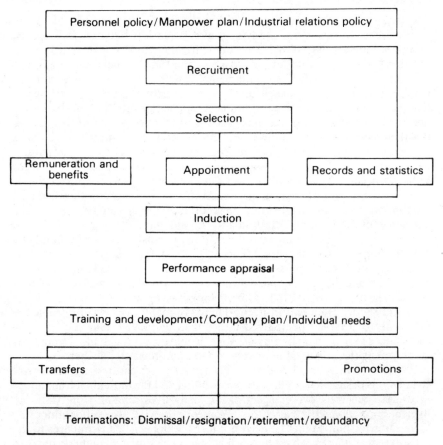

frequently cannot be measured accurately in monetary terms, management should not be able to visualize doing its job effectively without the support of such policies. Figure 2.1 shows the main functions and responsibilities normally covered under personnel management.

Personnel policies do not develop in a vacuum, however. They are, as said earlier, an expression of the 'style of management' of an organization. They should be dynamic, both changing with and bringing about changes in the behaviour of the workforce and the organization. In order to arrive at a clearer understanding of the relationship between personnel policies and the style of management of an organization, it is necessary for managers and students of management to look at the findings of those who have studied the behaviour of people at work.

One of the problems in attempting such a task is the amount of published work available and also the wide variety of opinions. As a result only what are considered (by the author) to be the most important points have been selected. (Anyone wishing to study the subject should refer, as a starting point, to the reading list at the end of this chapter.)

People at work

The study of people at work falls within the province of the social sciences which are concerned with studying the relationship between individuals, groups of individuals and their environment. The knowledge obtained can be used in two principal ways, namely to understand and predict changes and also to bring about changes. The fundamental conclusion to be drawn from the work of recent behavioural scientists, and Abraham Maslow in particular, is that man is a satisfaction-seeking animal motivated primarily by his biological needs. Hotel and catering managers should be more conscious of the truth of this than most others. In addition, and unlike most other animals, once man's biological needs are satisfied further needs emerge — mainly of a social nature. This manifests itself in the pursuit of power, status, security and other outward signs of 'success'. Most people are not conscious of these needs which drive or motivate them. If, however, management can recognize them, they can take appropriate steps to ensure that these driving forces can be used to the advantage of both the organization and the individual.

The first need, the need for bodily comfort, is satisfied relatively simply by adequate meals and housing. The welfare state, recognizing that the satisfaction of this need is essential to the survival of individuals and of society ensures by and large that no one needs to go without food and shelter. Individuals in our society, therefore, no longer accept that working merely for food and shelter is an end in itself. There are many cases where people are financially better off unemployed rather than employed, and consequently they choose to remain unemployed. Most people expect much more from their employment than being able merely to purchase food and shelter.

Physical security is also these days very largely assured by the State. Regulations designed to protect the community and the individual from injury or disease penetrate every aspect of our daily lives ranging from traffic to hygiene regulations. Even after this, if someone does fall ill or suffer injury, the State cares for him so that he need not fear the financial consequences to the same extent that he may have done a few years ago or that he might do today in many other countries. Therefore, seeking employment with low physical risk or with benevolent employers is no longer as important as it may have been a hundred or even fifty years ago. Consequently, because our biological needs are now largely guaranteed by the State they no longer provide the motivation that they once did. Instead, other and much more complex needs — the social needs — have emerged.

Satisfactory relationships with other people are among the highest of our needs. To work with and for people we get on with is something most of us like to do, and it is no doubt a major force attracting many people into the hotel and catering industry. In looking at staff turnover it should be noted that the greatest numbers leave in the earliest days of employment — the period when relationships have not developed. On the other hand, one of the main reasons why people stay in their jobs, when all other conditions should encourage them to leave is because of their relationship with those at work including colleagues, bosses, subordinates and customers.

In our society another aspect of our relationship with others which plays a significant part is our need for social acceptance. Frequently this depends on our job and our way of living. By certain indications society locates us on the social ladder but many people not content with their position attempt to move up. Social mobility has increased considerably even in the last thirty years and the main evidence is change of occupational status, type of housing, earning more money, obtaining a variety of other status symbols such as motor cars, longer holidays, thicker carpet in the office, etc., or even by changing from one occupation or employer to another with a higher social standing. This fact unfortunately deters many people from working in the hotel and catering industry because many jobs, in spite of being highly skilled, are not awarded the status awarded to other jobs demanding the same or maybe less skill. It is within this field that the industry's trade and professional bodies need to do a great deal more work. This problem is not unique to Britain. At the International Hotels' Association Conference in Geneva in 1985 the delegates resolved that national bodies worldwide needed to put greater effort into improving the perceived standing of hotel and catering work.

Next on the list of human needs comes the need to satisfy one's own ambitions and aspirations. This usually means making the maximum use of one's intellectual, social and manual skills. It may include the desire to be a company chairman or, more modestly, the wish to produce a satisfactory piece of workmanship. Today with the undoubted economic need for mass production and consequent simplification, whether it be the production of 'in-flight' meals or motor cars, a person's need for this satisfaction is constantly overriden. It is one of the strongest needs of working people and one for which they often make considerable sacrifices. People will put in long hours in difficult conditions even for low pay when intrinsic job satisfaction is high.

Finally — having satisfied all these needs — security of their continuing satisfaction is itself another and, these days, a growing need. Mergers and acquisitions along with automation now threaten many more people than ever before, and even those who a few years ago could feel secure no longer do so. Seeking this security now plays an important part in labour relations and many people leave insecure employment for what they believe to be a secure alternative position. It is usually found that where job security is high, such as in banking or insurance, labour turnover is low — completely unlike the rate of labour turnover in some sectors of the hotel and catering industry, where job tenure is often short and notoriously precarious. Job security normally leads to a stable and skilled labour force with many of the consequent efficiencies. On the other hand, job security can be such that it can work against the best interests of the organization with abuse abounding, such as excessive absenteeism and the protection of the grossly inefficient.

When all these needs are satisfied, it is argued that an employee is more likely to offer stable and competent service, but, if any one of these needs remains unsatisfied, he or she will almost certainly behave in one of a variety of ways, some of which are contrary to the business interest.

First, he may seek employment elsewhere which offers more likelihood of a satisfying job. Second, he may seek other compensations, such as extra money or more time off. If he has leadership qualities, he may become the focus for group, rather than individual, dissatisfaction or aspirations and this may lead him to play an active part in trade union affairs or other similar activities. Third, he may just opt out and seek his satisfaction outside work, for example, at home or in club activities. This last is unfortunately not often the case, since evidence indicates that those who obtain most satisfaction at work also play the biggest part in social or community affairs. In between these three distinct patterns of behaviour there are many degrees that most managers will recognize including absenteeism, lateness, waste, pilferage and, of course, lack of co-operation or even sheer obstructionism, not all of which can be laid at the door of management.

The behavioural scientist F. Herzberg developed a theory that suggests two largely independent sets of factors which influence work behaviour. One set of factors, the 'hygiene' factors (such as work conditions), influences mainly the level of dissatisfaction. Improving the hygiene factors only removes causes of dissatisfaction without motivating the worker. Room temperature illustrates the point: ideal temperature goes unnoticed and does not motivate a person; a temperature which is too hot or too cold creates discomfort and demotivates.

The other set of factors are known as motivators (achievement, praise, work itself). These actually make people feel positive about their work and have to be built into work in order to motivate the workforce. Ideally the hygiene factors should be put right first.

The theories of Maslow and Herzberg are described by Campbell *et al.* (1970) as 'content theories'. Campbell also describes 'process theories' which concentrate on more complex explanations of job satisfaction and performance. Leading 'process' theorists include Vroom,* and Lock.†

In such theories distinctions are made between job satisfaction and performance. Concepts of 'fairness' related to inputs are considered which do not appear directly in Maslow's or Herzberg's theories.

Human resource management and styles of leadership

Another finding of considerable importance, highlighted by Douglas McGregor in his book *The Human Side of Enterprise*, is that most people behave in the way expected of them and consequently 'live up' or 'down to' their superiors' expectations. Therefore the relationship between employee and boss can be described as a dynamic one — the higher the expectations made (within reason) of an employee, the higher the performance, and consequently even higher expectations can and will be made of and met by him or her in the future. Unfortunately some managers expect the worst from all their subordinates and by making this apparent they inevitably achieve the worst results.

The 'style' of management is therefore of vital importance in an organization because this determines to a large extent whether employees obtain satisfaction from their jobs and whether managers will achieve their business objectives.

The 'authoritarian' manager generally manages by issuing orders and instructions leaving little or no opportunity for discussion or even explanation.

*Vroom, V. H., *Work and Motivation*, Wiley, 1964
†Locke, E., Towards a theory of task motivation and incentives. *Organisational Behaviour and Human Performance*, Vol. 3, 1968

Figure 2.2 *Ten management theorists of crucial importance to the development of manpower policies*

1841–1925 Henri Fayol
(France)

Claimed to be the earliest known proponent of a theoretical analysis of managerial activities. He defined management as having five functions:

to forecast
to organize
to command
to co-ordinate
to control

1856–1915 Frederick W. Taylor
(U S A)

The founder of the movement known as 'scientific management'. He proposed four 'great underlying principles':

The development of a true science of work
The scientific selection and progressive development of the workman
The bringing together of the science of work and the scientifically selected and trained man
The constant and intimate co-operation of management and men

1868–1924 Frank Gilbreth
(U S A)
1879–1972 Lillian Gilbreth
(U S A)

Followers of F.W. Taylor, whose combined work emphasized that in applying scientific management principles it is essential first to understand the needs and personalities of workers

1880–1949 Elton Mayo
(U S A)

Often referred to as the founder of the Human Relations movement. His work demonstrated the importance of groups in affecting the behaviour of individuals at work. He is most famous for the Hawthorne investigations which led to a fuller understanding of the 'human factor' at work

1903–1981 Rensis Likert
(U S A)

Showed that effective supervisors and managers tended to be 'employee centred' rather than 'job centred'. Likert distinguished four systems of management:

exploitive/authoratitive
benevolent/authoratitive
consultative
participative

He favoured the participation system although other systems could also produce high productivity

1906–1964 Douglas McGregor
(U S A)

Famous for theories X and Y. In theory X people are assumed to dislike work and need direction and control. In theory Y people are assumed to enjoy work and external control is not necessary. Managers' assumptions about their subordinates shape their behaviour

Frederick Herzberg
(U S A)

Famous for demonstrating that factors which led to dissatisfaction ('hygiene' factors) were quite different from those that led to satisfaction (motivators).

Determinants of job satisfaction	Determinants of dissatisfaction
Achievement	Company policy and administration
Recognition	Supervision
Work itself	Salary
Responsibility	Interpersonal relations
Advancement	Working conditions

Abraham Maslow
(U S A)

Maslow saw human needs in a form of hierarchy, for which he is famous; as one set of needs was satisfied another emerged. Their order is:

physiological needs
security and safety needs
affiliation, or acceptance needs
esteem needs
self-actualization

Peter Drucker
(U S A)

Famous for developing the concept of Management by Objectives (MbO). When used properly MbO harnesses the aspirations and energies of managers in striving to meet the aims of the employing organizations.

Today, with strong pressures for more participation, this type of manager is finding life increasingly difficult. Very similar to this style is the 'unitarist' style which is based on a reliance on traditional market forces and hierarchical systems with a clear split between the responsibilities of management and those of the workforce.

There are also the 'democratic' managers, who recognize that they are not only leading, but are also part of a team and that this requires the others in the team — the staff — to be involved in decisions through discussion and explanation. Evidence generally indicates that nowadays this style is the more acceptable. The expression 'pluralist' is often used nowadays to describe such a style of management which recognizes that the aspirations of all sections of the workforce are to be taken into account in the decision-making process.

Unfortunately some managers of the older authoritarian school feel that to consult subordinates is a sign of weakness and that democratic management is a way of sharing, ducking or abdicating responsibility. It should be clear though that democratic management should in no way be abdication. Democratic management is a recognition that most co-operation and the best results are achieved by pooling knowledge and experience and by involving people in the decisions that affect them.

The third manager, the *laissez-faire* type, abdicates responsibility — leaving his or her staff to face the problems that are rightly the manager's. This fact was referred to in a Commission on Industrial Relations report on hotels and restaurants and it is evident that far too many hotel and catering managers consciously or unconsciously avoid the high-pressure points, such as the restaurants, kitchens or reception areas, during busy periods. The staff are left to face complaints from customers without the authority to rectify or overcome causes of disruption. These three very simplified descriptions of styles of management have been included to illustrate that there are several different ways of managing which are complex interactions between the individuals, the tasks and the environment which usually determines a particular style of management.

There also exist different attitudes or orientations towards the workforce. Amitai Etzioni has produced a useful classification of the power used by managers to ensure compliance, and as with McGregor's theory, it can be shown that particular styles have particular effects. Etzioni states that there are three principal management orientations to workers.

First, there is the *coercive* power used by managers in which fear of the consequences is the main motivator. Those managers who bewail the passing of the 'divine right of dismissal' most probably fall into this category. The second category is the *utilitarian* use of power. This depends upon the manipulation of material rewards, such as wages, and is commonly seen in large manufacturing industries where the only reward for work done is money. It is also seen in the hotel and catering industry, particularly in the way seasonal and casual workers are employed. Etzioni's third category is *normative* power. This rests largely upon the use of prestige, esteem and social acceptance. The managers of many organizations are motivated very much in this way, seeking titles, bigger cars, admission to prestige-carrying committees, etc.

Etzioni goes on to argue that each management type has an appropriate worker involvement. First, there is an *alienative* involvement which signifies that the employee has strong negative attitudes towards the employer. Normally, this would probably persist only where no reasonable employment alternatives exist, but such an attitude would be manifested probably by various forms of sabotage, theft, or worst of all, arson (which does occur in hotels). Second, Etzioni identifies a *calculative* involvement which is based on money or material exchange. Casual workers in catering are very likely to have this attitude towards their employers. Third, there is a *moral* involvement which signifies that the employee identifies closely with the employer's and colleagues' values and objectives. He or she will carry out their work because they value the objectives of the work. Many hotel and catering staff will hold this attitude to their work because they believe that it is worthwhile to make people comfortable and to help them enjoy themselves.

There is, of course, one other crucial perspective which needs to be considered — the Marxist one. Professor V. L. Allen, of Leeds University, wrote in *Personnel Management* (December 1976) that both the unitarist and the pluralist relationships are 'protective of the status quo' (the capitalist system). He went on to write that Marxism provides the alternative form of analysis of industrial relations and that the industrial relationship is one of permanent conflict between the buyers and sellers of labour power. He wrote, 'The conflict . . . is permanent . . . it is pervasive and influences every aspect of people's lives', and he suggested that in accepting such a perspective social relationships will be better understood. In considering such statements of course it is vital to be clear that in the case of Marx there is still considerable debate as to whether it is a scientific method or an ideology.

Having given these brief outlines of some important contributions to our understanding of work people's behaviour, it must be emphasized that there are many other important contributions which, perforce, have had to be omitted. The purpose, however, is to show that there are different, often mutually supporting, explanations of behaviour which state that different styles of management engender different worker attitudes.

Associated research also demonstrates that there is no such thing as a universal leadership or management quality. Instead, successful management and leadership is dependent, or contingent, upon the interaction of a whole variety of factors, of which the nature of the goods and services being offered and the market itself are vital. A steady, non-seasonal trade, as encountered in much industrial catering, will call for a style of management very different from that required by a busy seasonal hotel. Circumstances and time, therefore, can make a manager who would have been a failure in one situation, a success in another.

The human resource policy

Taking many different factors into account, including those just mentioned, management attempts to design its recruitment, training and reward systems in order to shape the workforce in such a way that it matches management's expectations. It is this process that is the organization's human resource or personnel policy. In some cases a personnel policy need not be in writing, particularly in smaller establishments. Increasingly, however, with pressure from legislation, for example, to release more information to employees, to provide written health and safety policy statements and training policy statements, it is good practice for organizations to produce written policy statements.

Further reading

Armstrong, M., *A Handbook of Personnel Management Practice*, 2nd ed., London: Kogan Page, 1984

Campbell, J. P., *et al.*, *Managerial Behaviour, Performance and Effectiveness*, London: McGraw-Hill, 1970

Etzioni, A., *Modern Organization*, Englewood Cliffs, N. J.: Prentice-Hall, 1980

Handy, C. G., *Understanding Organisations*, 2nd ed., London: Penguin, 1981

Herzberg, F., *Work and the Nature of Man*, St Albans: Crosby Lockwood, 1975

Koontz, H., O'Donnell, C., and Weihrich, H., *Management*, 8th ed., McGraw-Hill: Tokyo, 1984

McGregor, D., *The Human Side of Enterprise*, New York: McGraw-Hill, 1960

Pratt, K. J., and Bennett, S. C., *Elements of Personnel Management*, 2nd ed., Wokingham: GEE, 1985

Pugh, D. S., Hickson, D. J., and Hining, C. R., *Writers on Organisations*, 3rd ed., London: Penguin, 1983

Rothwell, Sheila, In search of excellence, *Personnel Management*, London: 1984

Thomason, G., *A Textbook of Personnel Management*, 4th ed., London: Institute of Personnel Management, 1981

Torrington, D., and Chapman J., *Personnel Management*, 2nd ed., London: Prentice-Hall, 1983

chapter 3

Job design

Although the term *management* (in its abstract sense) has almost as many definitions as there are managers, it is generally understood to refer to the art or skill of achieving required results through the efforts of others. There is today, however, considerable debate regarding what precisely it is that motivates people to achieve the results required of them. On the one hand there are those of the scientific school of management (see Chapter 2), who believe that all that is necessary is to select the right people, give clear directions and enough money and the required results will be achieved. On the other hand there are those from the human relations school (see Chapter 2) who believe that organizational objectives will only be achieved by recognizing to the full the needs and expectations of working people. Whichever view prevails, however, it is generally held that people produce their best performances when they know clearly what is expected of them. Consequently if an undertaking's objectives are to be achieved it follows that all its managers and work people must know clearly the results they are expected to produce. Such a statement of an organization's expectations of its employees can be made either orally or in writing, but experience proves that the written word is less likely to be misunderstood and that the need to think carefully before putting words to paper generally produces more logical and effective results than oral statements.

It is for such reasons that clear, precise job descriptions should be given to everyone at work, because once a job is clearly described on paper there should be little room for subsequent misunderstandings. As a result a job should be performed more efficiently.

However before producing job descriptions it is essential to realize that the job description should be the result of a process referred to as job design.

In the past job design was seen as the process by which the employer set out to maximize the output of the workforce. For many employers this remains the sole objective. However, there is an increasing recognition that if job design is to be effective, the resulting jobs must satisfy the individual worker's needs also.

This second approach recognizes Drucker's view that it is important to distinguish between efficiency and effectiveness. Designing jobs for short-term efficiency may result, for example, in high labour turnover with a drop in customer satisfaction and hence in long-term effectiveness.

Figure 3.1   *Aspects of job design*

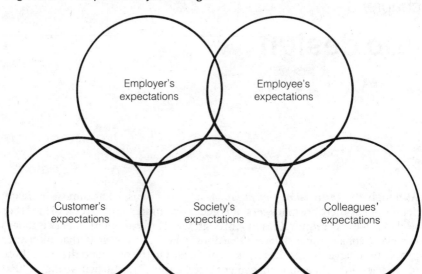

Third, of course, job design must result in customer satisfaction. Fourth, most people work in teams or groups, so colleagues' expectations have to be considered. And, finally, the job must be designed in such a way that society's expectations (e.g. health and safety) are satisfied.

Approaches to job design

In setting out to design any job therefore it is essential to recognize the expectations of everyone involved. The actual approach adopted will depend on the amalgam of these sets of expectations; for example where customers and employers want fast service, with minimum personalized contact, such as in many fast food operations, the resultant job may emphasize speed at the cost of job satisfaction. The consequence will be a high labour turnover, which may well be acceptable to the employer where there is a steady supply of replacement labour.

Job specialization

This approach to organizing work has been around for thousands of years and has led to civilization as we know it today. However, as an approach to organizing modern industrial production it was developed by a number of theorists including F. W. Taylor, the founder of scientific management. Major principles resulting from the scientific management approach are as follows.

Science of work The need for scientific methods of observing, measuring and analysing work activities to replace existing unsystematic approaches.

Standardization Using the resulting knowledge, efficient working methods and performance levels can be set for work.

Selection Systematic and scientific approaches to selecting workers with relevant qualities and abilities, together with planned training for the work involved.

Specialization Both management and workers should concentrate upon specific functional activities, involving a limited range of tasks for which the individual's abilities and training enable expert performance. (Reproduced from Torrington and Chapman 1983.)

There have been two main consequences of the application of these ideas. First, areas of expertise and responsibility have become much more specialized, particularly in the management areas. There are now many more specialists in management than there were fifty years ago, even ten years ago. The hotel and catering industry has been no exception to this trend with a considerable recent growth in the range and numbers of those involved in middle and senior management. Second, and particularly at an operative level, job content is simplified by reducing the number of tasks each operative performs to a very limited number so that the need for skill and training is minimized.

The apparent benefits of job simplification, however, were accompanied by many problems, such as industrial strife, the causes being put down to that same job simplification. In contrast, the findings of behavioural scientists were showing that work people could not be treated as mere components of machines: instead they had a range of needs to be met by the work they performed. As a consequence other approaches to job design became necessary.

Job rotation

One reaction to job simplification was job rotation. This provides individuals with some variety in either the working conditions (i.e. where or when the basic job is done) or in the actual tasks performed. The jobs, however, remain simple, provide little stimulation and do not satisfy esteem needs.

Job enlargement

Job enlargement, in contrast, extends the range of tasks performed and is aimed at reducing boredom, increasing interest in work and increasing self-esteem. Job enlargement, however, brings about the very problems that work simplification sets out to eliminate, such as the need for greater knowledge, skill and training.

Job enrichment

Job enlargement extends 'horizontally' the range of tasks to be performed by an individual by adding tasks of a similar nature. It does not, however, meet the more complex expectations such as the need for autonomy. Job enrichment instead extends 'vertically' the range of tasks by increasing an individual's responsibility and autonomy through adding elements of the job which may have been the responsibility of supervisors or management, such as planning, organization and control.

Sociotechnical systems

This approach to job design sets out to bring together an employer's technical system (e.g. buildings and equipment) and the social system comprising the work people. This is because the scientific school aimed to maximize the technical system, seeing the work people as components. In contrast, the human relations theorists concentrated on maximizing the satisfaction of human needs. These two approaches can be seen to be incompatible. It is necessary to look at an organization as a sociotechnical system which compromises between technical efficiency and group needs.

In the sociotechnical system of job design three major factors are considered. These are: first, the need to recognize the needs that are met by formal and informal groups; second, work is allocated to groups who are able to identify clearly with the work; third, the group is given a high degree of autonomy over its work.

Job design, therefore, is the process which sets out to harness the energies of the human resource in order to achieve an organization's objectives. In turn job descriptions are the written results of the process of job design.

In some cases brief descriptions only may be sufficient, whereas in others quite detailed and complex documents are called for. The degree of detail needed in describing the various elements of a job varies from job to job and from organization to organization. There are, however, two main documents: job descriptions and job specifications. Job analysis is also sometimes considered to be a document describing a job in detail, but it is more commonly used when referring to the technique of examining jobs in depth. Job descriptions and job specifications are described below. In addition a brief description of Management by Objectives is included in this chapter because it describes a methodical and systematic approach to the design and description of jobs and setting of objectives.

Job descriptions

Job descriptions are a broad statement of the scope, purpose, duties and responsibilities involved in a job. Their main purposes are to:

1 Give employees an understanding of their jobs and standards of performance.
2 Clarify duties, responsibilities and authority in order to design the organization structure.
3 Assist in assessing employees' performance.

Figure 3.2 *Job descriptions: the 'hub' of personnel management*

4 Assist in the recruitment and placement of employees.
5 Assist in the induction of new employees.
6 Evaluate jobs for grading and salary administration.
7 Provide information for training and management development.

There are two distinct but equally important parts to the full description of jobs. The first is the statement of conditions for which employees contract to do work; some time ago in the United Kingdom it was recognized that the clear definition of conditions was not generally adequate, with the result that the Contracts of Employment Act became law in 1963. This Act with recent amendments requires that certain information regarding conditions of employment, such as hours of work and length of notice, be given to employees. This subject, together with other legal reasons for producing and issuing comprehensive job descriptions, will be dealt with in subsequent chapters.

The second part of describing jobs requires the provision of information to employees which specifies clearly what results are expected of them and indicates how their performance will be measured.

Job descriptions should contain the following main elements.

Job identification   This section identifies the job by title, department, level in
   the hierarchy.
Scope of job   A brief description of the scope of a job.
Content   This section is a detailed statement and normally includes a list of
   duties and how these are performed, and what standard of performance is
   required.
Conditions   This section describes any particular conditions which make the
   job more or less difficult; for example, if a public house is situated in a rough
   area, this will need to be highlighted.
Authority   This section describes any limits to his or her authority such as:
   cash limits; authority to make contracts on behalf of the employer; authority
   to engage or dismiss subordinates.

   Figure 3.3 shows a typical job description for a chef and Figure 3.4 shows
one for a counter assistant.

Figure 3.3   *Job description for a chef*

Title	Chef
Department	Food and Beverage
Scope	All hotel food preparation operations
Responsible to	Food and Beverage Manager
Responsible for	1 Personnel: all kitchen staff including kitchen manual staff
	2 Equipment: all kitchen fixed and removable equipment and kitchen utensils
Lateral communication	Restaurant Manager, Front Office Manager, Head Housekeeper
Main responsibilities	The planning, organization and supervision of food preparation in the hotel including:
	1 Menu compilation according to agreed costed recipes
	2 Purchasing of foodstuffs, kitchen materials and equipment from nominated suppliers within agreed budget levels
	3 Portion and waste control
	4 Control of labour and other variable costs within budget levels
	5 Arrangement of staff rosters
	6 Training of new staff
	7 Hygiene and cleanliness
	8 Fire precautions
	9 Security of all kitchen supplies, equipment, utensils and silverware
Limits of authority	1 Engagement and suspension of all subordinates until circumstances can be reported to the Food and Beverage Manager

Figure 3.4   *Job description for a counter assistant*

Title	Counter Assistant
Department	Depot General Canteen
Scope	To assist in the preparation of meals, to keep the kitchen and dining areas in a clean and tidy state and to serve customers
Responsible to	Assistant Manageress
Responsible for	No subordinate staff
Lateral communication	Cashier, cooks
Main responsibilities	1 Prepare foodstuffs according to directions
	2 Clean and lay up canteen dining area
	3 Stock up and replenish service points as necessary
	4 Serve customers during service periods
	5 Clear away used plates, utensils, trays, and wipe down tables and working surfaces during and after the service period
	6 Clean and polish service equipment and kitchen areas after service periods
	7 Comply with company standards and statutory hygiene regulations
Limits of authority	No authority to authorize or make expenditure
	No authority over other staff

Job design in hotel and catering operations

At one extreme job design can simplify work so that little skill and training is needed. Trends in this direction are very apparent in the hotel and catering industry in several sectors including fast food operations, the use of cook–chill and cook–freeze in many different operations including schools, hospitals, banqueting and 'in-flight' catering. A major reason is the process sometimes referred to as 'de-coupling', whereby the production and service elements are totally separated — pre-prepared meals being produced away from the service point. Such systems are concerned mainly with the 'production elements' of hotel and catering products. However, because of the significant 'customer contact' element, it is difficult to 'simplify out' many of the tasks which customers expect as part of the service and which employees themselves find rewarding, such as social interaction. Consequently while some jobs are being simplified many other jobs in the industry remain rewarding because the very nature of the industry, small units, socio-interaction, autonomy all meet the requirements of what appear to be major contributions to effective job design.

Job specifications

In many cases more detail than is normally contained in a brief job description may be necessary for a job to be performed satisfactorily. A detailed statement

Figure 3.5 Extracts from a job specification for a waitress

Duties	Knowledge	Skill	Social skills
1 Preparation			
1.3 Preparation of butter, cruets and accompaniments	1 Correct accompaniments for the dishes on the day's menu	Operation of butter pat maker. Preparation of sauces, e.g. vinaigrette	
3 Service of customers			
3.3 Taking orders	1 Procedures for taking wine and food orders 2 Menu and dish composition 3 Procedure for taking requisitions to kitchen, bar dispense and cashier		1 'Assisting customers with selection in order to maximize sales 2 Informing customers of composition of dishes
8 Wine dispense	Product knowledge 1 Suitable wines for dishes on the menu 2 Suitable glasses for different wines 3 Correct temperatures for red, white and rosé	1 Presenting bottle 2 Opening bottle 3 Pouring wine	1 Assisting customers with selection 2 Dealing with complaints
	Licensing law 1 Young persons 2 Drinking up time		1 Refusing service 2 Asking people to 'drink up'
11 Preparation for cleaners after last customers have left			
11.3 Stripping tables	1 Safe disposal of ash tray contents 2 Disposal of cutlery, crockery, linen, cruets		

of the job may be required specifying the precise skills and knowledge needed to carry out the various component tasks of a job. This information may be contained in a document often referred to as a job specification. Alternatively, the information may be contained in such documents as manuals of operation, operating instructions and the like. Extracts from a job specification for a waitress are shown in Figure 3.5.

Within the last few years, however, job descriptions and specifications have become much more highly developed in the hotel and catering industry. Several companies are now using training booklets which serve several important purposes including the provision of:

Job descriptions
Trainers' programme
Trainees' aide-mémoires
List of duties
List of tasks
Standards of performance
Interviewing attainments checklist
Training checklist

Not only are these booklets very useful for selection, induction and training purposes, they are also useful from a discipline point of view. If someone has been trained to do something, and the fact is recorded, then certain standards can be expected.

Preparation of job descriptions and job specifications

Some managers like to prepare job descriptions and other such documents with the employees concerned, and generally speaking this is by far the best approach. Frequently, however, this principle can only apply to supervisory and management grades because the jobs of operative grades are often so clearly defined that discussion, apart from explanation, would only raise hopes that would be disappointed when it became apparent that no changes were forthcoming. Furthermore, it is not always possible to involve the employee concerned because the need for job descriptions often does not make itself apparent until a person has to be recruited.

The preparation of job specifications normally requires a more skilled approach than that needed for the preparation of job descriptions. The uses to which such documents are to be put should determine who prepares them; for example, if job specifications are to be used for training purposes, they should be prepared by training specialists and the line management concerned. On the other hand, if they are to be used as a basis for work measurement, work study specialists should work with line management.

Whatever form the description of jobs takes, however, vague terms such as 'satisfactory levels of gross profit' should be avoided and, instead, actual quantities or levels should be specified, such as 'a gross profit of 58 per cent is to be obtained'. It is good practice also to incorporate budgets and forecasts into job descriptions as it sets specific and quantified targets. Additionally, documents such as manuals of operation or training booklets may be directly related to job descriptions.

Because of the vital part played by job descriptions and specifications, particularly in such things as induction, training, job evaluation and performance appraisal, their preparation should be monitored by one person or department to ensure consistency. They should be regularly updated and a copy held by the job holder, by his or her superior, sometimes by the superior's boss as well, and, of course, by the personnel department, where one exists.

Management by Objectives (MbO)

Management by objectives is an approach to management which, if operated effectively, influences all levels and activities of an organization. It usually relies heavily on specially designed job descriptions and similar documents. MbO seeks to integrate all of an organization's principal targets with the individual managers' own aspirations. By concept it is typical of a *democratic* style of management although, in practice, it is often introduced by other types of manager.

MbO requires the establishment of an undertaking's objectives, the development of plans to achieve these objectives, and the methods for monitoring progress. At the same time each manager must be personally involved in the preparation of his or her own department's targets and in the means of achieving these targets. Objectives should not be handed down by superior to subordinate, but should be agreed between the two after all factors have been considered.

Figure 3.6   *Management by objectives (MbO)*

Figure 3.7 *Management by objectives: example of performance standards and improvement plans*

Manager, White Hart Restaurant: Objectives for six months ending 30 June

Key result area	Performance standard	Current level of achievement	Control information	Improvement target	Improvement plan
1 Gross profit (a) catering	63%	58%	Monthly stocktake	Achieve budget	Review selling and purchase prices, introduce more high-yield dishes, by 30 April
(b) liquor	55%	42%	Monthly stocktake	Achieve budget	Alter sales mix, introduce premium-priced beer, discontinue sale of cheaper draught beer
2 Sales volume	£60,000 per month	£66,000	Takings sheets	Increase to £84,000	Promote new private function room, spend £2000 on promotion during first quarter
3 Labour	23%	26%	Weekly wages sheet	Reduce to budget, 23%	Increase staff only for booked functions, no more staff to be recruited except to replace those who leave

The critical areas only of each manager's job are defined, the objectives where possible are quantified, the means of checking results, of identifying obstacles and of achieving objectives are developed. Planning and improvement goes on continuously through review meetings being held at regular intervals between superiors and subordinates. The procedure is illustrated in Figure 3.6 and an extract from an MbO job description is shown in Figure 3.7.

Where MbO concepts have been used in hotels and catering to set standards, generally speaking it is found that the performance standards of operative staff are 'guest centred', that is, they are concerned with identifying the standards of service to be provided to the guest. The performance standards of heads of departments, on the other hand, are 'profit centred', that is, they identify the cost criteria for producing the services to the guest. Heads of departments are, however, directly responsible for ensuring that the operational performance standards are met by department staff, so their performance standards may incorporate quality control standards as well as the 'profit centred' standards.

Recent developments in setting standards

In recent years, attempts have been made in the industry to introduce the basic MbO concepts to most levels of management, supervisory and operative staff. In 1977 the Hotel and Catering Industry Training Board commissioned a study* of the standards-setting field following some pioneering work carried out by several companies and management consultants operating in the industry. The result, at the time of writing, is a slow but emerging recognition that standards' definition can make a useful contribution to the industry's efficiency. This will require, however, the recognition and adoption of management tools, such as work study, which are still used rarely in many of the traditional sectors of the industry but which are essential, underscoring the rapid and successful development of the international branded fast-food operators.

Too many of the traditional employers in this industry expect results without defining clearly what these should be or how they are to be achieved. Instead they expect employees to know intuitively what is wanted of them, at the same time leaving them untrained, unsupervised and undirected for long periods. This lack of job description results in new staff often being dissatisfied because the job is not as was described in the first place. Furthermore, lack of careful and methodical job description results in poor training so that service to the customer is frequently inconsistent and unsatisfactory. On the other hand, employees' jobs could be made more easy, more satisfactory and the results of their work more predictable and efficient if their jobs were defined clearly.

Further reading

Armstrong, M., *A Handbook of Personnel Management Practice*, 2nd ed., London: Kogan Page, 1984

*Nightingale, M. A., *A Quest for Quality and Profitability*, London: HCITB, 1978

HCITB, *A Quest for Standards*, London: 1978

Humble, J., *Management by Objectives in Action*, London: McGraw-Hill, 1970

Kewney, Eustace, *How to Write a Job Description*, London: Institute of Personnel Management, 1981

Nightingale, M. A., *A Quest for Quality and Profitability*, London: HCITB, 1978

Pratt, K. J., and Bennett, S. C., *Elements of Personnel Management*, 2nd ed., Wokingham: GEE, 1985

Thomason, G., *A Textbook of Personnel Management*, 4th ed., London: Institute of Personnel Management, 1981

Torrington, D., and Chapman, J., *Personnel Management*, 2nd ed., London: Prentice-Hall, 1983

chapter 4

Recruitment

The hotel and catering industry has had a notorious reputation for high labour turnover and its problem of attracting the right people, even when unemployment is running at very high levels. In recent years, however, turnover in some sectors has reduced, probably as a result of several different factors, such as high unemployment, improving induction and training methods and the unfair dismissals legislation. Even so, turnover, to some observers, remains high. In looking at some individual establishments there are cases where statistically it appears that the complete staff changes several times a year. Statistics, of course, can be misleading and closer examination will show that such high rates of turnover generally are confined to certain sectors only of the industry and to the more junior and less-skilled employees. In spite of this, however, it must be recognized that the high turnover among employees, such as waiters, waitresses, bar staff and kitchen staff, is a very heavy drain on the time of the managers concerned, as they are called upon to recruit and train newcomers.* Apart from this, the continuous fluctuations in standards of service cause irritation and dissatisfaction to customers which can only damage the undertaking.

Recruitment advertising in the hotel and catering industry

The quality of recruitment advertising in the hotel and catering industry varies considerably. At one end of the scale, the large companies such as Trusthouse Forte and Bass are able to employ the best of expertise in designing recruitment advertisements. At the other extreme are the small operators who, with no expertise and very limited resources, have to design advertisements which, not surprisingly in many cases, are totally ineffective.

There are those who feel that the industry's recruitment needs considerable improvement; for example Peter Roberts of Leisure and Hotel Appointments

---

*Angus Fisher of Reading University is reported to believe, however, that the retraining costs in the hotel and catering industry are relatively low because of its low technology and minimum skill requirements (*Catering Times*, October 1980).

was reported in *Caterer and Hotelkeeper* (March 1985) as saying that the existing recruitment system does not work, 'It has failed to computerise its services, to take detailed job specifications, to standardise the presentation of curricula vitae, to provide a short list of candidates matched to the "job spec", and to have interviewers with operational experience in the industry.'

On the other hand Peter Morrison, Employment Minister in 1985, pointed out that 20% of all vacancies on the Manpower Services Commission's national computer network of job vacancies (NATVACs) were in the hotel and catering sector. Even so, considerable numbers of employers still do not have confidence that Job Centres can provide them with the quality of applicants they are seeking. The fault frequently rests with the employers who do not provide adequate job descriptions or personnel specifications.

By itself, good recruitment cannot overcome the problem of high labour turnover. This has to be tackled by keeping all conditions of employment under constant review and by making appropriate improvements to conditions as circumstances permit. The nature of the hotel and the catering industry, however, is such that most people holding management or supervisory positions are going to be faced frequently with the need to recruit people to fill vacancies.

Labour markets

In order to recruit successfully, however, it is important to have an understanding of labour markets, in the same way as in promoting products and services it is essential to know the nature of the target markets.

There are two principal labour markets and each has very different characteristics, particularly from a recruitment point of view.

Primary labour market

The primary labour market consists of those people who through education, training and experience are committed to an industry, sometimes even a sector of an industry. In the hotel and catering industry these would include hotel managers, chefs, hotel receptionists, hall porters and cocktail bar staff. Such people intend to develop their careers in the industry and in many cases see their opportunities nationally, even internationally. As a consequence they are mobile, both geographically and organizationally.

Secondary labour market

The secondary labour market consists of people, on the other hand, who have skills of use to an employer, but who do not feel committed to a career in a particular industry. They probably attach more importance to a geographical area than to a career. Typically the secondary labour market contains housewives, students and unskilled working people who choose to work in a particular industry in order to earn a living rather than because of a strong commitment to that industry. The secondary labour market also includes people with skills which may be common to many industries, such as secretaries, maintenance people, book-keepers and accountants.

Employment legislation

In some cases recruitment is the result of, or reaction to vacancies arising, in others it may be related to diversification or expansion and part of a manpower plan. Whatever the reason recruitment plans have to be prepared in the context of employment legislation, which covers issues such as the employment of young people and women, sex and race discrimination and the employment of disabled people (see Chapter 16).

In any event, recruitment is the art of attracting suitable applicants from whom the most suitable person may be selected. It depends upon adequate information being available including full details regarding the conditions of employment and the job to be performed — preferably in the form of a job description.

Personnel specification

From these details a 'personnel specification' can be prepared which is a description of the type of person most likely to be able to carry out the job described by the job description. The precise nature of a 'personnel specification' will depend upon the degree of sophistication or otherwise of an organization, but a comprehensive one should contain the following:

Job title
Sex (see pages 177–8)
Age range
Qualifications
Experience
Personal qualities including such traits as adjustment, motivation and intelligence
Personal circumstances

'Personal qualities' are discussed in Chapter 5.

From the job description in Figure 3.3, therefore, a 'personnel specification' could be drawn up and might look something like Figure 4.1. If considered necessary or useful, distinctions could be made between 'essential' and 'desirable' attributes.

From the information in the job description and personnel specification subsequent recruitment steps can be decided upon.

Figure 4.1 *Personnel specification for a chef*

Job title	Chef de cuisine
Sex	Male/female
Age range	28–50

ESSENTIAL
Qualifications

(a) educational	No formal requirements
(b) technical	City and Guilds of London 706/1/2 or formal apprenticeship
Experience to include	(a) experience in all corners, but in particular in the larder
	(b) experience of controlling a brigade of not less than five
	(c) recent experience of good quality à la carte service (up to 200 covers a day)
Personal qualities	(a) able to control mixed staff of English, Continental and Asian nationalities
	(b) stable employment record (e.g. no more than three jobs over the last ten years)
	(c) above average intelligence
Personal circumstances	(a) able to work late (11 p.m.) about three nights a week
	(b) will have to live out

DESIRABLE

Qualifications	HCITB on job trainer
Experience	Large-scale banqueting

Internal recruitment

The first step always in filling a position is to consider promoting or transferring existing employees. Considerable dissatisfaction can be caused by bringing newcomers in over the heads of present staff, which is often done with the intention of causing as little disturbance as possible to the organization. Unfortunately, because the hopes of some individuals in the organization may be frustrated, they may leave or behave in other unsatisfactory ways and the long-term effect is therefore far more damaging.

It is good management practice, therefore, for all vacancies in a company, and particularly those that may be seen by existing employees to be promotions, to be advertised internally on the staff noticeboard or by circulars. Circulating details to supervisors only is generally not satisfactory as some employees may fear that their supervisors will not put them forward for various reasons.

External recruitment

The next step, if no existing staff are suitable, is to go onto the labour market. This is where most problems arise and where most money and effort are wasted.

The numerous and varied means of recruitment include:

1   Newspapers: national, local and trade.
2   Agencies, including the Department of Employment and the Youth Employment Offices.
3   Executive selection and management consultants.
4   Posters, e.g. on London Underground, in one's own premises, postcards in local Post Office windows.
5   Colleges of Further Education.
6   Armed forces.

The choice of media is critical to success and always depends on the type and level of vacancy and whether prospective employees are part of a local, a national or a trade labour market. Generally speaking the higher level appointments will be advertised nationally; for example, if a company is seeking to appoint an area manager for a group of hotels, the national press such as the *Daily Telegraph* or *The Sunday Times* could be used in conjunction with the trade press. On the other hand, if a waiter or waitress is required, local employment agencies and the local press will probably be adequate.

The likely mobility of applicants is of course vital and in this industry, where accommodation is provided, even less qualified categories of employees are often part of a national labour market and hence are prepared to move large distances. Because of this the trade press can be used effectively. If, for example, a living-in bar cellarman is required, this can be advertised in a trade paper such as the *Caterer and Hotelkeeper* and the *Morning Advertiser* as well as in the local press, and through agencies. Figure 4.2 illustrates some suitable sources.

Advertising

From Figure 4.2 it is evident that a large part of any recruitment can be expected to rely on advertising and, therefore, apart from the choice of media, the drafting of advertisements is important. To recruit successfully these days, in the face of expert competition from other employers, it is no longer enough just to place an advertisement. It has to be a good advertisement. The rules for creating an effective advertisement are:

1   Be honest.
2   Catch likely candidates' attention with a suitable headline.
3   Hold a person's attention by giving clear, factual information including:
    (a)   locality
    (b)   job content
    (c)   prospects
    (d)   qualifications
    (e)   experience
    (f)   conditions of employment
4   Describe what action has to be taken in order to apply.

Figure 4.2 Recruitment sources and media

Staff to be recruited	Sources and/or type of media	Examples
Senior executives, e.g. area managers, regional managers, hotel managers	National press Trade press Consultants Agencies	*Daily Telegraph* *Caterer and Hotelkeeper, Catering Times* Executive selection consultants, 'head hunters' Alfred Marks, Job Centres, Professional and Executive Register
Departmental heads, managers of small units and public house managers	Trade press Specialized sections of national press Agencies Armed services Local radio	*Caterer and Hotelkeeper, Catering Times,* HCIMA Journal *Daily Telegraph, Lady* (for housekeepers, etc.), *Daily Mail* Alfred Marks, Job Centres, Professional and Executive Register Resettlement officers of armed services Capital Radio
Skilled employees, e.g. cooks, waiters	Local press, including London evening papers and Common Market local Press Local colleges Agencies Government Training Centres Rehabilitation Centres BHRCA (foreign employees) Local radio and TV	*Evening Argus, Evening Standard* Alfred Marks, Job Centres
Unskilled employees, e.g. cleaners, porters, kitchen hands, part-timers	Local press Agencies Local colleges Notices and posters Social Services, e.g. probation officers Regional Development Authorities Local radio and TV Salvation Army YMCA YWCA Redundancy areas	*Daily Echo* Alfred Marks, Job Centres, Universities, Colleges of Technology (students) Displayed in local Post Office windows or in own premises

5   Keep the language simple if it is directed at unskilled applicants.
6   Stimulate interest in the employer and promote his image, but remember that the priority is to fill a vacancy, not to advertise the establishment.
7   Avoid box numbers.
8   Avoid meaningless statements such as 'attractive wage' or 'salary according to qualifications'.
9   Test the advertisement on others before finalizing it.
10 Stimulate the reader to act by telling him to call in, write or telephone.

Advertising a vacancy should be the method by which an employer communicates to potential employees that he is seeking to fill a vacancy. If the advertisement is loosely or vaguely worded, it may encourage too many unsuitable applicants or, worse still, it may not attract the most suitable people.

A well-designed advertisement will do more than just communicate basic information, in words; it can, by its graphic design, say a lot about the employer and his style. Bob Payton's advertisement designed by a professional advertising agency illustrates this (Figure 4.3).

Figure 4.3   *Display advertisement*

There is an often-quoted law of recruitment advertising which states that the ideal advertisement attracts only one applicant and that application will be successful. This is obviously overstating the case but it does illustrate the need to think carefully about the choice and content of advertising. After all, the money wasted on ineffective advertising could well have been spent on new equipment, redecorations or even increases in salaries, and others in the organization will not be slow to point this out.

The Chef's position described in Figure 3.3. could be advertised in the form shown in Figure 4.4. This illustrates an advertisement for a skilled person whereas advertising for unskilled people needs a different approach; for example, if advertising for a barman or barmaid it may well be that the person appointed will need no experience, but some personal qualities instead, such as 'good appearance and personality'. For this reason the headline should be directed at *young people* not *barmen or barmaids* (see Figure 4.5).

There are three main ways of inserting advertisements in newspapers: display, semi-display and classified. The examples in Figures 4.3, 4.4 and 4.5

Figure 4.4   *Display advertisement for a chef de cuisine*

An example of an advertisement which sets out to create a good impression of the employer. It says a reasonable amount about the job and encourages people to apply in the simplest way.

Figure 4.5   *Display advertisement for a barman or barmaid*

Local Press

THE SPLENDIDE HOTEL

situated in the centre of Newtown and catering for a busy commercial trade requires

A SMART YOUNG PERSON

to work as a part-time assistant in the cocktail bar. The successful applicant, aged 18 – 30, will assist the cocktail barman on Tuesday to Saturday evenings each week. Once the person appointed is familiar with the work he or she will stand in for the cocktail barman on Sunday evenings. Hours will be 5.45 p.m. to 10.45 p.m. (The Hotel is on several convenient bus routes which run up to about 11.00 p.m.)

No previous experience in bar work is required as training will be given, but the ability to get on with people will be essential. A meal will be provided during the evening and the rate of pay will be £2.50 per hour.

If you are interested telephone Mr A. Smith, Food and Beverage Manager.

Splendide Hotel
Newtown, Newtownshire
Telephone: Newtown (0021) 12345

are 'display' and because they take up the most space and involve the most work they are the most expensive.

The second method is 'semi-display' which gives the advertiser some prominence in the classified section. Often this is all that is required to attract applicants. An example of semi-display is shown in Figure 4.6.

Classified advertising is the least expensive and usually the least effective. This is because a large number of job advertisements are lumped together and consequently are less likely to catch the reader's eye. This is most likely to be the case when trying to recruit unqualified part-timers, because these are often recruited from normal readers who are not looking for jobs and consequently they will not look up the classified columns. On the other hand, a good display advertisement may well attract their attention and prompt them to apply. Many people, after all, have never thought of themselves working in a bar or restaurant, but the advertisements in Figures 4.3 and 4.5 would probably prompt several to apply. Figure 4.7 shows a typical classified advertisement.

Recruitment agencies

In large organizations where recruitment costs run into thousands of pounds a year, it is advisable to retain a recruitment agency. Usually their services cost relatively little as they receive a commission from the newspaper owners.

Figure 4.6
Semi-display advertisement

Figure 4.7
Classified advertisement

**WORKING
HEAD CHEF**

required

for busy 60-bedroomed
Hotel.

Large banqueting suite,
100-cover restaurant
and pub food operation.

Ideal candidate will be
required to form five
commis into a cohesive
team, maintain strict
food cost control and
attain percentages.

Candidate will be
totally responsible for
kitchen cleanliness.

Apply in writing to:
**Managing Director
Osterley Hotel
764 Great West Road
Isleworth, Middlesex**

CVCR25-017

COOK REQUIRED at Sussex House Nursing Home for alternate weekends, hours 8 a.m.-1 p.m. If you are a kind, capable person interested in good home cooking then you may be the person we are looking for. Telephone for an informal chat on Horsham 65356 and speak to Mrs. Stepney, S.R.N., our Director of Nursing. T2 25/26G

Smaller firms, on the other hand, will not be able to offer recruitment agencies enough business for them to be interested, but in this case the newspapers themselves will always give advice and guidance.

Word of mouth

One particular method of recruitment has been purposely left until last because of the unique and important part it plays in recruitment. People in this industry know well the value of 'word of mouth' recommendation. Many highly successful hotels, restaurants and public houses do not need to spend a penny on attracting customers. Their reputation is enough. This applies equally to staff and there are many successful managers who never have to spend a penny to recruit new staff. Consciously or unconsciously, their existing employees recruit newcomers for them.

This method of recruitment is particularly good because of the two-way recommendation. An existing employee is recommending someone as a good employer and the applicant is being recommended as a suitable employee. Recognizing the value of this method of recruitment, some firms actually stimulate it by paying bonuses to employees who successfully introduce newcomers to the firm.

However, for large organizations there can be a risk of running foul of Race Relations legislation, because word-of-mouth systems of recruitment have been found to be discriminatory.

Costs

Recruitment, like any other business activity, costs time and money. Most other business activities are measured in some way and standards or ratios are used to indicate the efficiency or otherwise of the activity.

This principle should apply equally to recruitment if it is a regular and substantial part of the running costs of the business. Where an agency is retained it will calculate the cost effectiveness of various media, but if an agency is not used this should be calculated internally. Figure 4.8 shows a simple form for the analysis of such costs.

Analyses can be much more complex but something along the lines of the form shown in Figure 4.8 will prove sufficient for the average organization to recognize which means of recruitment is the most effective and which involves the least interviewing, correspondence and other administration.

Figure 4.8   *Recruitment costs analysis*

Media	Daily Globe	Evening Star	Evening Star	Blue Agency	Dept. Employment
Job	Chef	Receptionist	Waiter	Waiter	Porter
Cost	£120	£40	£40	£70	
Number of applicants	8	20	4	7	16
Number interviewed	5	12	3	6	9
Cost per applicant	£15	£2	£10	£10	
Number of successful applicants	1	4	2	2	2
Cost per successful applicant	£120	£10	£20	£35	

Recruitment code

Apart from costs, a manager also has wider responsibilities. As a result the Institute of Personnel Management has drawn up the 'IPM Recruitment Code', the main points of which are as follows:

1 Job advertisements will state clearly the form of reply desired (for example *curriculum vitae*, completed application form) and any preference for handwritten applications.
2 An acknowledgement or reply will be made promptly to each applicant. Where consultants are acting mainly as forwarding agents for companies, the parties will agree who will acknowledge applications.
3 Candidates will be informed of the progress of the selection procedure, what this will be, the time likely to be involved and the policy regarding expenses.
4 Detailed personal information (for example religion, medical history, place of birth, family background) will not be called for unless and until it is relevant to the selection process.
5 Recruiters will not take up any reference without the candidate's specific approval.
6 Applications will be treated as confidential.

The full code is contained in Appendix 3.

A manager, as was said earlier, achieves results through the efforts of other people. Without the right people working under them managers are unable to achieve their objectives and therefore it is vital that they spend time choosing the right people. Recruitment is not a chore to be squeezed into the 'normal' working day; it is a vital part of that working day because if it is done properly most of the other tasks become easier.

Further reading

Armstrong, M., *A Handbook of Personnel Management Practice*, 2nd ed., London: Kogan Page, 1984

Courtis, J., *Cost Effective Recruitment*, 2nd ed., London: Institute of Personnel Management, 1984

HCITB, *How to Recruit and Select Young People*, London: 1983

Plumbley, Philip, *Recruitment and Selection*, 4th ed., London: Institute of Personnel Management, 1985

Pratt, K. J., and Bennett, S. C., *Elements of Personnel Management*, 2nd ed., Wokingham: GEE, 1985

Ray, Maurice, *Recruitment Advertising*, London: Institute of Personnel Management, 1980

Selecting Managers, London: joint publication of Institute of Personnel Management/British Institute of Management, 1980

Thomason, G., *A Textbook of Personnel Management*, 4th ed., London: Institute of Personnel Management, 1981

Torrington, D., and Chapman, J., *Personnel Management*, 2nd ed., London: Prentice-Hall, 1983

chapter 5

Selection

One of a manager's major responsibilities is to initiate action but to do this he or she has to receive and interpret information in order to arrive at conclusions that will lead to the right action. The further up the hierarchy of management a person moves the more he exercises the skills of judgement and the less he carries out routine and supervisory tasks. In fact, a senior manager's job is normally devoted almost entirely to making decisions that implement action and to designing systems that enable better decisions to be made. The skill of selecting staff is concerned entirely with this same process. In filling a vacancy a manager obtains information, sorts it, compares it, makes conclusions and implements action. This is illustrated in Figure 5.1.

A manager will use the selection procedure normally for three different occasions:

1 To choose the most suitable person from several applicants to fill one vacancy.
2 To choose the right job from several for an applicant or several applicants.
3 Where there is only one applicant for a vacancy, to decide whether or not to appoint the person and, if so, to know his strengths and weaknesses so that additional supervision or appropriate training can be given, or so that the job can be modified.

In order to do this he should go through the procedure (described in Chapters 3 and 4) which requires a comprehensive job description and personnel specification to be prepared. Correct advertising will have attracted candidates and it is then the manager's job to ensure that information is obtained from candidates in a way that enables a comparison to be made with the personnel specification. From this procedure the most suitable applicant will emerge.

To assist in selection there are a variety of tools available to the manager including letters of application, application forms, interviews, group selection procedures, assessment centres and a range of tests sometimes referred to as psychological tests.

Selection procedures attempt to predict, as accurately as possible, a person's likely performance in a particular job or, where there are several vacancies, the job in which he is most likely to be successful. Most selection methods are of an 'historical' nature, that is they base their predictions on a person's past.

Figure 5.1 *The selection procedure simplified*

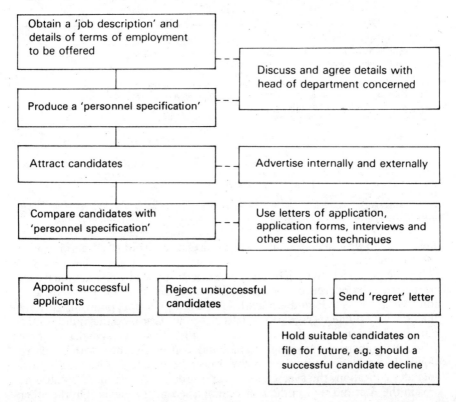

However, most people accept that, economic and human considerations apart, the best method would be to employ a person for a period of time and then, if he proved satisfactory, to offer him the job. This is obviously not a practical method, although 'trial periods' are used both consciously and unconsciously in most industries. Selection procedures, instead, need to be designed in order to elicit the most useful and appropriate information in the most economical way.

In attempting to assess or to measure a person's suitability for a job it is important to know what characteristics are to be measured. The range and descriptions of these characteristics can be vast and in many cases almost meaningless. Some interview assessment forms contain a long list of items including charm, punctuality, honesty, integrity, ability, etc. Many of these are supposed to be assessed (or guessed at) at an interview.

Most characteristics or patterns of behaviour, however, can be grouped under several broad headings and two methods of assessment in particular are of interest. The National Institute of Industrial Psychology has a system that uses seven broad headings and J. Munro Fraser's plan uses five (see Figure 5.2). Both systems are excellent but the five-fold system in particular merits examination here, due to its simplicity. The five-fold system is a technique for

Figure 5.2   *A summary of two of the most popular approaches to staff selection*

THE SEVEN-POINT PLAN (ROGER). The seven-point plan covers:

1 *Physical make-up* — health, physique, appearance, bearing and speech.
2 *Attainments* — education, qualifications, experience.
3 *General intelligence* — fundamental intellectual capacity.
4 *Special aptitudes* — mechanical, manual dexterity, facility in the use of words or figures.
5 *Interests* — intellectual, practical: constructional, physically active, social, artistic.
6 *Disposition* — acceptability, influence over others, steadiness, dependability, self-reliance.
7 *Circumstances* — domestic circumstances, occupations of family.

THE FIVE-FOLD GRADING SYSTEM (MUNRO FRASER). The five-fold grading system covers:

1 *Impact on others* — physical make-up, appearance, speech and manner.
2 *Acquired qualifications* — education, vocational training, work experience.
3 *Innate abilities* — natural quickness of comprehension and aptitude for learning.
4 *Motivation* — the kinds of goals set by the individual, his consistency and determination in following them up, his success in achieving them.
5 *Adjustment* — emotional stability, ability to stand up to stress and ability to get on with people.

---

measuring to what degree an individual possesses each of five points or groups of characteristics.

The degree to which each of these points is possessed by an individual may be measured by reference to the normal curve of distribution. This is divided into five grades, A to E, and subdivided into a total of twenty points. Figure 5.3 illustrates this. The average person falls into grade C around the middle of the curve. Those individuals possessing a higher than average degree of a particular point move into a higher grade and, conversely, those with less move down the scale; for example, in the aspect headed 'Qualifications' which includes education, the average man scores around the ten mark because he was in the A or did well in the B stream of a secondary school. On the other hand someone who obtained three 'A' levels would score about sixteen, and someone who could not do better than average in the B stream in a secondary school would probably score no more than seven. The same principle of measurement can apply to all the points.

Figure 5.3   *The normal curve of distribution*

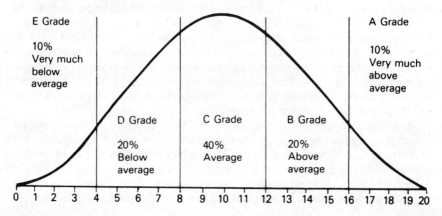

In producing a personnel specification, therefore, inclusion of these aspects with indications of desirable grades or precise requirements would considerably improve the 'pen picture' of the person required. Then during the subsequent selection procedure, candidates should be assessed or measured in the same way, making it a simple task to identify the person with the assessment nearest to the personnel specification. He or she should be the most suitable of the candidates.

This necessarily brief description of the two plans is intended to illustrate broadly two popular techniques that enable a manager about to recruit an employee to indicate and grade specifically the personal characteristics needed to perform a job satisfactorily, thus producing a detailed 'personnel specification'. Readers with a particular interest in interviewing should certainly read the books mentioned at the end of this chapter.

The next step in the selection process is to obtain information from candidates so that this information may be compared with the personnel specification, thus enabling the most suitable candidates to be identified. The least expensive way administratively would be to talk to someone on the telephone and to make an offer at the end of the telephone conversation. It is surprising, in an industry that requires personal characteristics such as tidy appearance and cleanliness, that anyone could be appointed in this way, but they still are. At the other end of the scale are group selection procedures and assessment centres that can last for thirty-six hours or more and involve the employer in very high selection costs. These procedures, however, are normally only used for management or trainee management appointments. Their success rate is usually considerably higher than less expensive methods. 'Success' in this context is measured by labour turnover figures, including 'survival rates' that show how long employees stay with an employer.

Letter of application

Generally speaking it is not possible to use letters of application as a selection method any more than the telephone without the support of an interview. However, well-designed advertisements can ask applicants to give sufficient information from which some candidates can be invited for interview. A typical sentence at the end of an advertisement would read:

> 'Kindly write giving full details including age, education, training, experience, and earnings to . . . .'

To attempt to make an appointment purely on the strength of information contained in a letter is very risky, but if done, references should certainly be taken up first.

Application forms

The application form is used primarily to gather together relevant details so that the selector has this information at his finger-tips and can make fair comparisons with the personnel specification and with other candidates' applications.

When designing an application form it is important to remember that it may have to serve several purposes, such as:

1   Deciding whom to invite for an interview.
2   Being used as an interview assessment form.
3   Documenting employees and obtaining referees' names and addresses.
4   Providing a reserve list of potential employees.
5   Measuring the effectiveness of various recruitment media.
6   Analysing the labour market.
7   Obtaining agreement for medical examination, reference enquiries, etc.

The information required on an application form will, therefore, include some or all of the following:

(a)   Position applied for.
(b)   Personal data: name, address, telephone number, age, sex, marital status, children, nationality.
(c)   Education: schools, subjects studied, exams passed, and further education.
(d)   Professional qualifications.
(e)   Experience: jobs, duties, responsibilities, employers, earnings, reasons for leaving.
(f)   Military experience: branch of the service, rank attained, experience.
(g)   Personal circumstances: when available, prepared to travel or to move, current holiday plans.
(h)   Medical history.
(i)   Interests, hobbies, sports, other activities.
(j)   Record of offences. (Note: This is subject to the Rehabilitation of Offenders Act.)

The exact nature and extent of the information asked for will depend on the type of job and the employer's administrative requirements, but it should be confined as far as possible to information necessary for sound assessments to be made.* It is not appropriate, therefore, for one 'blanket' type form to be used for all job categories. The type of form used for senior executives which asks about professional qualifications and total employment history would not be suitable for an unskilled worker, such as a room-maid, where the last five years' work history may be quite sufficient.

The interview

The next step after candidates have completed and submitted their application forms, or discussed their qualifications on the telephone is to invite selected candidates in for interviews. The interview is the most commonly used method of selection. It is also the most abused because few people are trained in the

*See the recruitment code in Appendix 3.

Figure 5.4 *Application form for non-management positions*
(This is an example of contents — but not of spaces provided)

Application form

Surname

Full Christian names

Address

Dependants

Splendide Hotel
Newtown, Newtownshire
Telephone: Newtown (0021) 12345

Telephone no.   Nationality

Are you a Registered Disabled Person? If yes please give your registration
number

Have you ever been convicted of any criminal offence? If so please give details:

Education *Only complete this section if your full-time education ended less than
5 years ago*

School *last attended*   Exams passed

Details of Further education   Course and exams passed
Other training courses including HCTB courses

Have you been previously employed by this Company? YES/NO If yes please give
dates and position held

Date available   How did you learn of this vacancy?

Details of previous employment — last three positions. If this covers a period of
less than five years give details of other positions held

Name and address of employer	Date		Position	Wage	Reason for leaving
	From	19..			
	To	19..			
	From	19..			
	To	19..			
	From	19..			
	To	19..			
	From	19..			
	To	19..			

I agree to being examined by the company's doctor should a medical
examination be required

I understand that incorrect or misleading information may render me liable to
instant dismissal and that any appointment is subject to satisfactory references

Applicant's signature   Date

Figure 5.5 *A typical application form for management positions*

Confidential

Application form

Job applied for

Reference

Splendide Hotel
Newtown, Newtownshire
Telephone: Newtown (0021) 12345

We realize that to complete this form will involve you in time and effort, but this will help us to be as objective and accurate as possible in considering your application. Information will be treated confidentially and no reference will be made to your present or past employers without prior permission.

Surname   First names
Block letters please

Degrees, professional qualifications, etc
Please state dates obtained

Address

                                  Home telephone number
Place of birth   if convenient

Date of birth   Age

Height

Weight

Marital status   Ages of children, if any

Education

Schools attended	Dates	Exams passed	Year

Further Education: Full-time and part-time

College/University attended	Dates	Exams passed	Year

Present/Most recent appointment

Name and address of employer

Nature of business

Title of appointment   Location   Date appointed

Current basic salary   Bonus   Fringe benefits
including pension, cars, etc.

Please outline your responsibilities, stating to whom your are responsible and
who is responsible to you.

Other appointments commencing with the appointment before that described
above.
Please explain any gaps in employment history.

Year and month from to	Name and address of employer and nature of employer's business	Position held	Reason for leaving	Salary and benefits Starting	Leaving

Medical history   Please give details of any serious accidents, illnesses or
disabilities:

Please set out any further information which you think should be taken into
account in considering your application, including professional, trade or
community activities.

How soon could you be free to take up a new appointment?

What salary do you expect to receive?

Signature   Date

skills of interviewing or take the trouble to develop these skills. Consequently many bad appointments are made because the candidates have not had the opportunity to show their paces, or because the interviewer could not interpret rightly the available information. It is not possible in this book to discuss interviewing in depth, but several excellent books have already been written on the subject (see the list of Further reading at the end of this chapter). In conducting an interview, however, it is important to keep to a plan, see Figure 5.6 for an example, and the simplest method is to follow chronological order — starting at childhood and working up to the present day. Questions normally become more searching as one approaches current or more recent experiences, and must therefore be designed to test fully a person's claimed level of competence and likely level of achievement.

Main types of interview

The most common method is the individual interview, i.e. one interviewer interviews one candidate at a time. Whilst this method usually enables the candidate to relax more quickly, there is the risk of bias or preference — particularly if the interviewer's decision is made independently of other colleagues.

The second method is a panel interview or selection board — very common in the public sector. This will usually consist at least of the line manager concerned and a personnel specialist. This approach reduces the risk of bias, particularly as the panel increases in size. The approach can be varied by candidates being seen individually in turn by each member of a selection panel.

There is one type of interview sometimes referred to as a 'stress' interview. The intention is to create a stress situation to see how an applicant reacts. It is only valid if a person is likely to encounter stress situations, e.g. difficult customers, regularly and such interviews should only be administered by trained interview specialists. Even so there are serious doubts about the ethics of conducting such an interview without giving the candidate prior notice — in which case much of the effect of the stress interview will be lost.

If necessary make notes during an interview, but do explain to the candidate that this is necessary so that nothing of importance can be forgotten. The following *do*s and *don't*s will be useful.

Do
1 Have a clear job description, personnel specification, details of conditions, and an interview plan that contains prepared technical questions.
2 Use a quiet, comfortable room.
3 Suspend all phone calls and other interruptions.
4 Introduce yourself, be natural and put the candidate at ease.
5 Explain clearly the job, conditions of employment and prospects.
6 Ask questions that begin with When, Where, Why, Who, What and How. This avoids receiving 'Yes' and 'No' as an answer and encourages the candidate to talk.
7 Avoid asking unnecessary questions already answered on the application form.

Figure 5.6 *An example of what can be included in an interview plan*

Interview plan

Part 1

Introduction — Introduce oneself, describe position held and responsibilities, give brief description of unit, company, job, conditions, prospects, reasons for vacancy, hours of work, rate of pay.

Part 2

Facts — What made applicant decide to come into the industry? Any connections with the industry, e.g. brought up in hotels?

Life — Where did applicant go to school, college, university? What qualifications did he or she attain? Special interests at school, college, both academic and non-academic. What was the first job after leaving school?

All jobs — Reasons for joining. Reason for leaving. Responsibility when first appointed and upon termination. Earnings when appointed and upon termination. What did applicant think of employer, manager? What was the most important lesson learnt there? What changes could be made? Main problems there. Main achievement there.

General — What is applicant's most important achievement? Hobbies and interests. What is ambition in life — next year, five years, ten years?

Technical expertise — A series of questions to test an applicant's technical knowledge should be asked.

Attitudes (towards, e.g.) — College training/informal training. Recent legal changes. Unions, customers, work, management.

Family — Any domestic responsibilities at home? When available to start? What hours/days prepared to work? Mobility.

At present — Working? Type of job, duties, progress made in that job. Prospects, wages, benefits, reason for leaving, reason for coming to this position. Health, personal and of family. Criminal convictions.

Part 3

Close — Answer applicant's questions. Explain next step in selection procedure. Check on travelling expenses.

8　Listen and let the candidate talk freely, but at the same time guide and control the interview.
9　Encourage the candidate to ask questions.
10　Close the interview firmly and explain the next step in the procedure.

Figure 5.7 *Selection interview appraisal report (for a senior appointment). Source: Croner's Personnel Records 1/86, with kind permission of Croner Publications.*

NAME .... AGE .... APPRAISED FOR ....

INTERVIEWED BY .... DATE ....

1　PRESENT CIRCUMSTANCES:

Firm .... business .... size ....

Position held .... location ....

Salary .... benefits .... pension .... holidays ....

Availability .... preferred location ....

Notice given/received .... other appointments pending ....

Salary expectation ....

Responsible to: ....

Responsible for: ....

a)　no. and type of staff ....
b)　duties ....

Prospects: ....

Reasons for leaving: ....

Reasons for wanting this appointment: ....

2　PERSONALITY AND APPEARANCE:

Appearance: ....

Dress: ....

Self-expression, accent, voice: ....

Manner: ....

Acceptability: ....

3　FAMILY BACKGROUND:

Origins .... married/single .... children ....

Views of candidate and his/her spouse on conditions of employment, including travel: ....

4　EDUCATION:

Type of education .... achievements ....

11 Treat all candidates as though they are potential employees and customers.
12 Write up your assessment immediately after each interview (see Figure 5.7 for an example).

Figure 5.7 *cont.*

5 PROFESSIONAL QUALIFICATIONS:

Type .... place ....

Method of achievement; number of attempts:
....
....

6 EXPERIENCE:
....
....
....
....
....

7 APPRAISAL

Intelligence and ability
....
....
....

Knowledge and experience:
(breadth and depth) ....
....

Career development — salary progression:
....
....

Motivation, personal relationships, adjustment, stability:
....
....
....

Health, outside interests, etc.:
....
....
....

8 RECOMMENDATION:
....
....
....
....
....

Don't
1   Keep the candidate waiting.
2   Oversell the job.
3   Conceal unpleasant facts about the job.
4   Interrupt or rush the interview.
5   Preach to the candidate.
6   Read out to the candidate what is on the application form: he filled it in and knows it already.
7   Ask questions that indicate the answer.
8   Ask questions that only get 'Yes' or 'No' for an answer.
9   Allow the first impression to influence the whole interview.
10 Ask unnecessary personal questions.
11 Raise hopes unnecessarily.
12 Leave candidates with a bad opinion of your organization; they may be potential customers in other contexts.
13 Wait until the end of the day or even till the following day to write up your assessments.

The three 'C's — Contact, Content, Control

Some interviewers evaluate the quality of interviewing by referring to the three 'C's — Contact, Content, Control.

Contact refers to the ability to 'make contact' with the candidate, to develop a rapport. This is achieved by setting out to enable the candidate to relax so that the 'real' person comes through. This is a difficult situation to achieve because for many candidates the interview can be very nerve-racking. However, a number of techniques, usually combined, can help, such as:

Interview in an informal setting, e.g. in a lounge bar but where there are no risks of disturbances or of being overheard

Avoid having a desk between the interviewee and yourself — a desk creates a psychological barrier

Offer a cup of tea or coffee

Invite a candidate to smoke if he or she wishes

Discuss common ground, e.g. a hotel or manager known to both

Use body language, e.g. move towards the candidate to emphasize that you are interested in what is being said

Use encouraging statements such as, 'That's interesting', or, 'Tell me more about that'.

Content refers to the need to ensure that the interview covers all the important ground, including a person's technical competence, ability to get on with others and maybe the ability to take on increased responsibilities. It is particularly difficult to judge a person's future potential but one useful piece of information can be provided by a person's perspective of what is challenging. The question, 'What is the biggest work-related responsibility you have ever had?', can be very informative. One person may answer, 'To have catered for 5,000 at an agricultural show', whereas another candidate may answer, 'To

Figure 5.8 *Comparative career progression charts*

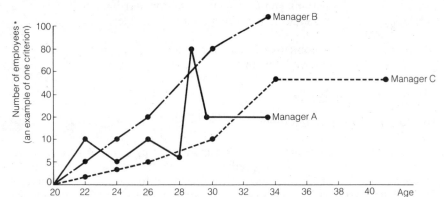

have prepared a cold buffet for 200'. Such answers enable the interviewer, having checked the facts, to determine which of the three applicants is more likely to fit in with the employer's scale of expectations.

Another important piece of information useful in predicting a candidate's growth potential is his career progression chart. From this one can look for growth in responsibility, such as size of establishment, number of subordinates, increase in standards (e.g. star rating) and earnings over a period of time. Figure 5.8 shows three career paths.

Manager A (aged 33) has had an erratic career, manager B (aged 33) appears to be on a growth path whilst manager C (aged 40) has 'plateaued out'. If all three were applying for a positon with, say, around 150–200 subordinates, everything being equal, then manager B appears to be most likely to be suited. Obviously many other factors have to be considered such as the number of job changes or promotions in each person's career and the reasons for the changes.

Another important aspect of 'Content' is to ensure that the interviewer communicates all the necessary information to the candidate, pleasant and unpleasant (e.g. unsocial hours). The interview is, after all, a two-way process.

Control refers to the interviewer's ability to ensure that the interview plan is completed in the time allocated. This will require the skill to guide the candidate through the career and technical questions and to bring the candidate back if he or she begins to wander from the subject without changing the 'Contact' or rapport being built up.

One final rule and a useful one by which an interviewer's skill can be measured is to estimate the amount of time devoted by the interviewer to listening and to talking. Generally speaking the less the interviewer talks, the better he or she is at formulating questions, listening and making the right assessment.

Group selection procedures and assessment centres

These are the specialized techniques and should always be conducted by people trained in their design, operation and interpretation. The purpose of a group selection procedure is to observe candidates' behaviour in a situation or in a variety of situations similar to those they would have to face in the organization. A group selection procedure could include:

1 The analysis of problems with written and verbal reports.
2 Group discussions and debates.
3 Business games.
4 Individual interviews.
5 Tests.
6 'Informal' drinks and dinner.

Group selection procedures and assessment centres are normally used to identify personality traits and to predict behaviour or personality traits that are difficult to assess in an interview or from personal history. These traits may include leadership ability, persuasiveness, self-confidence, ability to stand up to pressure, mental flexibility. They are used both for recruiting new employees (usually senior) and for assessing promotion potential of existing employees.

Psychological tests

The testing of individuals in education, at work and in other aspects of our lives has been going on in various forms for many years. Its main industrial purpose is to help to predict future performance in particular fields by understanding individual and group behaviour. As with other selection procedures testing assists in identifying the most suitable person for a job, and in identifying the most suitable jobs for individuals. As the HCITB's magazine *Service* stated: 'Much of the disappointment arising from failures and drop-outs in training could be eliminated by the use of simple tests of the ability and potential of applicants.'

Most tests can normally only be administered under the supervision of a trained person registered with the National Foundation for Educational Research.

The five main groups of tests are:

1 *Intelligence (IQ) tests* These measure the stage of development of intelligence in children and the intelligence of adults relative to the general population. The mean score is 100. Such tests are commonly used to determine if a person will be able to cope with certain intellectual tasks.
2 *Attainment tests* These measure the degree to which a person has acquired knowledge or skill. A craft test such as the City and Guilds of London Professional Cookery examination is typical. Applicants for jobs such as cashiers, book-keepers or other clerical staff could be given simple attainment tests which could easily be devised by supervisors along with a personnel or training specialist. But it is important, in designing such tests, to recognize that failure to do the test may not indicate total unsuitability, but only a need for training. Many more skill or attainment tests, including those shown in Figure 5.9, could be used in this industry.

Figure 5.9 *Attainment tests — examples of uses*

Example of category of employee	Nature of test
Chefs and cooks	Demonstrate knowledge of recipes and practical skill in making up certain dishes
Waiters and waitresses	Demonstrate knowledge of recipes, the accompaniments for certain dishes, and the service of some complex dishes
Barmen and barmaids	Demonstrate knowledge of and ability to prepare certain of the more popular drinks Demonstrate the ability to compute the cost of rounds of drinks
Cashiers and receptionists	Demonstrate knowledge of some common reception routines, the ability to operate appropriate office machines and to compute typical cash transactions

3 *Aptitude tests* This group of tests identifies an individual's innate suitability for particular types of work and can indicate whether a person would be more suited to one type of work rather than another.

4 *Interest tests* These tests indicate broadly which type of work an individual would prefer, such as: indoor, outdoor, computational, gregarious, individual, routine, creative.

It is important to stress that an interest in, or preference for, particular work need not indicate an aptitude for that work. However, where an aptitude for a certain type of work is supported by an interest in the same type of work the chances of that individual succeeding are much higher.

5 *Personality tests* These tests determine an individual's reactions to different situations from which general conclusions can be drawn regarding likely future behaviour. They are concerned mainly with measuring non-intellectual characteristics. In particular most attempt to measure how a person relates to the world around him and they do this by measuring the degree to which a person possesses certain personality traits, such as drive, stability, persuasiveness, self-confidence, introversion, extroversion. Some personality tests, such as Cattell's 16 PF,* are claimed to be extremely comprehensive, covering all possible aspects of personality encountered in normal individuals. The Brewers Society has commissioned research in this field and tests designed to predict success as a licensee can be validated.

Test batteries

It will be clear that each of the groups of tests mentioned above, with one or two possible exceptions, attempts to measure limited aspects of an individual.

*Raymond Cattell, *Sixteen Personality Factor Questionnaire* (16 PF).

These are intelligence, attainment, aptitude, interests and personality. Each individual employed, however, needs levels or aspects of each of these characteristics and one type of test only may not do him justice. As a result some selection specialists use a battery or variety of tests that measure several of those aspects of a person that may be considered of importance. Additionally, a test battery may be only part of an overall procedure incorporated, for example, into a group selection procedure.

References

It is important to remember that references are only as reliable as the judgement of the person giving them, and because of the fear some employers have of putting a bad or indifferent reference in writing, many written references are worthless. The best procedure for obtaining references, therefore, is to telephone referees and to discuss a candidate's application on the telephone. This discussion should be written up afterwards so that it can be

Figure 5.10   *A reference inquiry letter*

Splendide Hotel
Newtown, Newtownshire
Telephone Newtown (0021) 12345

Dear Sir,

We have received an application for employment from Mr   who says that he was employed by you. It would be very helpful to us if you could answer the questions at the bottom of this letter and return it to us in the enclosed pre-paid envelope. The information will of course be treated in the strictest confidence.

If at any time we can be of similar assistance please do not hesitate to contact us. We hope that this enquiry does not cause you too much inconvenience.

Yours faithfully,

Please delete one

Full name

Position held   Correct/Incorrect

Dates employed from   to   Correct/Incorrect

Reason for leaving   Correct/Incorrect

Would you re-employ him if you had a suitable vacancy   Yes/No

Would you prefer us to telephone you   Yes/No

Would you care to add any comments regarding suitability for the job applied for:

put into the person's file.* Alternatively, a standard letter or questionnaire asking previous employers to confirm certain details can be used, see Figure 5.10.

References must only be sought after a person has been offered an appointment subject to references, as he may not have informed his current employer of his plans to move; unless, of course, he has given specific permission for references to be applied for before being offered an appointment.

Successful selection, that is, placing suitable people into the right jobs, is vital to the prosperity of an organization. But selection can only be successful if it is carried out methodically, and this requires a clear job description and personnel specification, plus a system which ensures that the most suitable candidates are attracted and identified. This will require well-designed advertisements and application forms that elicit appropriate information. Interviews and other selection techniques, as outlined above, will then have to be conducted enabling the assessor to predict, as accurately as possible, a candidate's performance if he were to be appointed. This will involve knowing which characteristics are desirable and it will also involve using techniques that identify or measure those same characteristics.

Careful selection is an investment in team building and while it is more time-consuming than haphazard recruitment, the reduction in labour turnover which normally results, together with the consequent improvement in efficiency and customer satisfaction, make it worthwhile.

Further reading

Armstrong, M., *A Handbook of Personnel Management Practice*, 2nd ed., London: Kogan Page, 1984

BIM Checklist no. 9, *Selecting Staff*, London: British Institute of Management, 1977

Higham, M., *The ABC of Interviewing*, London: Institute of Personnel Management, 1979

IPM, *Towards Fairer Selection*, London: Institute of Personnel Management, 1978

Mackenzie, Davey D., and McDonnell, P., *How to Interview*, London: British Institute of Management, 1975

Pratt, K. J., and Bennett, S. C., *Elements of Personnel Management*, 2nd ed., Wokingham: GEE, 1985

Thomason, G., *A Textbook of Personnel Management*, 4th ed., London: Institute of Personnel Management, 1981

Torrington, D., and Chapman, J., *Personnel Management*, 2nd ed., London: Prentice-Hall, 1983

*Remember that under the Data Protection Act the subject may have the right to see this if the data is on computer.

chapter 6

Appointment and induction

First impressions are often the most lasting impressions, and the first impressions formed by many employees upon starting employment with a new organization are unfortunately not often good. While they may be false, the employee is not to know this. Impressions have been shaped by the advertisement, the interview and interview arrangements, treatment of travel expenses, etc., and new employees arriving to start work are in many cases thrust straight into the job without even minimal introduction to the employer's methods and rules, let alone introductions to colleagues and management. The first hours and days are critical and if properly dealt with can create the right relationship that contributes to employees' staying with an employer. Figure 6.1 shows information from the National Economic Development Committee's research into the industry's manpower and shows the low level of formal induction. This shows that less than 10% of hotel and restaurant managers in the industry actually carried out a formal induction of new employees.

Induction has been defined in the Department of Employment, Glossary of Training Terms (HMSO) 1971 as, 'Arrangements made by or on behalf of the

Figure 6.1   *Induction in the hotel and restaurant industry*

Method	Per cent
None	24
Introduce and show around	13
Introduce, show around, explain rules	30
Introduce, show around, explain rules, give supervised job trial	14
Brief chat	2
Take through booklet describing job	3
Supervised job instruction	3
Special induction course/procedure	8
No response	3
	100

Source: EDC manpower survey — interviews with managers

management to familiarize the new employee with the working organisation, welfare and safety matters, general conditions of employment and the work of the departments in which he is to be employed. It is a continuous process starting from the first contact with the employer.'

As this definition shows, the process of correctly inducting an employee starts even before the formal offer of employment. Even in times of high unemployment there is still competition for well-qualified employees so it is necessary to handle these issues efficiently and with sympathy. When the employer has made a decision, the successful applicant should be told immediately that the employer wishes to make an offer. This should be done, if possible, at an interview (not at the selection interview) or by telephone so that agreement can be reached on the spot about details such as starting date, outstanding holiday arrangements, etc.

Letter of appointment

A formal letter should then be sent off incorporating all conditions of employment and also the job description. An example of a typical letter of offer is shown in Figure 6.2.

This letter satisfies several requirements.

1 It gives the new employee full details concerning the job and conditions.
2 It fulfils the requirements of Employment Legislation by giving the employee details of certain conditions of employment and obviates the need to do this within thirteen weeks of his or her joining.
3 It demonstrates an efficient, businesslike and, by its tone, sympathetic approach that should make the person feel he or she is joining a worthwhile organization.
4 It obtains written acceptance of the offer and also written permission to write off for references.
5 It states exactly when and where the person is to come, and what to bring on the first day.

Documentation

The next step is to arrange that when the employee arrives all documentation proceeds smoothly. This includes obtaining the P45 and, where the employee is to be paid through a bank, the bank's address. A personal file or dossier will have to be opened which will contain all relevant correspondence and documents including the application form and acceptance of offer, and in time a variety of other documents. In larger companies an engagement form should be completed to ensure that no documentation procedures are missed out. This could look like the one illustrated in Figure 17.5 (page 188) and would be produced with sufficient copies for each interested department, including the wages department.

Figure 6.2   *Example of a letter offering employment*

Splendide Hotel
Newtown, Newtownshire
Telephone: Newtown (0021) 12345

Mr J.L. Cook
3 Seaside Gardens
Newtown
Newtonshire

Dear Mr Cook   29 September 1986

Appointment as chef de cuisine

This letter is to confirm the conversation that we had yesterday in which I was very pleased to tell you that your application for the position of chef de cuisine has been successful.

I should like to confirm that you will be commencing employment on Monday 6 October next and that the following are details of the conditions of employment that we agreed.

Your pay is at the rate of £1,000 per month, paid monthly in arrears. All meals will be provided whilst on duty. The company undertakes to ensure that any future changes in the agreed terms will be communicated to you in writing within one month of the change.

Your normal hours of work are forty-five over a five day week. The actual hours will be agreed on a weekly basis with the food and beverage manager. As this is a management appointment there is no entitlement to overtime payments.

Your entitlement to holidays (excluding public holidays) and holiday pay (including accrued holiday pay on termination of employment) is four weeks per annum. Your holiday will fall within the period 1 May–30 September each year, the actual period to be fixed in accordance with the rota drawn up by the hotel manager.

You are covered by the company's sick pay and pension schemes, details of which are set out in the accompanying handbook.

You are entitled to receive one week's notice of termination during the first four weeks of employment, then four weeks for up to four year's service, and thereafter an additional week for each year of service up to a maximum of twelve weeks. You are required to give the company similar notice.

If you have any grievance regarding your employment, you should raise it with your departmental supervisor, either orally or in writing. If the matter is not settled at this level, you may pursue it through the company's grievance procedure, details of which are set out in the accompanying handbook.

This offer is subject to satisfactory references and satisfactory medical report from the company's doctor.

A copy of this letter is attached for you to sign and return to me. I shall treat it both as an acceptance of the offer and permission to write to your referees.

You will find attached a copy of the job description which we discussed at the interview, and if you have any queries do not hesitate to contact me.

In the meantime I should like to wish you every success and happiness with the company and look forward to seeing you in my office at 9.30 a.m. on 6 October. Would you kindly bring your P45 with you.

Yours sincerely

JE Jones

J.E. Jones
General Manager

Enclosures: Job description, details of company schemes covering sickness, pensions, discipline, grievances, health and safety.

Introduction to colleagues, rules, etc.

The second part of inducting new employees is concerned with ensuring that they know and understand what is required of them in order to do their jobs satisfactorily. This includes telling them or preferably showing them the layout of the place of work, introducing them to colleagues and explaining to them the function of other relevant departments. It will also be necessary for them to know about house rules such as 'no drinking' and relevant laws such as licensing hours and 'no smoking' in food areas.

Training needs

The third aspect is concerned with determining the employee's ability to do the job itself effectively and this will depend upon a person's training and experience. No training may be needed, or merely working under close guidance and supervision for a few days may be adequate. On the other hand, detailed training may be required and this is often the case in larger organizations that are prepared to employ untrained people and have standard methods common to many branches.

Induction checklist

Whatever the level of competence, however, it is advisable to use a checklist to ensure that an induction procedure deals adequately with all necessary aspects of induction. In this context it is important to remember that what may not appear important to the employer may be very important to employees. A checklist is illustrated in Figure 6.3.

Where it is discovered that some items mentioned on the list are not provided for in an induction programme, the latter may need to be amended. At the same time this example of a checklist is not claimed to be complete and further items could be added to it.

Induction — each employee is an individual

Introducing staff into an organization inevitably involves some of the mechanistic processes just described, but it has to be remembered that each member of staff is an individual. Precisely how one introduces or inducts each new individual to an organization depends upon many factors, such as the newcomer's experience and knowledge, and the type and level of job he is to undertake. It is vital, however, if induction is to be successful, to try to put oneself in the new employee's place. As Rafael Steinberg writes, 'He arrives unknown. His face is not recognized. His interests and idiosyncrasies are ignored by people he meets. He has suddenly become a number, an anonymous replaceable cog. Quite naturally, without thinking about it, he

Figure 6.3   *Checklist for induction programmes*

When? *e.g. 1st day or 1st week*	*By whom?* *e.g. sponsor or trainer or manager*
1 Documentation Are the following points covered?	Name Address Tel no. Next of kin Name Address Tel no. P45 Bank address
2 Information Are the following departments informed?	Wages/Pensions/Insurance/Personnel/Training/ etc.
3 Terms of employment Are the following explained and understood?	Hours of duty/Meal breaks/Days off/Method of calculating pay Holiday arrangements/Sick leave/Pension scheme/Grievance procedures Rights regarding Trade Unions and Staff Associations Additional benefits such as Group Insurance rates or other discounts
4 History and organization Are the following explained and understood?	Origin and development of the organization Present situation/Objectives
5 Establishment organization Are the following explained and understood?	Layout of establishment including toilets, showers, etc. Names of relevant supervisors and colleagues
6 Rules and regulations Are the following explained and understood?	(a) Statutory: licensing laws and hours, food hygiene, Innkeeper's Liability Act, etc. (b) Company rules: punctuality, drinking, smoking, appearance, personal business, use of employer's property, etc.
7 The job Are the following explained and understood?	Purpose/Methods/Training needs
8 Review of induction	Interview at end of programme to check effectiveness

resists this depersonalization and strives to introduce a measure of humanity to his strange new world.'*

Probably the simplest and most common method of induction is a short discussion in a supervisor's office followed by informal chats. This may be quite practical where a person's superior is readily available. However, where this is not the case, unless a checklist is used, many points may remain unclear for a considerable time.

Another method is the 'sponsor' method in which a newcomer, after an initial talk with his own supervisor, is introduced to an established employee who will 'show him the ropes'. This should not be confused with 'sitting next to Nellie' which is concerned primarily with training and not induction. If this 'sponsor' technique is used, however, the sponsor should be carefully selected to ensure that he knows what his duties are and has the necessary knowledge to carry them out. These would include many of the items listed on the induction checklist. In addition, however, a well-chosen sponsor will introduce the new employee to 'the inner face' of the organization, i.e. informal systems, unwritten rules, etc. A copy of this list should be given to the sponsor who would return it to the newcomer's supervisor once everything had been completed. This might take as little as a few minutes, or could be spread over several days.

Finally some induction programmes make use of formal training techniques in classroom situations. This is normally only used by larger employers that can afford the facilities and these programmes, apart from the initial documentation, may include talks, discussions and films on the company's history, organization, rules and regulations. In addition, a large part of the programme may be devoted to job training.

The advantage of formal systems such as the 'sponsor' and the classroom methods is that because one person is clearly responsible for the induction of newcomers it will normally be organized and conducted properly.

Induction can be considerably simplified by the preparation of clear 'handouts' or manuals elaborating aspects of employment that may need some explanation. Pension schemes and grievance procedures, for example, are ideally explained in written form owing to the amount of detail involved. Many other subjects, too, can be included in manuals such as trade union or staff association agreements, suggestion schemes, holiday arrangements, sick leave and fringe benefits.

What a 'job' consists of

Induction is not something that takes place on the first morning of a new job, it can be a relatively long process, with some people taking many weeks to settle in. This is because every job has two parts to it. First there is the work itself and second there are all the peripherals to the job including conditions and social contacts.

People will not be able to cope with the *work* part of their job unless they

*Rafael Steinberg, *Man and the Organization* (Time-Life International, 1977).

Figure 6.4   *The main elements of a job*

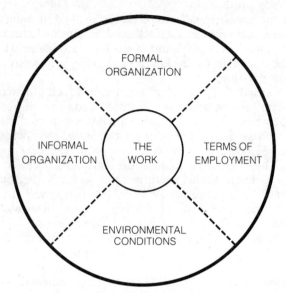

understand and are reasonably happy with the surrounding elements. These include:

Location and physical layout
Colleagues and informal relationships
Management, supervision and formal relationships
Customers
Conditions of employment and contracts
Company and house rules

The induction process is concerned with introducing an employee to all these elements as quickly as possible so that he or she need not worry about them any more. This enables him or her to concentrate on the work which is the main purpose of the job rather than having to learn and worry about all the elements surrounding the work.

Benefits of induction

The employer benefits from effective induction by:

1   Reducing staff turnover.
2   Improving staff efficiency and work standards.
3   Improving staff morale.

The employees benefit by:

1   Fitting in and feeling part of the team.

2 Being accepted as part of the team.
3 Becoming competent and hence confident in the shortest possible time.

Measuring the effectiveness of induction programmes

The purpose of induction procedures is to introduce new employees into the workforce and, with most employers, to reduce the likelihood of the new employee leaving. The effectiveness of induction can be measured by measuring labour turnover in three specific ways. These are:

1 The survival curve which measures an employer's ability to retain its entrants. It shows employee wastage as a curve which can be divided into the induction crisis, differential transit and settled connection.
2 The labour turnover rate, which measures leavers as a proportion of the labour force.
3 The length of service distribution which shows the employer's ability to build a stable team.

These are discussed in detail in Chapter 14.

In meeting the individual's needs it is important to recognize features of the employer's organization and the industry. The hotel and catering industry has a number of features which distinguish it from many other employers and these should be borne in mind when induction programmes are being prepared. These include:

1 The industry employs a large number of people from the 'secondary' labour market, i.e. people who have not trained specifically for employment in the industry such as housewives.
2 The industry has its own traditions and jargon, much of it either based on a highly specialist use of normal words or, in the case of kitchen work, based on French.
3 Immediate customer contact, frequently with little, if any, supervision.
4 Complex interdependent operations, which can be seriously interrupted by one person not performing his or her role properly.

In the obviously difficult field of managing people, comparing human beings with machines should be avoided, but in the use of induction a very useful parallel can be drawn. Time spent in carefully installing and running-in a new piece of machinery usually results in that machinery giving long reliable service. It is as well to remember that in this context most human beings behave in very much the same way as machines.

Further reading

BIM Checklist no. 7, *Induction*, London: British Institute of Management, 1976

BIM Checklist no. 25, *The Employee Handbook*, London: British Institute of Management, 1978

Hornsey, T., and Dann, D., *Manpower Management in the Hotel and Catering Industry*, London: Batsford Press, 1984

Marks, W., *Preparing an Employee Handbook*, London: Institute of Personnel Management, 1978

Wright, A., *Contracts of Service*, London: British Institute of Management Report, 1980

NOTE: The HCITB publishes a large number of useful publications, including: *Staff Induction.*

chapter 7

Appraisal

The appraisal of people at work goes on continuously. Every time a supervisor issues a good word or a reprimand some form of appraisal has taken place. From time to time, however, it becomes necessary for a supervisor to get away from the hurly-burly of the work place and to examine objectively the performance of his or her subordinates. The supervisor needs to do this because the employer should know the strengths and weaknesses of the employees and because employees need to know how they stand. The supervisor should examine each employee's performance against expectations and at the same time consider the person's potential as well. He or she should then decide what steps should be taken in both the employer's and the individual's best interests. This process has several titles but is commonly called 'performance appraisal' and should be an essential part of any worthwhile human resource policy.

The appraisal of employees has one overriding objective and that is to improve the performance of the organization. However, the problem with many schemes is that the appraisal *system* itself takes over and considerations such as salary reviews or training needs analyses override what performance appraisal should really be about, i.e. improved performance. This is acheived by:

1 Identifying both individuals' and group weaknesses and strengths so that weakness can be corrected and strengths developed and built upon.
2 Identifying each individual's hopes and aspirations so that, where these do not conflict with the organization's objectives, they can be satisfied. This is necessary because when most individuals' hopes and aspirations are frustrated for too long they will begin consciously or unconsciously to work against the employer's interest.

From a properly conducted appraisal programme an employer should obtain the following:

1 An analysis of training needs which enables individual and group training programmes to be produced.
2 A succession plan and management development programme that earmarks individuals for promotion and identifies their particular development needs.

3   A reasonably objective basis for salary review.
4   Improved communications.

The individual also benefits by knowing:

(a) How he or she stands and what help is to be given to improve performance.
(b) What his or her career prospects are. (It is advisable not to discuss salary increases during an appraisal interview as this may well reduce the objective note that has to be aimed for.)

There are three main steps in conducting appraisals correctly:

 (i) Having an up-to-date and objective job description, and performance targets.
 (ii) Comparing the person's performance with the job description and targets.
(iii) Communicating and discussing the supervisor's and the person's views regarding his or her performance, and the recording of both the supervisor's and the subordinate's views.

Job descriptions have already been discussed in Chapter 3 and it now becomes apparent why they should contain as many objective, measurable items as possible; for example, if the word 'satisfactory' is used, superior and subordinate may interpret the word differently. On the other hand, if an objective term such as '60 per cent gross profit' is used, neither person can dispute the interpretation of this figure so long as each is clear about what is included in the calculation. In comparing a person's performance with his or her job description, therefore, it is necessary to bring together as much relevant information as possible such as budgets, forecasts and other records.

The appraisal form
The type of form used to record the appraisal is incidental to the interview itself although a well-designed form can help in preparing for and conducting the interview. In cases where the form itself is of more importance than the interview — which is unfortunately only too common — the approach to the management of people is likely to be mechanistic rather than human. It enables the employer to achieve some of his objectives without fully considering the individual's own needs and aspirations. The design of the form, therefore, should be dependent on the purposes of the appraisal, but should contain at least some of the following:

1   Personal details, e.g. name, length of service, job.
2   Performance report covering:
    Knowledge
    Skill
    Application

Initiative
Expression, written and spoken
Ability to plan and to organize
Ability to work with others
Ability to direct others
Specific job targets or objectives and the measure of achievement.
3 Training needs in present job.
4 Potential.
5 Training or development needs if promotable.
6 General salary recommendation.
7 Employee's comments.

Types of appraisal scheme

Some schemes require the manager making the assessment to place ticks in graded boxes, or to award points, as judged appropriate. They are relatively easy to operate, but just how reliable or fair they are is very debatable. They are particularly difficult to use for the assessment of non-quantifiable factors such as personality traits.

In 'written assessment' schemes much greater importance is attached to a freely written report. These types of schemes have the advantage of encouraging the manager making the assessment to think broadly about his or her subordinates rather than limiting them to a form full of boxes.

There are systems that compromise between these two extreme types and which ask the manager to fill in boxes and to write a broad statement as well. One such scheme is shown in Figure 7.1.

Pratt and Bennett (1985) describe three commonly used techniques for rating performance. The first is the 'linear rule' which requires the appraiser to place a tick along a numerical scale or in a box which represents a rating for the characteristics. They point out the distinction which needs to be made between measuring *results*, such as quantity of work, and *traits*, such as reliability. The second technique is known as BARS (Behaviourally Anchored Rating Scale). In this technique people familiar with a job select appropriate aspects of a job and describe examples of behaviour ranging from ineffective to effective along a scale for each aspect. An appraiser can then identify individual performance on the scale. Third, Pratt and Bennett describe management by objective (MbO) which is described in Chapter 3 of this book.

Ideally a system of assessment should reduce the non-quantifiable to a minimum and should concentrate the assessment on objective criteria, so that facts rather than opinions are used as a basis for the interview and report.

The appraisal interview

The next, and the most crucial, aspect of appraisal is the conduct of the interview itself. Some managers find that asking their subordinates to examine and complete an appraisal report themselves makes the situation easier. This is

Figure 7.1   *Example of an appraisal form*

Performance review: Part 1   Confidential
Name of employee   Job   Branch
Completed by   Name   Position
Overall assessment *Put tick in*   Whichever grade you award please
appropriate boxes   elaborate here on this person's
                                              performance:

    Excellent   ☐   Satisfactory   ☐
    Good   ☐   Poor   ☐

Detailed assessment

		Excellent	Good	Satisfactory	Poor	Remarks
For all staff	Technical competence					
	Application					
	Initiative					
	Relations with: Supervisor					
	Colleagues					
	Customers					
For supervisory staff	Ability to direct others					
	Planning and organizing ability					
	Expression: Written					
	Oral					

Performance review: part 2   Confidential

1 Is this person promotable, and if so, what type of job would most suit his/her abilities and aspirations?
2 List what training can be given, or other action taken, to assist in improving performance or preparing for promotion
3 What salary increase would you recommend? Give reasons

    High   ☐   Low   ☐
    Standard   ☐   None   ☐

4 Have you discussed this appraisal with your subordinate? Yes/No
   If no, why not?
   If yes, what were his/her comments?

known as 'self-appraisal' and enables a supervisor to study beforehand a person's views concerning his or her own performance. This obviously means that the supervisor is better equipped to get the best results out of the interview as he or she knows where the person is likely to be most sensitive. At the same time, if the person has identified known weaknesses, the supervisor can concentrate on means of improvement and on the future without dwelling on shortcomings and the past.

Many managers, however, find this approach too liberal and prefer to maintain a more 'normal' superior–subordinate relationship. Unfortunately this can involve the manager in playing two roles — judge and counsellor. This and the associated problems were referred to in Charles Margerison's article 'A constructive approach to appraisal', in *Personnel Management* (July 1976) when he wrote:

Of course, they (managers) recognize that appraising a subordinate's performance and helping him improve it in the future is important. However, for many managers the appraisal interview is embarrassing. They are put in a position of having to make an evaluation of their subordinates and this act in itself hardly leads to a genuine discussion of performance. Once an evaluation has been made, the subordinate is left either agreeing or disagreeing with it. If he agrees, there is little to be said. If he disagrees, there are serious implications.

If I as a subordinate disagree with your evaluation, then I am in danger of becoming a mutineer — I am rebelling against your assessment and in the process putting myself on the side of the revolutionaries. Is it possible for me to contradict my superior when I know that he has the power to influence my future rewards and career?

This conflict in the conduct of appraisal interviews is very difficult for many to overcome, as McGregor (1957) wrote, 'Managers are uncomfortable when they are put in the position of playing God' (Harvard Business Review, 1957), but if the manager can concentrate on the *counselling and problem-solving* rather than making judgements and examining shortcomings, this problem can be overcome to some extent.

Experts in performance appraisal have various ideas on the different types of approach to performance appraisal interviews.

Appraisal styles

Pryor and Mayo (1985) suggest that there are six styles on a continuum consisting of dominating, telling, advising, joint, self-assessment and abdicating. These relate to the interaction between the appraiser and the appraised and can be seen on their Appraisal interaction model in Figure 7.2.

As with selection interviewing, appraisal interviewing is a skilled technique and those responsible for conducting these interviews need training and practice, along with the ability to examine and criticize their own performance. Here are some useful rules to follow:

Do
1 Plan the interview by obtaining all necessary information and by giving the person to be interviewed prior notice of the interview and its purpose.

Figure 7.2   *Appraisal styles*

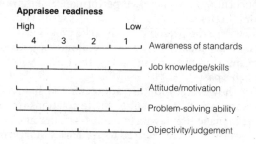

Appraisal interaction model

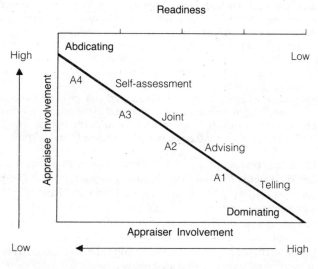

Source: Personnel Management, June 1985

2   Remember that interviews are a means of two-way communication and that the best interviewers do little talking themselves.
3   Suspend phone calls and other interruptions and allow plenty of time for the interview.
4   Put the interviewee at ease and try to make the occasion an informal one. (For example, avoid having the desk between yourself and the interviewee.)
5   Make the interviewee feel that the main purpose of the interview is to benefit him or her.
6   Start by praising strong points. Remember a person's 'ego' and that any subsequent criticism will be rejected as unfair or even untrue unless the balance is maintained by acknowledging good points.
7   Ask for interviewee's reasons for any shortcomings and ask for suggestions for improvement.

8 Finish the interview firmly on a positive note reiterating what performance is expected and what assistance the employee can expect in the form of training or other help.
9 Remember always that giving a person a poor appraisal can be a reflection on the manager's own ability.

Don't
1 Rush the interview. It is one of the most important occasions in a person's working year.
2 Prejudge the outcome of the interview and therefore don't finalize the form until afterwards.
3 Read out the printed form. Your appraisal should come over in your own words.
4 Preach or be pompous. This is an occasion to discuss how a person's performance can be improved with your help.

Small organizations

In the smallest organizations with no more than a few employees a formal approach will be unnecessary and could even disrupt some healthy superior–subordinate relationships. Even so, those employees with potential and prospects should be told of this so that they are less likely, as a result, to go to another employer for advancement.

Appraisal is one of the most personal and potentially unsettling situations that occurs in a working person's life. It is, after all, an examination and judgement of the main role in life and consequently it can be very damaging to the ego. It must therefore be positive, constructive and helpful. It should not be an occasion for apportioning blame or responsibility for past shortcomings or failures. If these are discussed, they should be used as examples to illustrate points from which both sides can learn in order to take steps to build for the future. Appraisal must be creative and must result in new objectives and in agreement on the means by which these objectives can be achieved.

Further reading

Armstrong, M., *A Handbook of Personnel Management Practice*, 2nd ed., London: Kogan Page, 1984
McGregor, D., *Harvard Business Review*, 1957
Pratt, K. J., and Bennett, S. C., *Elements of Personnel Management*, 2nd ed., Wokingham: GEE, 1985
Pryor, R. and Mayo, A., *Personnel Management*, June 1985
Randell, G., *et al.*, *Staff Appraisal*, 3rd ed., London: Institute of Personnel Management, 1985
Thomason, G., *A Textbook of Personnel Management*, 4th ed., London: Institute of Personnel Management, 1981
Torrington, D., and Chapman, J., *Personnel Management*, 2nd ed., London: Prentice-Hall, 1983

chapter 8

Training

One of the features of working life today is that whatever training is obtained at the start, it will almost certainly become redundant or obsolete during the same working lifetime. The need to train, to acquire new knowledge and new skills has become an everyday aspect of each individual's working life. In some cases this may merely be an updating process, but in others it will require a complete change from one occupation to another.

Some jobs and whole industries will disappear and others will emerge. Fortunately for the hotel and catering industry there is no likelihood of the main services it provides becoming redundant in the immediate future. Jobs within the industry may change, but the industry itself is predicted to continue to flourish.

The responsibility for ensuring that working people are equipped to cope with these changes is threefold. The State carries a part of the responsibility, particularly in providing training for school-leavers and for those who need retraining owing to the decline of their own industries, nationally or regionally. This responsibility is discharged by the provision of a variety of training facilities ranging from technical colleges and training centres to numerous types of grant.

From the hotel and catering industry's point of view the government has been instrumental in a number of important initiatives aimed at improving the industry's standards. The most important probably was the establishment in 1966 of the Hotel and Catering Industry Training Board (HCITB), now known as the Hotel and Catering Training Board (HCTB). While many industrial training boards were disbanded in the 1980s, the government decided for a number of reasons to retain the HCITB. These reasons included the obvious growing, even vital, importance to the economy of tourism, and also the tremendously fragmented and still predominantly untrained workforce in hotels and catering generally. The Education and Training Advisory Committee for the hotel and catering industry demonstrated that less than 40 per cent of the workforce, including management, had any appropriate training and that the output of all the college courses would not keep pace with replacement needs, let alone needs generated by the growth of the industry.

Apart from the traditional training work of the HCITB, the government also set up a national scheme for the development of open access and distance learning programmes designed for anyone wishing to acquire technical expertise without having to have prior qualifications and without having to attend conventional college courses. A number of courses have now been developed for the industry, principally by the HCTB and the British Institute of Inn-keeping. These open learning programmes aimed mainly at managers and supervisors without prior qualifications include:

Computing studies
Supervisory skills
Food and beverage management
Licensed house management.

Employers, too, have their share of responsibilities and they discharge these by providing training intended to suit their individual needs, or by participating, as do some employers in the hotel and catering industry, in group schemes, which generally provide a good standard of training quite economically. Some employers provide excellent training, whereas others are quite content to recruit trained individuals from the labour market without putting any trained people into the market themselves. The Industrial Training Act of 1964 recognized this and attempted to stimulate industrial training and to spread the burden over most employers.

Within the hotel and catering industry staff training is steadily becoming more effective. However, the generally high labour turnover still reduces the effectiveness of the training effort, although companies such as McDonald's cope well with the problem. They do this by using extremely well thought out and well supervised training programmes. In addition, like many of the best of the large retailers, they budget for and plan training time into all recruits' work. Their 'crew members' only progress to more responsible roles when they have completed satisfactorily the preceding training.

In contrast many of the industry's traditional employers, particularly the smaller, privately owned businesses, do not implement proper training for a number of reasons:

1   Many proprietors and managers have had no formal training themselves and, therefore, are unaware of the standards that can be achieved and of the benefits of training.
2   Many employers are concerned constantly with immediate operational problems and do not plan ahead.
3   Many are undercapitalized and cannot afford the investment.
4   Many believe that it is the responsibility of others, such as colleges, to provide them with trained staff.

At the same time, however, there is a constant up-grading in the industry and a move towards both 'High Tech' (modern technology) and 'High Touch' (high customer contact) each demanding more training, with the leading employers now putting more resources into training.

The industry's willingness to participate in new schemes of training is encouraging also; for example ten top companies offered 1,600 places on Youth Training Schemes in the year 1983–84. Admittedly only 42 per cent of these were taken up — maybe the result of the industry's image. Other important initiatives include the participation of a number of companies in developing and implementing 'Open Learning' management development programmes. On the other hand major employers do not emulate many other industries in terms of collaboration between themselves and educators; for example sponsorship schemes in the industry are extremely rare.

The third part of the responsibility rests with individuals. No amount of training will be effective unless an individual wishes to make the most of what is available. The State and employers may provide the best of facilities, but it remains ultimately for the individual to make the most effective use of these facilities for the benefit of himself, his employer and the community.

Industrial training is concerned primarily with bridging the gap between individuals' and groups' actual performance and the performance required to achieve an undertaking's objectives. These objectives may include such things as expansion, increasing sales, increasing profitability and improving standards. On other occasions training may be needed merely to maintain the employer's position in the market. However, there are some useful signs, or symptoms, that may indicate a need for training and these include:

1   Failure to attain targets such as gross profit on food or liquor, turnover, net profit.
2   Dissatisfied customers.
3   Slow service.
4   High labour turnover, low morale.
5   Friction between departments such as restaurant and kitchen, or house-keeping and reception.
6   High accident, breakage, wastage rates.
7   Staff unable or unprepared to adapt to changes.

It is not suggested that training alone can solve all these problems. If a hotel or restaurant is badly planned or wrongly situated, no amount of training (apart from training the executive responsible) can rectify this. However, training can often provide the solution or part of the solution.

Training should also consciously try to help individuals to reach the limits of their capabilities and realistic aspirations — so long as these do not conflict with organizational goals.

The main components of training

There are three main components that an individual requires in order to do a job effectively. These components are knowledge, skills and attitudes. Each of these can be developed or improved upon (from the organization's point of view) by effective training. Each component, however, needs a different training approach. Knowledge, for example, can be imparted by talks, lectures and films, but these techniques would prove almost valueless in imparting the second component, skill, such as handling a knife. In this case, practice is necessary. The third component, a person's set of attitudes, is the most difficult to impart or to change, even with soundly based training, and it requires deep understanding of human behaviour by those responsible for training. Training techniques in this field may include discussions, case studies and role playing.

It is agreed, however, by many behavioural experts that because attitudes are extremely difficult to modify it is better to select people with the right attitudes rather than attempt to train people who have wrong attitudes.

In order to design effective training programmes the following principles must be known and understood:

1 Training can only be successful if it is recognized that learning is a voluntary process, that individuals must be keen to learn and consequently they must be properly motivated; for example, if trainee waiters are losing earnings in the form of tips in order to attend a course, they may well begrudge the time and therefore may be unwilling to participate actively.
2 People learn at different rates and, particularly in the case of adults, often start from different levels of knowledge and skill and with different motives and attitudes.
3 Learning is hindered by feelings of nervousness, fear, inferiority, and by lack of confidence.
4 Instruction must be given in short frequent sessions rather than a few long stints; for example, if a trainee is being instructed in the use of kitchen knives, ten lessons lasting forty-five minutes are obviously far better than one lesson lasting seven and a half hours.
5 Trainees must play active roles — they must participate; for example, lecturing puts the trainees into a passive role, whereas discussions or practical work give them active roles.
6 Training must make full use of appropriate and varied techniques and of all the senses, not just one, such as the sense of hearing.
7 Trainees need clear targets and progress must be checked frequently.
8 Confidence has to be built up by praise, not broken down by reprimand. Learning has to be rewarding.
9 Skills and knowledge are acquired in stages marked by periods of progress, 'standstill' and even a degeneration of the skill or knowledge so far acquired. Instructors must know of this phenomenon ('the learning curve'), as it can be a cause of disappointment and frustration for many trainees.

These principles of learning illustrate and emphasize that it is both difficult and wasteful to treat individuals as groups. So far as possible training needs to be tailored to suit individual needs. The techniques to be used depend on a variety of factors, including whether it is knowledge, skills or attitudes that are to be imparted and whether individuals or groups are to be trained. The two main approaches are 'on the job' and 'off the job' training.

On the job training

In the hotel and catering industry much of the staff's work is performed in direct contact with customers. For this reason much of the training of new staff has to be performed 'on the job' so that experience of dealing with customers can be obtained. 'On the job' training, therefore, plays a vital part in the industry's approach to training. If handled correctly, it can be very effective for the teaching of manual and social skills, but it requires that training objectives are clearly defined and that those responsible for instruction are proficient in training techniques. Unfortunately, newcomers are often attached to experienced workers who are not in any way equipped to train others. This is often referred to as 'sitting next to Nellie'. Apart from not having a suitable personality, they may not even have been told what to instruct and what not to instruct. Instead, if experienced workers are to be entrusted with the training of newcomers they should be chosen because of their ability to deal sympathetically with trainees, because of their knowledge of the job itself. They should then be given appropriate instructor training* before being asked to train newcomers. The progress of trainees should be checked from time to time by the person responsible for training. Responsibility for training should not be abdicated to the instructor. An example of an 'on the job' training programme for a cocktail barman is shown in Figure 8.1.

Note that the programme in Figure 8.1 is in progressive stages. It requires each phase to be completely covered before the next is started. In addition, this particular programme is only a checklist and therefore presupposes that the instructor already has the detailed knowledge. Because of this, in many cases it will be necessary to expand this type of list by specifying in a document such as a training manual exactly what has to be instructed under each new heading. Appendix 7 is an abridged version of a short book on training 'on job' or staff trainers.

Off the job training

'Off the job' training takes place away from the working situation. A variety of methods and techniques may be used but the particular choice will depend on what is to be imparted. The main methods are listed below:

1　*Talks* are best used for imparting knowledge such as company history and policies, legal matters, regulations, recipes, and an outline of methods and procedures. In giving a talk, progress must be checked frequently by use of questions and answers.
2　*Discussions* are best used to elaborate on and to consolidate what has been imparted by other techniques.
3　*Lectures* often mean little more than talking at trainees and are therefore to be avoided as there is usually little trainee participation.
4　*Case studies, projects, business games* are best used to illustrate and to consolidate principles of management such as planning, analytical techniques, etc.
5　*Role playing* is best used to develop social skills such as receiving guests, handling customer complaints, selling, interviewing or instructional techniques. Ideally this should be supported by tape recordings and closed circuit television recordings, if possible.

*Generally with the HCTB or on an HCTB approved course.

Figure 8.1 *Example of an 'on the job' training programme for a cocktail barman. (This is basically a list of duties and tasks)*

First stage

1 Bar preparation and cleanliness (a) Washing down of bar counter, bottle shelves
(b) Polishing of mirrors, glass shelves
(c) 'Bottling up'
(d) Use of counter towels, drip mats and trays
(e) Preparation of accompaniments including lemon, olives, cherries
(f) Use of beer dispense equipment

2 'Cash' (a) Price lists
(b) Use of cash register
(c) Cheques and credit cards
(d) Charging to customer accounts
(e) Computation of costs of rounds and 'change giving'

3 Main points of law (a) Licensing hours and drinking up time
(b) Hotel residents and guests
(c) Adulteration
(d) Weights and Measures Act

4 Service of simple orders (a) Beers, wines by the glass
(b) Spirits and vermouth with mixers
(c) Use of accompaniments such as ice, lemon, cherries
(d) Cigarettes, cigars

Second stage

1 Bar preparation and cleanliness (a) Requisitioning of stock
(b) Cleaning of beer dispense equipment
(c) Preparing weekly liquor and provisions order

2 'Cash' (a) Checking float
(b) Changing till roll
(c) 'Off sales'

3 Further law (a) Betting and gaming
(b) Young persons
(c) Credit sales of intoxicating liquor

4 Service of simple mixed drinks (a) Shandies
(b) Gin and Italian, gin and French

Third stage

1 Bar preparation and cleanliness (a) Rectification of faults such as 'fobbing beer', jammed bottle disposal unit
(b) Preparation for stock taking

2 'Cash' Cashing up

3 Service of all drinks contained in house list (a) Knowledge of recipes
(b) Use of shaker and mixing glass

6 *Films, charts, and other visual aids* should not normally be used as instructional techniques by themselves, but should support talks, discussions, case studies and role playing. Films on a variety of hotel and catering subjects are obtainable from several training organizations.

7 *Programmed texts and teaching machines* have a considerable future because they satisfy many of the principles of learning (mentioned on page 107). In addition, they can be used by individuals at any convenient time — not requiring the presence of an instructor. They cannot, of course, be used to teach some things such as manual skills and they can be very expensive to design.

An example of a fairly typical 'off the job' programme for cooks is shown in Figure 8.2.

Figure 8.2   *Example of first day of an 'off the job' training programme for cooks employed by a firm with many establishments offering standardized service*

Time	Subject matter	Method of instruction
9.00 / 9.45	Company history Present organization and objectives Personnel policies	Talk, discussion and film
9.45 / 10.30	Kitchen equipment; cleanliness, safety, uses	Demonstration and discussion
10.30 / 11.00	Hygiene	Film and discussion
11.00 / 11.15	Coffee	
11.15 / 12.00	Principles of cookery; grilling	Demonstration and discussion
12.00 / 1.00	Portioning, preparation and presentation	Demonstration and practical work
1.00 / 2.00	Lunch	
2.00 / 4.00	Practical cookery	Practical preparation of simple dishes
4.00 / 4.15	Tea	
4.15 / 5.00	Costing and portion control	Talk and discussion
5.00 / 6.00	Clearing up	

Training needs analysis

Having looked at what training attempts to do, at the main principles of learning and at the main techniques available, the next step is to consider the design of training programmes. This starts with an identification of training needs, sometimes referred to as a 'training needs analysis', which is conducted by the person responsible for training in consultation with line managements. It should attempt to identify those *problems and opportunities* that line management could solve and exploit with the assistance of appropriate training. It should be produced by studying the training needs of individuals as identified in 'appraisal reports', and by detailed discussions with the line managers. The individual's job description, actual performance and potential should be the basis for these discussions together with organizational plans for the future.

From the consolidation of individual training needs will emerge organization or corporate training needs. Some will be 'essential' and some 'desirable'. These priorities should be laid down by senior management and will consequently fit in with the undertaking's business objectives.

In the case of an industrial catering contractor or of a group of restaurants, for example, there may be plans to expand the number of units and in order to do this a variety of key staff for the new units will be needed over a given period of time. It will be important, therefore, to identify those people who can be transferred or promoted and the training that will be needed in order to prepare them. This may range from preparing some assistant managers for full management to preparing junior kitchen hands to take over some more skilled responsibilities such as cooking.

The question of having sufficient trained personnel to fit into expansion plans is a critical one to the successful growth of an organization and it is one area where the training function together with effective recruitment can prove to be of considerable value to a company.

All training needs obviously do not emerge from the annual training needs analysis. They also arise from unexpected changes in trading conditions or business emphasis; for example, many restaurant operators do not pay sufficient attention to the profits that can be generated by liquor sales. In this case, if a company decides that sales of drinks are to be promoted, effective training of waiters and waitresses in product knowledge, service and selling techniques can play a big part in boosting sales and profits. Likewise, a brewery may change its emphasis from running tenanted houses to running managed houses. In this case it will have to recruit and train managers to run the public houses; it will also have to train district managers in the supervision of managed houses.

The identification of training needs process may identify training needs in three broad areas. The first is the organization's needs; for example, improved customer relations. Such a need may affect all employees. The second need is a group need; for example a particular group of employees such as head receptionists may need training in maximizing room occupancy. The third is that of individuals; for example the proposal to computerize the payroll could result in the need for the payroll clerk to be trained in appropriate computer skills.

Figure 8.3　*Identifying training needs*

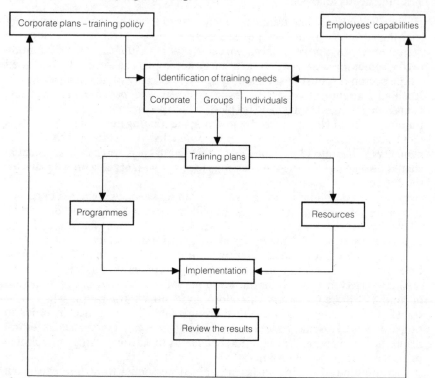

Line management support

It is vital that line management is seen to support training by participating in it as far as possible, because if all instruction is left to the training staff an undesirable gap can develop between line management and the 'teachers'. The best way to overcome this is to ask line management, such as unit and departmental managers, and the most skilled operators, such as chefs and wine-waiters, to be trained to take some teaching sessions. This ensures that the instruction given is in line with working requirements and conditions, but, of more importance, it persuades line management that training personnel are working with and for line management.

The subject of training is very extensive and because of this in some cases it becomes an 'end' in itself rather than a means to an end. It is therefore vital for it to be seen in perspective.

Training is one of the tools of management that should be used to increase an employer's efficiency. It enables the undertaking's goals to be achieved by properly equipping its personnel with the knowledge, skills and attitudes necessary to achieve those goals. But at the same time training should also enable individuals to achieve whatever realistic aspirations they have in their work by enabling them, through increased competence and confidence, to earn more and to gain promotion.

Organizations that can be of assistance in the training field are listed in Appendix 5.

Further reading

Armstrong, M., *A Handbook of Personnel Management Practice*, London: Kogan Page, 1984

Boella, M. J., *Effective Staff Training*, Brighton: Brighton Polytechnic, 1986

Donnelly, E., Kenny, J., and Reid, M., *Training and Development*, London: Institute of Personnel Management, 1986

Pratt, K. J., and Bennett, S. G., *Elements of Personnel Management*, 2nd ed., Wokingham: Van Nostrand Reinhold, 1985

Singer, E., *Training in Industry and Commerce*, 2nd ed., London: Institute of Personnel Management, 1977

Thomason, G., *A Textbook of Personnel Management*, 4th ed., London: Institute of Personnel Management, 1981

Torrington, D., and Chapman, J., *Personnel Management*, 2nd ed., London: Prentice-Hall, 1983

NOTE: The HCITB publishes a large number of useful publications, including:

1 *Planning Your Training*
2 *Implementing Your Training*
3 *Reviewing Your Training*
4 *Staff Induction*
5 *Health and Safety*
6 *On-the-Job Training*
7 *A Guide to Systematic Training*
8 *Training Your Staff*

chapter 9

Management development

As we saw in the preceding chapter on training, one of the main concerns of senior management is to improve continuously the performance of those employed in the undertaking, but it should go without saying that training can only be effective if the right people are available to be trained. The well-being of any undertaking depends upon its staff and, in particular, on its management. Senior managers, therefore, have a vital responsibility to ensure that suitable people are available and are being developed to succeed to management posts as they arise.

Management development may be defined as those activities designed to provide the organization with a competent management team which is able to meet its short-, medium- and long-term objectives. These activities should include:

The improvement of managers' techniques in planning and controlling the organization's structure and resources.
The acquisition of new information on the environment.
Helping managers adapt their attitudes or mental modes.
(After Dr Graham Milborrow, *Management News*, June 1985.)

In addition an organization needs to plan for natural replacement caused by retirements, resignations, deaths, etc., and it needs to ensure that sufficient competent management is available for expansion plans. However, in a healthy organization these plans must also extend to satisfying an individual's reasonable aspirations; for example, if an employer stands in the way of an employee's trying to obtain a recognized qualification by not allowing adequate time off, the employee will almost certainly place his qualification before his job and will seek an employer who will assist him. Plans that only accommodate the employer's needs will result in dissatisfaction, frustration, low morale and high labour turnover.

The senior management of an organization must therefore ensure that adequate plans and resources exist to recruit, motivate, train, develop, and retain its existing and future management. This is all part of the management development role, but in this chapter only the planning of management succession and the development of individual management skills will be discussed. Other aspects of the full management development function such as recruitment, induction and appraisal have been dealt with in other chapters.

Figure 9.1 *A management succession or replacement form*

Position	Present job holder	Most suitable replacement *Put present job in brackets*	Second recommendation *Put present job in brackets*
Hotel Manager (Splendide)	J. Jones	A. Smith (Food and Beverage Manager, Splendide)	R. Barker (Front Office Manager, Grand)
Promotion potential		Ready for promotion	Promotable with training
Training and/or development needed		None	Food and beverage experience needed
Signed by	J. Jones	Date	20/1/86
Approved by	J. Walker	(Area Manager)	

A succession plan

This is produced simply by comparing future management requirements with currently available management. In order to do this, organization charts should be drawn up which show the structure of the undertaking at the present time and at various future dates, for example, three months, one year, three years, five years. Each job shown may have two boxes immediately next to it or under it in which the names of suitable successors can be inserted. A replacement form is shown in Figure 9.1, and a succession chart in Figure 9.2.

The names shown in Figures 9.1 and 9.2 would result from discussions between the most appropriate levels of management, using appraisal reports as a basis. This emphasizes the need for a section on promotion potential to be included in the appraisal report.

So long as the basis for discussion is that replacement will be due to normal retirement, accident or the voluntary departure of the incumbent, the most appropriate levels of management to be involved in discussions will be:

1 The present holder of the job for which a replacement is being discussed.
2 The present job holder's superior.
3 The superiors of those proposed as replacements.
4 A member of senior management fully aware of future plans.
5 A personnel specialist (if one is employed).

Figure 9.2   *A succession chart*

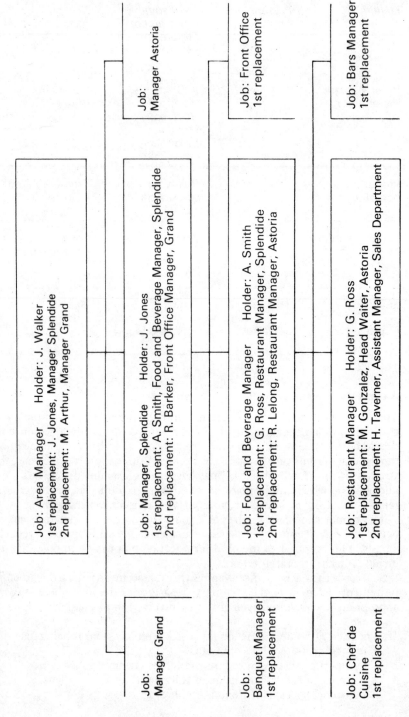

Job: Area Manager   Holder: J. Walker
1st replacement: J. Jones, Manager Splendide
2nd replacement: M. Arthur, Manager Grand

Job:
Manager Grand

Job: Manager, Splendide   Holder: J. Jones
1st replacement: A. Smith, Food and Beverage Manager, Splendide
2nd replacement: R. Barker, Front Office Manager, Grand

Job:
Manager Astoria

Job: Banquet Manager
1st replacement

Job: Food and Beverage Manager   Holder: A. Smith
1st replacement: G. Ross, Restaurant Manager, Splendide
2nd replacement: R. Lelong, Restaurant Manager, Astoria

Job: Front Office
1st replacement

Job: Chef de
Cuisine
1st replacement

Job: Restaurant Manager   Holder: G. Ross
1st replacement: M. Gonzalez, Head Waiter, Astoria
2nd replacement: H. Taverner, Assistant Manager, Sales Department

Job: Bars Manager
1st replacement

In some cases one person will fulfil more than one of these roles. The final plan, particularly for the more senior levels, must carry the approval of senior management.

In order to identify likely successors in the first place it is usual to ask each member of management to nominate those he or she considers to be most suitable as successors. However, where this is done it must be recognized that there may be the danger of rigid departmental career paths, whereas in some cases, interdepartmental transfers and promotions will be more desirable in order to broaden experience.

In the largest organizations which are broken down into regional or functional operating companies, the danger of 'sitting on' talent, consciously or unconsciously, has to be avoided. This can be achieved by all management above a certain level of seniority being dealt with as a 'group resource', in which case appraisals and other management development processes will be monitored by a central department.

Development of managers

As well as a succession plan, individual training and development programmes have to be designed. It is here that an understanding of how a manager acquires his knowledge, skills and attitudes is vital. People do not become managers in a classroom, although they can acquire much of the necessary knowledge and basic skills there. Most of their expertise is obtained in the hard practice of managing people in the work place. A management development programme must therefore contain a balance of formal training and planned experience. It is not something that operates for one period only of a manager's life. It is updated every year and continues throughout a manager's working

Figure 9.3 *Example of a career path for a young executive*

Year	Approximate age	Position
1	21	Trainee management programme, various departments and establishments
2 3	22 23	Junior supervisory position, e.g. assistant manager/ess of a hotel or restaurant
4	24	Specialized function, e.g. new projects department, sales office, training department
5	25	Line management, e.g. unit management, food and beverage management
6	27	Specialist function, e.g. sales management, training officer
7	28	Assistant to area manager
8	30	Line management, e.g. manager of medium to large unit, area manager

life. Over a period of years, therefore, a programme may include spells in line management and in various specialist departments; for example, a young executive's first ten years with a company could be shown as in Figure 9.3.

During this period the executive may also attend a dozen 'off the job' courses on such subjects as:

Supervisory skills
Budgetary control and forecasting
Techniques of instruction
Interviewing and selection techniques
Project planning
Finance for non-financial executives

Whether these are internal or external courses depends on the needs of the organization and the individual. Generally speaking, internal courses are more precisely designed to satisfy the needs of the organization, whereas external courses have to be broadly based to appeal to a wider market.

The value of external courses lies to a great extent in the opportunity to exchange views with managers from other organizations, but this only has value if those attending can bring about organizational changes. This prerogative normally lies only with more senior managers and therefore the value of external courses probably increases with the seniority of those attending (so long as they are geared to their needs).

The more junior people will be mainly concerned with acquiring knowledge and skills appropriate to their employer's needs and, so long as the numbers justify it, these courses should be run internally which ensures that only relevant matter is covered.

The British Institute of Management in 1985 reported that, 'there is a growing body of opinion which favours in-company courses — they argue that the "grape-shot" approach to cover a multitude of interests is not cost effective.'

Trainee management courses

As the first step in a young manager's career, the design of trainee managers' courses is critical. It is in the first months that the basis of knowledge and skills and, in particular, an understanding of the employer's attitudes and values will be formed. During this period, however, unless worthwhile targets are set and some experience of supervision is obtained, most trainees will feel frustrated. For this reason there are many critics and opponents of the traditional 'Cook's tour' involving spells of training in the most important departments. In some cases this criticism is well deserved because no objectives are laid down and the trainees are merely used as cheap labour, or not used at all.

However, in order to be a successful manager, knowledge and experience of certain departments are vital and the well-designed 'Cook's tour' serves this purpose; at the same time objectives must be agreed with departmental supervisors and trainees must be given their training objectives in written form. They should not move from one department to the next until departmental training objectives have been attained. Trainees should maintain training logs or diaries and, in addition, they should be given projects. Regular progress interviews should be held to ensure that the trainees' objectives are being achieved.

In considering an individual's development programme, which is updated and modified year by year, it is vital to examine both 'strengths' and 'weaknesses', remembering that they may well be strengths and weaknesses only so far as the employer is concerned. In another type of organization the same characteristics may be seen in a completely different light. Ideally the weaknesses should be corrected and the strengths built upon. However, this will not always be possible because some 'weaknesses' may not be merely lack of knowledge or skill but of a 'personality' nature and these are often very difficult to correct even if it were in the individual's interest to do so. For example, a highly creative person may prefer to work as an individual. He or she may not enjoy or wish to work with others, nor to control them. The 'weakness', so far as the employer is concerned, is that he or she cannot direct or lead others, so the employer decides to give the individual 'a spell managing others' to make him or her into an 'all-rounder'. In some cases this may work out, but in others it could have disastrous results, with the person concerned eventually leaving. Equally damaging, the individual could unsettle subordinates, whom, it must be remembered, he or she may not have wanted to control in the first place.

It is vital, therefore, in designing management development programmes to recognize those 'weaknesses' that can be corrected and those that cannot. It is far better to build on strengths and to provide opportunities for these to be developed and exploited to the utmost, rather than to try to compensate for 'weaknesses' that may only be weaknesses in the employer's mind in any case.

The future of management development

Obviously management development will continue to be concerned with the development of an individual's functional skills. In addition, however, managers will need to develop their own 'cross-functional' abilities, learning more about other functions.

New subject areas are emerging; for example, there is the need to manage information, not just administratively or operationally, but also strategically; and, as change becomes the norm, managers need to develop their abilities to manage change.

Increasing competitiveness and employees' increased expectations too, demand that managers should be more professional in their human resourcing skills such as selection, appraisal, motivation and communication.

Management development itself is going through some radical changes but if it is to achieve anything, 'management development must be an exciting change agent. It must be a catalyst whose presence helps us to better exploit [sic] opportunities facing our enterprises more creatively, more quickly and more effectively . . .' (Dr Graham Milborrow — Director of BIM's Management Development Services Division).

Further reading

Armstrong, M., *A Handbook of Personnel Management Practice*, 2nd ed., London: Kogan Page, 1984

Pratt, K. J., and Bennett, S. C., *Elements of Personnel Management*, 2nd ed., Wokingham: GEE, 1985

Thomason, G., *A Textbook of Personnel Management*, 4th ed., London: Institute of Personnel Management, 1981

Torrington, D., and Chapman, J., *Personnel Management*, 2nd ed., London: Prentice-Hall, 1983

chapter 10
Job evaluation

In many industrial disputes the levels of pay, the methods of calculating payment or the pay differentials existing between jobs are the underlying causes, but in the hotel and catering industry industrial disputes are rarely identified as such owing to the limited extent of organized labour. There are few strikes, so that what industrial action there is takes a different form, showing itself in dismissals, dissatisfaction, resignations or walk-outs, and institutionalized pilferage.* In this industry wage levels are frequently determined by expediency rather than by any form of methodical approach. Newcomers are sometimes recruited and paid more than existing staff doing the same job. Also many staff leave jobs because their employers refuse to grant increases even though the employers know that they will have to pay replacements more than the employees who have left. It is only in the most recent times that any significant efforts have been made to introduce job evaluation, and it is probably the realization that the involvement of unions could cause havoc for employers where wages are determined unsystematically, which has caused some employers to turn to job evaluation.

A methodical, fair approach to the award of wages and salaries is vital to a harmonious relationship between employers and employees. In organizations of any reasonable size, this can probably only be achieved if the relative value of each job is recognized and to do this a system of ranking jobs in order of importance needs to be used. It is important that a person, such as a chef, who has completed an apprenticeship and has acquired knowledge and skill should be paid more highly than a person whose job needs little knowledge or skill. It is simple to distinguish between jobs with skill and those without, but the problem arises when comparing jobs which are less easily differentiated; for example, when comparing those of a cook and a waiter. Both demand particular skills and knowledge but management has to decide whether to award more, and how much, to one rather than the other. A system of comparison that embraces all jobs within an enterprise needs to be adopted to ensure that wages are distributed fairly. Such a system, usually called 'job evaluation', provides a sound basis for comparisons to be made. Some systems attempt to be objective and analytical, whereas others are somewhat

*See *Room for Reform*, Open University.

Figure 10.1a   *Job evaluation: non-analytical methods*

Title	Broad description	Advantages	Disadvantages
Ranking	A simple method whereby the relative importance of the total job is assessed. Jobs are put in order of importance and may then be divided into groups	Very simple to use	Assessors need to know all jobs in some depth
Grading or classification	A simple method in which a grading structure indicating relative job values is designed. Each job is then placed within the most appropriate grade	Very simple to use	Assessors need to know all jobs in some depth. Marginal jobs may be placed in higher or lower grade because system may not be sufficiently discriminating.

Figure 10.1b   *Job evaluation: analytical methods*

Title	Broad description	Advantages	Disadvantages
Points assessment	A commonly used and very acceptable method. Factors common to most jobs in the organization are identified such as knowledge and responsibility. Maximum points are allocated to each factor weighted according to importance. Each job examined is broken into the various factors. Each factor is then awarded points between zero and the maximum. The total of points awarded will give the score for the job and thereby its standing relative to other jobs. Bench-mark jobs will be used to assist in allocating points	Simple to understand and operate	Takes longer to implement than ranking or grading. It can lead to considerable discussion on weighting of factors

Figure 10.1*b* *Job evaluation: analytical methods — cont*

Title	Broad description	Advantages	Disadvantages
Factor comparison	Similar in some respects to points assessment but in some cases monetary values are used instead of points. Fewer factors, also, will normally be used than in points assessment. Bench-mark jobs will normally be used	Simple to operate once it has been designed	Difficult to arrive at monetary values
Direct consensus method or paired comparisons	A complex technique where evaluators representing all interested parties are asked to indicate which job of a pair or which factors within pairs of jobs they consider more important. The evaluators will probably deal with several or even many jobs. The paired comparisons of all evaluators may then be fed into a computer which will produce the ranking of all jobs considered.	Reduces individual subjectivity to a minimum	Complex, usually needs a computer
Time span of discretion	This technique measures one factor only: the length of time in which an individual's work or decisions remain unchecked, e.g. a typist four hours, a managing director four years	Simple, once the concept has been fully understood	Sometimes difficult to determine true discretion span

subjective, but if managed properly they can be equally successful. Job evaluation may, therefore, be defined as the process which establishes the relative value of jobs in a jobs hierarchy.

There are considerable benefits to be derived from introducing an effective job evaluation system and these include:

1   Less staff dissatisfaction caused by unfair pay and, consequently, lower labour turnover.
2   A logical basis for setting all wage levels, enabling the starting rate for newcomers and annual merit awards to be determined without upsetting existing employees.
3   A rational basis for differentials, that is the difference in pay for doing different jobs, making promotion and transfers easier.
4   Ease of producing labour cost forecasts. Where there is no methodical system it is more difficult to predict labour costs.

Symptoms that can indicate a need for methodical job evaluation can include:

(a)   Employees leaving because wages are not awarded fairly and, in particular, because some newcomers earn more than long-serving employees.
(b)   No formal periodic review of wages or salaries.
(c)   Difficulties, due to wage levels, in transferring and promoting employees.
(d)   A need to pay 'extras' or bonuses to get people to do what is, or should be, part of their normal job.
(e)   Some employees working excessive overtime.

In order to carry out effective job evaluation precise job descriptions and even job specifications are required because without these the comparison of jobs becomes difficult, if not meaningless. Also, because comparisons of jobs are to be made, the preparation of job descriptions, must be standardized throughout the undertaking, and the actual evaluation should be conducted by one specialist or the smallest possible number of people to ensure a consistent result.

As Figure 10.1 shows there are many different job evaluation techniques. The first type — the non-analytical — considers the total job when jobs are being compared. In the case of *ranking*, jobs are placed in order of importance. They may then be placed in clusters of closely ranked jobs.

In the case of *grading* or *classification*, a number of grades will have been decided upon. A typical job illustrating the grade will be chosen which is known as a 'bench-mark' job. All other jobs are then placed into the most appropriate grades using the 'bench-mark' job for guidance (see Figure 10.2).

Figure 10.2 shows a typical approach, which is the system devised by the Institute of Administrative Management, and demonstrates its application to jobs in the hotel and catering industry.

Points assessment   This method allocates points for each factor of a job. The points for all factors are added up and the total of points indicates the job's relative position in the job hierarchy.

Figure 10.2 *A job grading or classification system (using the Institute of Administrative Management method)*

Level definition	Example of jobs
1 Very simple tasks of largely physical nature	Porter* Cleaner
2 Simple tasks carried out in accordance with a small number of clearly defined rules, and which can be carried out after a short period of training of up to 2–3 weeks. The work is checked and closely supervised	Chambermaid* Lift attendant Counter assistant Barmaid Hall porter
3 Straightforward tasks, but involving more complicated routines and requiring a degree of individual knowledge and alertness, as the work is subject to occasional check	Commis waiter* Clerk
4 Tasks calling for the independent arrangement of work and the exercise of some initiative, where little supervision is needed. Detailed familiarity with one or more branches of established procedure required	Receptionist* Waiter Cashier Store keeper Florist
5 Routine work, but involving an individual degree of responsibility for answering non-routine queries and/or exercising some measure of control over a small group of staff	Head waiter* Senior receptionist Assistant housekeeper
6 Non-routine work, involving co-ordination of several lower grade functions, possibly some measure of control over small group of staff. Also non-routine work involving recognized individual knowledge and some responsibility without follow-up	Head housekeeper* Banqueting manager Restaurant manager
7 Work necessitating responsibility for sections involved on routine tasks and/or where there are also individual tasks to be undertaken, calling for specialist knowledge	Chef de cuisine* Front office manager

*Bench-mark jobs

The type of factors evaluated in each job may include:

1 *Knowledge* This may be simple knowledge acquired in a few days or, at the other extreme, may be acquired by several years of study and application.
2 *Skill* This refers mainly to manual skills. These may be acquired within a very short period, such as the skills needed to operate a limited range of simple equipment, or they may take many weeks, even months of practice such as typewriting, or the varied skills needed by a competent cook.

3 *Responsibility* This may be of the type where a person makes important decisions that are not checked for a long period; alternatively they may be simple decisions that are checked immediately. This factor may include responsibility for people, equipment, cash.
4 *Physical demands* Some jobs, such as cooking, are physically demanding, or they may make little physical demand such as book-keeping or typing.
5 *Mental demands* All jobs, to a greater or lesser extent, make demands on a person's mental abilities including the ability to concentrate and to apply oneself; for example, a senior receptionist's job will be much more demanding mentally than a porter's.
6 *Social skills* Some jobs require more social skill than others. A restaurant manager, for example, will require a high degree of tact and patience, whereas a chef may require little or no social skill.
7 *Working conditions* This includes physical and social inconveniences such as heat, long hours, and whether sitting or standing. This may also take into account hazards such as risk of burns, cuts or even physical violence.

These seven examples give a broad indication of the types of factors considered. Others may be used and, in addition, a breakdown into 'sub-factors' may also be desirable. The main methods of evaluation or how these factors may be measured are shown in Figure 10.1 (a and b).

The normal method of awarding points for each factor is to have a scale with 'bench-mark' jobs on it. When evaluating a particular factor of a job it will be placed at or between what appear to be the most appropriate 'bench-mark' job or jobs; for example, in evaluating one factor, such as knowledge, the list of bench-mark jobs is examined and the job being evaluated is then placed in the most appropriate position on the scale (see Figure 10.3).

Figure 10.3 *Example of bench-mark jobs (for one factor only)*

Points   *Bench-mark jobs for knowledge — maximum points: 30; minimum points: 0*

30	Hotel manager
24	Front office manager
18	Restaurant manager
12	Station waiter
6	Hall porter

In evaluating the knowledge required of a head waiter, for example, it would fall between the station waiter and the restaurant manager in Figure 10.3, consequently being awarded somewhere around 15 points. The same procedure would then be adopted for all other factors to be evaluated. The bench-mark jobs will not necessarily be the same for each factor. After this has been done for all factors the points are totalled and the job grade should be determined by reference to a grade table such as shown in Figure 10.4.

Figure 10.5 shows the technique applied to two jobs; a restaurant manager's and a commis waiter's. In this example the factors outlined on page 125 are used but in designing a scheme other factors entirely may be considered.

Figure 10.4 *Example of a grade table*

Grade	Points (Total of all factors)	Example of job
7	121–140	Chef de cuisine
6	101–120	Restaurant manager
5	81–100	Senior receptionist
4	61–80	Waiter
3	41–60	Clerk
2	21–40	Hall porter
1	0–20	Kitchen porter

Figure 10.5 *Example of a points assessment system showing the evaluation of two jobs*

Factor	Maximum points	Example evaluation of two jobs	
		Commis waiter	Restaurant manager
Knowledge	30	5	18
Skill	20	10	20
Responsibility	30	3	24
Physical demands	10	5	4
Mental demands	20	8	15
Social skills	20	12	18
Working conditions	10	5	3
Total	140	48	102

After totalling the points a look at a grade table will indicate the grades of the two jobs — refer back to Figure 10.4. The commis waiter's job, therefore, is a grade 3 and the restaurant manager's a grade 6.

This is a very simplified example of a points assessment system. Some systems may be much more complex than this, but no matter which technique is used, the principles of job evaluation are:

1 Job descriptions must be precise and up-to-date.
2 Because wages and salaries depend on the results, evaluation must be scrupulously fair and consistent.
3 It is the job, not the job holder, which is being evaluated.

People at work measure their value to their employer, to a large extent, by reference to the amount that they and their fellow workers are paid. If, therefore, there appears to be unfairness or injustice in the methods or level of payment, employees will lose faith and confidence in their employer and will react accordingly. Arriving at a fair distribution of wages is not easy and only too often in the hotel and catering industry it is the result of expediency rather than methodical planning and application. It is vital, however, to recognize the relative importance of each job and, if they exist, to remove any causes that can lead to dissatisfaction. In order to do this it is vital, therefore, to adopt a methodical system of evaluating jobs so that wages and salaries appear to all to be fairly distributed.

Having said this however, it must be recognized that while job evaluation can lead to fairness *within* an organization, relative earnings between industries, trades and professions are still determined by market forces and the relative power of negotiating groups. A consequence is that highly trained, expert and dedicated people may still earn less than the less-qualified people employed in other sectors.

Further reading

Burns, M., *Understanding Job Evaluation*, London: Institute of Personnel Management, 1978

Job Evaluation: Theory and Practice, London: British Institute of Management Report, 1979

Taylor, A., *Job Evaluation: A Practical Guide for Managers*, London: British Institute of Management, 1970

Thakur, M., and Gill, D., *Job Evaluation in Practice*, London: Institute of Personnel Management, 1976

Thomason, G., *Job Evaluation: Objective and Methods*, London: Institute of Personnel Management, 1980

chapter 11

The administration of wages and salaries

The main purpose of a business paying wages and salaries is to obtain the labour required for it to operate. Some employers will pay as little as they can but as much as they have to, while others will attempt to pay what they think they can afford. Obviously wage payment is a highly charged subject and in the hotel and catering industry it is a very contentious one owing to a variety of complications. Apart from lack of method in setting basic rates, in some sectors other factors such as tipping, service charges and the provision of meals and living accommodation, all have to be taken into consideration. Within a single establishment it is quite possible to find a complete permutation of all the various benefits received by employees. Some live in and earn tips, some live out and do not earn tips, some are provided with meals and some are not. In addition, in the largest organizations, some subsidiaries encourage tipping, whereas others do everything to eliminate it and also levy service charges. This may be even further complicated by some executives being provided with company cars and other benefits. On closer examination, however, it may well be found that these same executives are worse off (in cash and kind) than their own residential managers.

Mars and Mitchell claim the payment system in hotels has particular problems because it consists of:

basic pay and subsidized lodging and subsidized food;
tips and service charges (where applicable) and 'fiddles' and 'knock-offs' (Mars and Mitchell 1976).

It is because of the difficulty of evaluating this total package that comparisons with other workers are so difficult and generally so onerous. Mars and Mitchell attach particular importance to the 'fiddles' element because of the power it provides management with. They suggest that management lays down parameters within which 'fiddles' are acceptable, but at the same time if someone displeases them for other reasons, they can dismiss the person for fiddling. Undoubtedly, whether fiddling is institutionalized or not, it is a major source of income to employees, and causes headaches to the industry's employers. The head of the Metropolitan Police's Hotel Squad, in 1979, is reported to have claimed that if 'fiddles' could be eliminated London hotels' 'profitability would be so increased that hoteliers could, for the moment, abandon plans to put up tariffs'.* In one Paris hotel foreign exchange transactions were estimated to have earned staff £250,000 and it is only recently that many British hotels have started to close this loophole.

Types of employees

Within the hotel and catering industry, there are probably four main types of employee, from a payment or earnings point of view these are:

Salaried employees; usually paid monthly by cheque or credit transfer and usually consisting of managers and senior supervisors.
Full-time operatives; usually working around a 30–45 hour week and who know from week to week that they have guaranteed work; paid usually weekly in cash.
Part-timers; usually working fewer hours than a full timer and who generally know from week to week that they have guaranteed work; usually paid by the hour in cash.
Casuals; normally working on a 'session' by 'session' basis (e.g. one evening) with no guarantees about future work; usually paid by the session in cash.

Formal wages administration

A major responsibility of managers is to decide how to distribute fairly among all employees the money set aside for payment of staff. This may range from as little as 10 per cent of revenue in some efficient public houses to over 40 per cent in top-class hotels. This money may derive from normal revenue or may also come from retained service charges. Managers may decide by looking at what competitors are paying, what the wages council rate is, what has been historically the employer's practice and, in many cases, what is necessary to overcome the current crisis. The result is that considerable anomalies exist in many hotels, catering establishments and, indeed, in whole firms. As mentioned in the last chapter, newcomers may be paid more than similar staff with long service and more senior staff may earn less than some juniors. Such anomalies are not necessarily confined to the smaller employers.

The exact policy to be adopted by an employer with regard to his wage and salary systems will depend to a great extent upon his business objectives, his personnel policies and his style of management; for example, in organizations where labour turnover is not considered to be important, there may be little method or formality in setting rates of pay. In other organizations, however, where it is recognized that a stable labour force is a valuable asset, much more method will be applied to wage and salary matters. This is typically so in the public sector.

*Catering Times, 4 October 1979.

Where there are many employees with differing levels of skills, fair salary administration will depend upon sound job evaluation which measures the relative importance to the organization of different jobs. But after jobs have been evaluated, rates will have to be set for each grade to ensure that there are realistic differentials between grades so that more senior jobs and promotions are rewarded by worthwhile differences in earnings; promotion then becomes something to aim for. This is illustrated in Figure 11.1.

Figure 11.1   *Example of a grade and wage table*

Grade	Basic wage
1	£90 p.w.
2	£97 p.w.
3	£105 p.w.
4	£120 p.w.

Determining the rate for each job or for key jobs depends on many factors including the make-up of the workforce, statutory requirements, competitors' rates of pay, other industries' rates of pay, cost of living, and the location of the employer. Because of this, in order to establish or to maintain competitive rates of pay, it will be necessary to study advertisements in the press, to keep in touch with staff agencies and the local office of the Department of Employment, and with the local associations of hoteliers and caterers. In making decisions, as a result of this research, it is vital to ensure that all factors affecting rates of pay are taken into account, such as tips and service charges, actual hours worked, the provision or otherwise of meals and accommodation. Some employers with units in different regions may, in addition, require different rates or even entirely different structures for each branch or region.

Increments

In some situations, in order to encourage good performance and long service, it may be appropriate to provide merit and service increments and where this is done there will normally be overlaps between grades, enabling someone in a low grade, but with long service or high merit, to earn more than someone in a high grade with short service. This recognizes that a person's competence and value to an organization usually increase with service, and because of this the increment is granted both as an increased share of his overall contribution and to encourage the employee to stay. Figure 11.2 shows a scale for such a scheme.

In the example shown in Figure 11.2 an employee could anticipate, with satisfactory service, to move from the minimum to the maximum in a period of about four years giving an average annual increase of about 6 to 7 per cent. The exact rate would be determined by performance appraisals and by the employer's financial policy. The advantage of this sytem, if publicized, is that an employee knows what he can expect to earn by gaining promotion or by staying with his employer. In addition, some employers have age-related scales or rates of pay, usually for employees up to about 21 years of age. Increases in these cases would normally be granted on each employee's birthday.

Figure 11.1   *Example of an incremental wage scale*

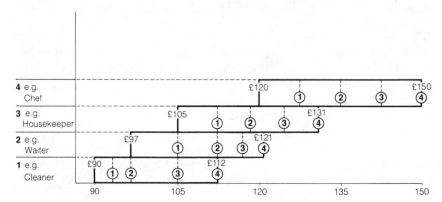

Starting wages or salaries offered to newcomers may not normally be more than 20 per cent above the minimum and this should only be permitted where appropriate experience in the type of job justifies it. Some trade unionists are opposed to incremental scales, saying that every job should have a set rate and that age and service are irrelevant if the job is performed satisfactorily. Furthermore, they claim that such systems can have an adverse effect on staff turnover because management, in order to keep payroll costs down, will encourage labour turnover, thus retaining a high proportion of employees at the lower end of the scales. This last argument, however, seems hardly tenable when the industry's need for the right manpower is considered, although it is reported that in the public sector lack of labour turnover, due to the recession, is having the effect of increasing costs.

Reviews should take place regularly and should fit into the employer's budgetary and financial cycle. In seasonal establishments reviews may take place towards the end of the season in order to retain those employees management wants to keep.

Communicating details of any increases should be done as soon as possible after the decisions have been taken, but, as mentioned in the chapter on appraisals, they should not be part of any performance review or appraisal. Where a person is promoted, the increase should take place upon promotion and not be subject to trial periods as this can indicate 'meanness' or, worse still, doubts about the person's ability to hold down the new job at the very time he or she needs the employer's fullest confidence. Nor should the individual concerned have to wait for the annual review, because a person should be paid the rate for the job being done.

Apart from increases for merit, service and promotion, some systems also allow for cost of living increases to be made from time to time. These will probably be related to some government data such as the retail price index, but where these are granted it is important to bear in mind that they have little positive motivational effect — unlike a promotion or merit award. This is because they are usually granted to all employees without discriminating between the good and the not so good. On the other hand it is important to keep in mind that the absence of 'cost of living' increases may have a negative effect — that is the employees' relative level of earnings may fall and force them to seek employment elsewhere. It can be said that although 'cost of living' awards have little positive, motivational effect, their absence may have a negative effect such as a higher labour turnover.

As with all systems, there is no need to adhere inflexibly to the systems described — systems should be servants not masters — but experience shows that once a systematized salary structure is operational the whole question of pay becomes less contentious and, in particular, where there are disputes or dissatisfactions over differentials management has a basis for dealing with these rationally.

Where systematic salary administration does not exist, on the other hand, there will almost certainly be anomalies, unfairness and, consequently, dissatisfaction. Staff turnover will be high not because of dissatisfaction with levels of pay, but because of some imagined or genuine grievance, such as learning that a newcomer is being paid more.

Further reading

Armstrong, M., and Murlis, H., *Salary Administration: A practical guide for the small and medium-sized business*, London: British Institute of Management Report, 1977

Genders, P., *Wages and Salaries*, London: Institute of Personnel Management 1981

Mars, G., Mitchell, P., and Bryant, D., *Manpower Problems in the Hotel and Catering Industry*, Farnborough: Saxon House, 1976

Philpot, N., *Remunerating Sales and Marketing Staff*, London: British Institute of Management Report, 1976

Redfearn, A., and Kenaghan, F., *Determining Company Pay Policy*, London: Institute of Personnel Management, 1979

chapter 12

Incentives

In addition to the normal wages or salaries which were looked at in the last chapter, it is common practice in many industries for some groups of employees to be able to augment their wages or salaries by earning additional payments in various forms. These payments are made largely to enable workers to participate personally in the success of the undertaking by rewarding individuals or groups for their contribution to the enterprise.

What motivates?

In Chapter 2 the contributions of a number of different theorists were considered. Most of these are crucially concerned with what motivates people to work. In spite of the vast body of knowledge coming from people like Taylor, Mayo, McGregor, Maslow and Herzberg there is still no consensus. Many managers still hold to the belief that money, because of what it can buy (including security and status), is a major motivator. Others tend to the more complex views of Maslow and Herzberg, arguing that people work for a composite package, including money, security, self-esteem, esteem of others, job satisfaction, etc. At a practical level this discussion obviously concerns the merits or otherwise of incentive schemes. Some people argue that employees should be given an adequate wage or salary and, so long as other prospects are adequate such as the regular review of earnings and the likelihood of promotion, people will give what they consider to be a 'fair day's work'. The prospect of incentives will not spur them to continued greater efforts. It is also argued that incentive payments are most effective when people are dependent upon them, that is, the nearer the basic pay is to subsistence levels, the more effective an incentive scheme. The effect of such an attitude on employer/ employee relationships, however, is hardly likely to be positive.

In work of a highly creative nature the prospect of incentive payments will not stimulate greater creativity. There are others, however, who argue that incentives will certainly influence productivity saying, for example, that in a selling situation the prospects of earning commission will definitely stimulate greater 'selling' effort. It is also argued that because of the growing interdependence of working people they can no longer increase their own earnings without the involvement of their colleagues. In many cases nowadays this is true, but in this industry there are still many opportunities for individuals to increase considerably their earnings — particularly in the 'selling' areas, such as waiting, bar work, hotel reception and function catering. Within the scope of this book it is not possible to consider further the arguments for and against incentive schemes. There are unfortunately innumerable examples supporting both viewpoints. It is intended here to look at the main forms of incentives operated in the hotel and catering industry including tips, the 'tronc', service charges, bonuses and commissions.

In other industries other forms of incentive payments are also used. These include methods such as piece rates or measured day work, which are usually based on work measurement techniques, whereas those commonly used in the hotel and catering industry are more normally related to financial targets such as gross profits, turnover, and variable costs (e.g. gas, electricity). In some cases they may be be entirely discretionary.

Although *tipping* and the *tronc* were mentioned along with other forms of financial incentive, it is probably better to think of them as part of normal earnings. Financial incentives are normally intended to stimulate and promote *extra* productivity, whereas tips, the tronc and service charges are considered by many employees as a matter of right and something without which they could not have a reasonable living standard.

Tipping is a form of payment that originated when many workers in the old inns were not employed by the innkeeper but were retained by guests to do particular jobs such as carrying bags, cleaning garments, etc. It also grew up in an age when it was normal to motivate people by fear. In the case of tipping the threat of a tip being withheld was used, and because there was probably no other income, the person's means of living was jeopardized. Many consider it an anachronism in this day and age and a view that has been expressed by many people for many years is that it needs to be eliminated as rapidly as possible. Professor Nailon of Surrey University, however, writes* that it is not necessarily a bad practice but that it may have profound effects on interdepartmental relationships. Also it removes from management an important area of personal control.

Service charges many argue, on the other hand, are quite acceptable methods for an undertaking to employ to raise revenue, so long as the sum allowed for distribution to the workforce is distributed on a fair basis. In many tourist countries it is common to find that tariffs are inclusive of taxes and service charges, and tipping is being eliminated.

Where the service charges are part of an employee's remuneration a minimum level should be specified so that a person can know how to regulate his affairs; for example, if an employer knows that his waitresses normally earn £20 a week from the service charge and £70 per week in wages, he could, without much risk to himself, offer a minimum guaranteed income of £90 per week. This guaranteed income could be paid weekly and the excess periodically, such as quarterly or half-yearly, thus spreading payment over good and bad spells of trade. Where a service charge is included in the bill, tipping is often actively discouraged and notices on bills, menus, brochures

*HCIMA Review, vol. 2, no. 4.

and in guest rooms discourage guests from giving tips in addition to paying the service charge.

Principles of incentive schemes

In designing an incentive scheme, whether for this industry or any other, there are several principles that should be adhered to for it to be effective in the long term. These are:

1   The undertaking's major business objectives should be promoted and their achievement assisted by incentive payments. These payments should enable individuals to identify with the success of the undertaking; for example, if food gross profit is vital, the chef and maybe his staff as well should be rewarded for achieving gross profit targets. But only elements over which a person exerts control should be included. A chef, for example, has no control over the rent and the rates, therefore there is no point in including these in a scheme for the chef.

2   When an incentive scheme is to be introduced *all* workers should be considered because of the effect the scheme may have on existing earnings differentials.

3   Payments should be related to results by comparing actual performance with forecasts, targets, standards, or budgets. This may be done individually or on a group basis.

4   Targets should be realistic, that is achievable with reasonable effort and agreed with the person or groups concerned.

5   Targets should be reviewed regularly, and at least annually, so that payments are something to be earned with effort rather than something which becomes a matter of right. They should also be reviewed if circumstances change considerably; for example, if a vast new office block opens next door to a snack bar, trade will probably increase greatly, through no effort of the manager. The turnover and other targets should, therefore, be reviewed at the same time bearing in mind that extra work will be created and that wages and salaries may have to be increased.

6   An incentive scheme should be simple and clearly understood by those within the scheme.

7   Payment of the incentive should be made as near as possible to the period in which it was earned. Long delays in payment cause irritation and reduce the incentive element.

8   All elements of a scheme and any rules should be objective. Management should not incorporate 'discretionary' rules such as 'management reserves the right to withhold payment without giving a reason'. Incentives, if earned, should be a matter of right, not for management to dispense on a discretionary basis, and the terms of the incentive scheme should become part of the 'Contract of Employment'.

Incentives are normally used to stimulate performance and particularly to increase sales and control costs. Figures 12.1, 12.2 and 12.3 are included as examples.

Figure 12.1 *Example of an individual incentive scheme (chef)*

1 *Job*	Chef
2 *Commission*	1 per cent of all 'gross profit' (for this purpose revenue less purchases and labour costs) in excess of £2000 per week, after achieving the following targets
3 *Targets*	1 Purchases not to exceed 45 per cent of revenue
	2 Kitchen labour not to exceed 15 per cent of revenue

4 *Example of calculation*
Period 7

Food cost	£6000	(37.5%)	Revenue	£16000
Labour cost	£2200	(13.75%)		
	£8200			
'Gross profit'	£7800	(48.75%)		

Gross profit £7800–£2000 = £5800 × $\frac{1}{100}$ =	£58.00
Commission to be	£58.00

Figure 12.2 *Example of a group incentive scheme*

1 *Department*	Front Office
2 *Commission*	£40 for every 1 per cent in excess of occupancy targets, distributed to all front office staff pro rata to salaries
3 *Target*	85 per cent occupancy

4 *Examples of calculation*
Week 41
Actual occupancy 90.4% therefore 5.4 × £40 = £216 to be distributed

Salaries: Head receptionist	£6400
2 Senior receptionists @	£4800
2 Cashier/receptionists @	£4000
Total salaries	£24,000

$$\frac{£108 \text{ commission}}{£24,000 \text{ salaries}} = 90\text{p per £ salary}$$

Therefore the following commissions will be paid

Head receptionist	£6400 × 90p = £57.60
Senior receptionists	£4800 × 90p = £43.20
Cashier/receptionists	£4000 × 90p = £36.00

Having looked at these examples, which are intended to illustrate principles only and which demonstrate that incentive schemes can be designed for many departments in an organization, it is vital to bear in mind that their introduction may have undesirable consequences which could exclude their being used; for example, the chef may well place commission above customer satisfaction and buy cheap materials or keep labour costs too low for efficient service. In the case of the receptionists they may overbook (more than is desirable) and consequently lose customers for the future. On the other hand, in looking at the restaurant manager's scheme, it can be seen that because the

Figure 12.3   *Example of an individual incentive scheme (manager)*

1 *Job*	Restaurant manager
2 *Commission*	5 per cent of net profit up to budget
	10 per cent of net profit between 101 per cent and 130 per cent of target budget
	20 per cent of net profit in excess of 130 per cent of target budget
2 *Target budget*	£20,000 net profit

4 *Example of calculation*

Year ended 31 December 1985   Actual net profit = £56,000

Commission rate	Qualifying net profit	Commission
5%	£40,000	£2000
10%	£12,000	£1200
20%	£4000	£800
TOTAL	£56,000	£4000

NOTE: In this example it is interesting to note that although the top rate of commission is 20 per cent and consequently well worth striving for, the actual rate of total commission is only just over 7 per cent.

commission is related to net profit, the manager has an interest in successfully controlling all aspects of the business, including turnover, purchases, wages, variables, and, of course, customer satisfaction. In designing an incentive scheme, therefore, one has to ensure that the benefits to the individual do not stimulate him or her to take measures that may not be in the employer's own interests. Incentives can cover such things as sales, profits, occupancy, suggestion schemes, new staff introduction bonuses, and new business introduction bonuses.

Financial incentives can reward individual employees or groups of employees through increased payment for their increased contribution to the enterprise. However, they can achieve little on their own. They must be part of a comprehensive, well-balanced personnel policy that is based upon offering every employee adequate wages and other conditions before incentives are offered.

Further reading

Armstrong, M., *A Handbook of Personnel Management Practice*, 2nd ed., London: Kogan Page, 1984

Lloyd, P., *Incentive Payment Schemes*, London: British Institute of Management Report, 1976

Pratt, K. J., and Bennett, S. C., *Elements of Personnel Management*, 2nd ed., Wokingham: GEE, 1985

Reilly, P., *Employee Financial Participation*, London: British Institute of Management Report, 1978

Thomason, G., *A Textbook of Personnel Management*, 4th ed., London: Institute of Personnel Management, 1981

Torrington, D., and Chapman, J., *Personnel Management*, 2nd ed., London: Prentice-Hall, 1983

chapter 13

Fringe benefits

The last few years have seen quite important developments in the value and type of fringe benefits that are offered by many organizations to their employees. Some of the major employers in the hotel and catering industry have not been slow to join this trend and nowadays the total number of fringe benefits available to a number of the industry's employees is considerable. There are still many employers, however, who could look into this area of employee compensation, which when properly considered can improve greatly the employees' standard of living — sometimes at little or no cost to the employer.

It is useful to bear in mind what *Catering Times* (June 1975) said on the subject:

The importance of fringe benefits should not be underestimated, because in a labour intensive industry involving a high degree of worker/customer contact, the contrast between the guest's environment and his own can become a major source of dissatisfaction to the employee.

The importance of fringe benefits in employment policies has grown, partly because of high levels of personal tax and partly because of pressure from other sources such as the rapidly increasing competition for employees. Fringe benefits are intended primarily to motivate employees to give better performance and to encourage them to stay with the employer. They include benefits that attract little or no tax such as meals, holidays, cars, and deferred earnings such as pensions. The total list of benefits offered today is considerable and is continually growing as employers look for new ways to woo employees. They can be divided into three main types: financial, part-financial and non-financial.

Financial benefits include: commissions, bonuses, profit sharing, share options.

Part-financial benefits include: pensions, meals, cars, subscriptions.

Non-financial benefits include: holidays, sick pay, medical insurances.

In considering fringe benefits it is vital to recognize that what may be considered an 'incentive' or 'motivator' today may lose its motivating effect with time. This may be because what is offered by only one or two employers to start with will be offered by many employers as they follow suit. Alternatively, what may have been offered as a reward for exceptional services one year becomes expected and a 'matter of right' within the next two or three years.

Having made this point, it is necessary to bear in mind also that although the presence of many fringe benefits in a 'compensation package' may not be a positive incentive to work harder or to perform better, the absence of fringe benefits, on the other hand, may be a disincentive and will leave an employer at a disadvantage in recruiting or retaining staff.

In some cases offering high salaries, commissions or bonuses may compensate for lack of fringe benefits, but owing to the fact that non-cash benefits are taxed lightly or not at all, these have been playing a bigger part in employee compensation in recent years. They can add another 25 per cent to the total payroll costs but a similar increase to salaries, due to high personal tax, would almost certainly not enable employees to purchase the same type of benefits, or to enjoy the same standard of living.

Fringe benefit programmes should be designed to further the employer's objectives and should, in particular, be designed to assist in manpower planning. Where, for example, it is desirable to have a stable, mature management team providing plenty of continuity, such as is required by many brewery companies, a very generous pension and life assurance scheme, along with loan facilities (for house purchasing among other things), will assist in retaining the management team. On the other hand a dynamic young organization will expect and will want a fairly steady flow of 'whizz kids', the majority of whom will not want to stay for long because there will not be room for all of them. In this case high salaries and good incentive payments will be preferable, as this type of person will not be so interested in pensions.

Figure 13.1   *A list of fringe benefits*

Staff restaurant/canteen

Living-in accommodation

Staff hostel/external accommodation

Register of local accommodation

Free uniform

Uniform cleaned/laundered free

Average working hours per week

Whether split duty

Holidays p.a.

Company pension scheme

Company life assurance

Sickness benefit paid

Medical personnel/facilities

Staff/management consultative committee

Company magazine/paper

Social club

Sporting activities

Discount buying scheme

Discount holiday scheme

Savings scheme

Money loaned, e.g. bridging loan for house purchase

Removal expenses paid

Disturbance allowance, e.g. for curtains, carpets

Long service award

Christmas bonus

Birthday gift

Incentive scheme

Suggestion bonus

Occupancy bonus

Language proficiency award

Employee introduction bonus

The differing needs of employers, along with pressures exerted by competing organizations and by statutory requirements, will all help to dictate what type of fringe benefits programme needs to be offered. There are many different components and the permutations can be numerous. The major ones, however, as listed in a survey published in *Catering Times*, are shown in Figure 13.1.

Financial benefits

Commissions and bonuses   These were covered in more detail on pages 134–138 but, as was said there, they should be directly related, as far as possible, to performance. Discretionary 'handouts' have little positive motivational value.

Profit sharing   Although many profit sharing schemes may not be justified directly on motivational grounds, because individuals do not receive a commission or bonus related to their own efforts, and because these awards may be expected as a matter of right, profit sharing may well be justified for indirect reasons. There is a growing view that employees have a proprietorial interest in the undertaking which employs them and that consequently, they should have a share of any increased profits. Awarding a bonus of this kind may not assist directly in increasing profits but withholding an award may have an adverse effect on employees' morale. Whether this share of increased profits should be in the form of a bonus or salary increase depends on current performance of the employer's business; for example, if there is a strong upward trend in profits an increase in salaries could be awarded, whereas if a year's performance was exceptional and not certain to be maintained, a bonus may be preferable from the employer's point of view, because it is a 'once only' payment and because it does not have a gearing up effect on future wage increases, pensions, etc.

Share option schemes   These enable executives to buy options on company shares with loans provided by the employer. The better the company performs, the more the value of the executives' shares increases. These schemes are strictly controlled by law; for example, they do not allow an executive to sell his shares until a certain number of years has elapsed. All of the above schemes are now offered in the hotel and catering industry.

Part-financial benefits

There are many benefits which may be awarded that can be described as partly financial. These are benefits that the employee cannot normally dispose of in cash or kind, but which enable him or her either to save spending personal resources on these benefits or to enjoy a higher standard of living. These benefits include such things as pensions and life assurance schemes, company cars, expense accounts. The major 'part-financial' benefits are as follows:

Pensions   Most schemes grant a fraction of final earnings for each year of service. The better schemes grant one-sixtieth of final salary (sometimes the average of the last few years) for each year's service, thereby enabling a person with forty or more years' service to retire on forty-sixtieths (or two-thirds of final salary), the maximum pension currently permissible. Provision is also normally made for a man's widow whether he dies in service or in retirement.

One of the benefits to employers of comprehensive pension schemes is that they enable employers to retire their older employees, particularly for health reasons, replacing them by younger people, knowing that the older ones will be well provided for in retirement.

Currently there are two main types of scheme. In the contributory schemes employees have a proprietory right, at least over their own contributions. Upon leaving an employer they can either have their own contributions frozen and take a pension upon retirement, or they may transfer their contributions to the new employer's fund. Contributions cost up to about 11 per cent of pay — divided between employer (6 per cent) and employee (5 per cent).

The other type is the non-contributory scheme in which only the employer pays a contribution and in which employees may not acquire any vested rights.

Life insurance In itself this is hardly a benefit that will persuade a person to join one employer rather than another. From the employer's point of view, however, the major value is that it provides for the dependants of employees who die in service. Without this provision the employer may feel that there is a moral, if not a legal responsibility to look after an employee's dependants, particularly if that person dies in the course of work. If no insurance is provided, some other provision may have to be made on a discretionary basis and, where large numbers of people are employed, cases may be treated inconsistently. Also, the burden may fall more heavily in one year rather than another and, worst of all, if the employer went out of business the dependants of ex-employees may be completely unprovided for.

Company cars Generally speaking these are provided for one of two reasons. First, it is because an employee needs a car in order to do the job. This would include a variety of people such as regional or area managers and stock takers. Second, cars are provided to improve a person's standard of living without incurring the full tax liability that paying an equivalent cash amount would impose.

The provision of company cars is a highly contentious benefit, however, for reasons such as these:

1 Cars are very nearly 'cash equivalent' and therefore if a car is provided to one employee in a particular job grade because it is needed, another employee of similar grade but who does not need or receive a car may well expect a cash equivalent. To complicate this further, if a cash equivalent were paid this would be taxed fully, whereas only part of the estimated value of the car to the other employee would rank for tax.
2 Cars are status symbols both within the organization and within the community at large and wherever status is concerned people are very sensitive and often irrational.

House purchasing Purchasing a house is usually the biggest investment that a person ever makes and often moving house is one of the biggest obstacles to employee mobility. (The fact that labour mobility in the hotel and catering industry is high while home ownership by the industry's employees is low are probably not unrelated.) By helping employees to buy a house employers can increase the stability of their labour force. At the top of the scale this assistance can take the form of cheap loans, but, more practically, it can be confined to the employer acting as guarantor for any amount a building society may feel is appropriate and with constantly rising property prices the risk is minimal.

Removal or relocation expenses These payments are intended to indemnify an employee for the cost incurred in moving home when being appointed, transferred or promoted by the employer. The amount allowed should be such that the employee is no worse off, financially as a direct result of moving house. The expenses included in this, however, can be extensive, including estate agents costs, legal fees, furniture removal, new school uniforms, temporary accommodation, etc.

The employer's responsibility should be confined purely to indemnifying the employee for the actual costs incurred in the employee's transfer from one home to another. Considerations of capital appreciation should be excluded.

These are the major part-financial fringe benefits offered by many employers. There are many others as well which enable employees to enjoy a better standard of living and these include advantageous purchasing of food, insurances, furniture, etc. These can all be arranged through the employer's own suppliers or agents.

Non-financial benefits

Although the main benefits in this category can cost the employer considerable sums of money, they do not normally provide employees with any direct financial advantages. Instead they afford employees other benefits such as a degree of security or more time for leisure.

Fringe benefits are often provided where it is recognized that financial incentives may have little effect due to heavy taxation. The main benefits in this category are:

Holidays These can be used as a stimulus to labour stability; for example, extra days over the minimum can be granted after a certain number of years' service. Extra holiday must be reasonably obtainable, however, because working for fifteen years, for example, for extra holiday entitlement will contribute nothing to retaining staff. It is much better to grant two to four extra days after two to four years' service, leading up to an extra week after five years. The table in Figure 13.2 illustrates one example.

Sick pay schemes As with several other conditions of employment details of payment during sickness have to be entered in the statement of conditions of employment. This is required by the Employment Protection (Consolidation)

Figure 13.2   *Example of a service-related holiday entitlement scheme*

Years of service	Holiday entitlement per annum
During 1st year	4 weeks (pro rata to actual service)
2nd year	4 weeks and 2 days
3rd and 4th year	4 weeks and 3 days
5th and 6th year	4 weeks and 4 days
7th year onwards	5 weeks

Act 1978 and, in the absence of such details, an employer may have to pay a sick employee the full wage or salary until dismissal of the employee having given full notice of termination.

It is for this reason as well as for normal human considerations that employers should formulate a sick pay policy that is consistent with their personnel management practices and which is affordable.

It is important to recognize that in some employment situations sickness leave, with pay, can increase considerably the incidence of absence. This appears to be particularly so in the public sector where sick leave may be seen as another form of holiday entitlement.

Private medical treatment   Private medical treatment is one particular fringe benefit that is being granted to many more employees these days. The direct advantage to the company is that employees can be treated at a time convenient to the company and not when it is convenient to the National Health Service. This is particularly appropriate to key members of the staff. Sometimes the cover provided by the company includes the employee's family as well.

Some employers may feel it is too expensive or even inappropriate to pay for this service, but even so employers can arrange 'group rates'* and monthly deductions of premiums from salaries enabling their employees to benefit from preferential rates at no cost to the employer. A combination of these two methods can be adopted where senior employees are paid for by the company and the remainder of the employees have the option of participating in the group scheme.

This chapter has dealt with the major benefits that can be offered to employees. All employees will not qualify for all these benefits automatically. Some benefits should be incentives to stay with the organization and to seek promotion; therefore they should be granted only for service and seniority. On the other hand some may be offered to all employees upon joining, for example, discounted purchasing facilities.

Fringe benefits play a vital part in an employer's personnel policy as the nature of all the benefits offered influences considerably the type of employees who will be attracted to the employer and who will stay. And since the cost of fringe benefits can add another 25 per cent to the payroll cost, it is essential that the range of benefits offered and their likely effects are fully considered.

*The HCIMA has negotiated a group rate with BUPA for its members who may not have the benefit of a company scheme.

Further reading

Armstrong, M., *A Handbook of Personnel Management Practice*, 2nd ed., London: Kogan Page, 1984

Murlis, H., *Employee Benefits*, London: British Institute of Management Report, 1978

Pratt, K. J., and Bennett, S. C., *Elements of Personnel Management*, 2nd ed., Wokingham: GEE, 1985

Thomason, G., *A Textbook of Personnel Management*, 4th ed., London: Institute of Personnel Management, 1981

Torrington, D., and Chapman, J., *Personnel Management*, 2nd ed., London: Prentice-Hall, 1983

chapter 14

Labour turnover and termination of employment

Labour turnover within the hotel and catering industry has provoked considerable discussion and debate over many years because at one extreme are critics who, using industries such as manufacturing as their yardstick, suggest that the turnover levels in some sectors are excessive, while at the other extreme are employers who take annual labour turnover rates of 200 per cent and more as quite normal and unremarkable.

One of the problems in considering the industry's turnover is that 'the industry' consists of many sectors and there are also many differences within sectors. Consequently we find tremendous differences both between and within sectors; for example, in the catering departments of five South of England universities and a European Community office complex in Brussels, the annual labour turnover figures in 1981 ranged from 5 per cent to 45 per cent. At the other extreme an annual labour turnover rate of over 550 per cent in the wash-up and kitchen portering areas of a very large London hotel was reported.

There are of course many factors influencing labour turnover. These include:

1 The nature of the industry itself: e.g. seasonal; limited career structures; fragmented; large number of small units; high proportion of 'secondary' labour force.
2 The nature of individual units: e.g. location; size; staff/work ratios.
3 The nature of individual managers: e.g. lacking formal management training; acceptance of high labour turnover.

These and many other factors are discussed in more detail by Mars *et al.* (1979), Johnson (1980) and Hornsey and Dann (1984).

For the industry as a whole the HCITB estimated labour turnover to be 95 per cent per annum (HCITB 1984). If one adds the vacancies arising from growth, in the region of 1.4 million vacancies arise each year. The pattern is shown in Figure 14.1.

In order to understand and control labour turnover properly at a unit level, not only is it important to analyse it by department as illustrated in Figure

Figure 14.1 *Annual number of recruits and sources*

Recruited from:				
	Outside the industry	Other sectors within the industry	The same sector (including promotions)	Total
Managers	19,000	22,000	12,000	53,000
Supervisors	17,000	15,000	30,000	62,000
Craftspeople	41,000	54,000	76,000	171,000
Operatives and others	718,000	180,000	193,000	1,091,000
TOTAL	**795,000**	**271,000**	**311,000**	**1,377,000**

Figure 14.2 *Labour turnover in three hotels*

Sampled departments	Two large London hotels A	B	Medium-sized county town hotel
Kitchens	140%	80% }	47%
Wash-up, porters	550%	135% }	
Coffee shop	125%	100%	17%
Hall porters	68%	105%	0%
Housekeeping	150%	146%	28%
Weighted average *all* departments	110%	105%	40%

14.2, but it is necessary to look at the 'survival curve'. This is a means of identifying when labour turnover is most critical; is it occurring during the early induction period, the subsequent 'settling-in' period or after employees have become settled? Such an analysis (see Figure 14.3) can indicate causes such as poor induction or a change of supervisor or manager. With such information the employer may be able to take appropriate measures.

Whilst labour turnover is analysed by department and by length of service, the actual reasons for employees leaving need to be determined also. Some employers do little or nothing about such an analysis while others obtain very detailed information. Figure 14.4 shows how one of the fast food companies analyses employees' reasons for leaving.

With such information management may then be in a position to consider changes and improvements to their personnel practices in order to reduce labour turnover. Causes of turnover may include:

1 Wage and salary rates falling behind the rates offered by competitors.
2 Better conditions generally (such as reduction in split shifts, or a five-day week) being offered by competitors.
3 The decline in quality of supervision and departmental managers.

Figure 14.3   *A survival curve*

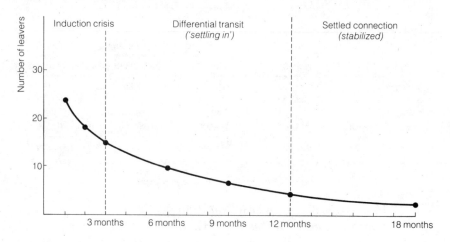

Figure 14.4   *A list of reasons for leaving an employer*

Codes:

1	Another job	11	Retirement
2	Returned to college or school	*12	Failure to return after leave of absence
3	Medical reasons	*13	Conclusion of temporary employment
4	Marriage	*14	Reduction in labour force
5	Relocation	*15	Unsatisfactory performance
6	Dissatisfaction with wages	*16	Misconduct
7	Undisclosed personal reasons	*17	Gross misconduct
8	Resigned without notice	*18	Absenteeism
9	Dissatisfaction with work	*19	Permanent disability
10	Dissatisfaction with conditions	*20	Death

*Involuntary leavers

4   Recruitment, selection, induction and training practices needing improvement.
5   Unfair or uneven work distribution.

The analysis of labour turnover is discussed further in Chapter 17. Both the staff turnover report itself and the information deduced from such reports are of a statistical nature, that is, they are mainly concerned with groups and numbers of people. The actual termination procedures adopted, however, are concerned with individuals and these are divided into two main types: voluntary, where the employees leave of their own free will, and involuntary, where the employer decides that employment should terminate.

Voluntary termination

Almost invariably this arises where an employee has the opportunity to take other employment that offers more attractive conditions, but, because employees leaving voluntarily have not been dismissed by the employer, they are probably the employees that an employer would most like to retain. It is for this reason that these employees should be interviewed to determine their reasons for leaving. The *exit* interview may reveal specific information regarding conditions of employment, competitors' conditions, the quality or otherwise of supervision, training and selection procedures. Finally, a well-conducted exit interview can ensure that employees leave on good terms. Ex-employees are, after all, to some extent an employer's ambassadors, broadcasting his reputation among other potential employees. In some cases it may be advisable to supplement an exit interview by talking to a departing employee's past supervisor in order to check the reasons given by the employee.

Involuntary terminations

In this industry, along with some others, dismissal is often used as the first remedy for a variety of ills, rather than being used as the last. In fact, in some sectors of the industry dismissals are quite indiscriminate; for example, it is common practice for complete bar staffs to be dismissed because of bad liquor stock results. The innocent suffer the same fate (dismissal) as the guilty.

One recognizes that pilferage in this industry is a serious problem, but other measures such as more methodical selection, checking of references, better conditions of employment, and better career prospects, along with stricter and more accurate means of control, are better solutions than indiscriminate sackings. Where pilferers are caught, however, they should be prosecuted rather than being allowed to get away with their crime, often because the employer wants no trouble or publicity.

The dismissal of an employee is a very serious measure particularly now that the law provides employees with protection against unfair dismissal. The law on dismissals is dealt with in more detail in Chapter 16.

The vast majority of terminations, however, are not a consequence of pilferage, and in most cases are as unwanted by the employer as by the employee. The most common reasons are:

1   Lack of ability.
2   Continual late arrival, absenteeism, or disobedience.
3   Personality.

In all these cases when contemplating dismissal other remedies should be considered first; for example, lack of ability may well be the fault of the employer because he did not select or place the employee carefully enough, or because he did not provide appropriate training. In the second case tighter discipline could possibly overcome the problem and a discussion with the employee to discover the underlying causes would possibly be helpful. In the third case, if it is a 'clash of personalities', and if the organization is big enough, a transfer may be the solution. On the other hand, once a decision is made to terminate employment it must always be borne in mind that the employer may have to prove in an industrial tribunal that the dismissal was 'fair' as laid down by the Employment Protection (Consolidation) Act 1978. Documentary evidence, therefore, of unsatisfactory work or behaviour, and of warnings given may be vital in proving the case. It is important, therefore, to operate a formal system of warnings that can be used as a last resort by the employer should he be called to an industrial tribunal. Typical warnings could look like those shown in Figure 14.5.

Figure 14.5   *Examples of written warnings*

Memo   1 April 1987

To: A.N. Other   From: T. Boss

Further to my discussion with you this morning I should like to confirm that your constant late arrivals for duty must cease; otherwise I shall be forced to consider terminating your employment.

Memo   1 May 1987

To: A.N. Other   From: T. Boss

Further to my memorandum of April 1 and our discussion this morning I should like to confirm that if there are any further occurrences of late arrival within the next six months your employment with the Company will be terminated.

In the case of written warnings it would be unreasonable for a final warning (particularly for something like unpunctuality) to have an indeterminate life. It is therefore advisable to state the period of time during which the warning is considered final. In addition, although a final warning for one type of unsatisfactory conduct, for example, rudeness, cannot normally be used as a reason for dismissal, following other types of unsatisfactory conduct, for example unpunctuality, a catalogue of warnings (none of which is final) for different reasons may well provide sufficient grounds for fair dismissal.

Redundancy

The other main form of involuntary termination is of course redundancy. This is where a job is eliminated owing to such things as changes in methods, or mergers. In this case the law lays down certain minimal payments to be made to the employee. In addition to this payment some employers, recognizing the inadequacy of the amounts awarded by the redundancy legislation, allow what is known sometimes as 'severance pay'. This is additional to redundancy pay and is usually calculated by using some formula that recognizes age, service and present earnings. Employers must recognize, however, that redundancies are sometimes the fault of their own lack of forward planning. If planning, and this includes manpower planning, is conducted thoroughly, many redundancies can be avoided by allowing natural wastage to reduce the labour force. But once it becomes apparent that redundancies are unavoidable this fact should be discussed with employee representatives so that plans for a properly phased run-down can be agreed.* This may include voluntary early retirements and compensation payments for voluntary terminations. In some cases it may be essential to keep employees working to a certain date in which case special 'incentive payments' to stay in the job will have to be agreed.

Retirement

The last type of termination is, of course, when a person goes into retirement and these days some of the more enlightened employers recognize that their responsibility extends beyond providing a pension and a gold watch. In fact, they provide some form of pre-retirement preparation that enables an individual to adjust to completely changed circumstances, because not only does he or she suddenly have greatly increased free time, but income may drop considerably and contact with friends and colleagues may be reduced. This may take the form of a steadily reducing working week with attendance at a pre-retirement course.

Exit interviews

The importance of interviewing employees when they leave was touched upon briefly earlier in this chapter, but it cannot be overemphasized that the numbers and types of people leaving an organization are one critical indication of the success or otherwise of an employer's personnel and employee relations policy. Employees leaving can be a valuable source from which to learn where improvements in personnel practice can be made. With few exceptions, therefore, all employees should be interviewed before their departure, in order to:

1 Learn the real reasons for their departure (unless these are patently obvious).
2 Pin-point trouble spots and causes of irritation and frustration.
3 Inform employees of all their benefits and rights, such as pensions, and insurances. In the case of pensioners they will need to know what rights they retain such as insurances, holidays and discount purchasing facilities.
4 Explain the make-up of the final pay cheque including such items as holiday pay.
5 Hand over the P45 or obtain a forwarding address.
6 Collect any company property that may be outstanding such as cash advances, equipment, uniforms, protective clothing.
7 Part on friendly terms, if possible, so that ex-employees act as 'ambassadors'.

*This is laid down in Employment Protection legislation.

Who dismisses?

The question of who actually dismisses employees is a contentious one. Many line managers feel that they need to have this right as a support to, and indication of, their authority. Others, on the other hand, would dearly like to abdicate the responsibility to someone else such as a personnel officer. However, because line managers, in the last resort, are responsible for the results of their departments they should carry this burden and they should make the decision assisted and guided by specialists, where they are employed, such as personnel officers. In many circumstances it is best for the 'grandfather' principle to be applied to dismissals. This means that no person can dismiss subordinates without the approval of his own superior. Furthermore, in large organizations the approval of the personnel officer or department should also be obtained because they will know if any opportunities exist for an employee about to be dismissed or if legal consequences are likely. It has now become common practice in many companies for the right to dismiss to be held by the unit manager only, with the subordinate having the right to suspend and no more.

The industry: labour turnover

Many managers in the industry hold the view that the industry's high turnover rate is not as costly as some claim. Instead they maintain it has some beneficial effects.

First, some turnover is the inevitable result of the seasonal nature of the industry, although past patterns are now altering in many places as a result of such factors as increased tourism and conference business; for example, Brighton's season is very different from what it was twenty years ago and London has two peaks and two troughs.

Second, turnover, it is claimed, provides job variety and satisfaction for the industry's many semi-skilled and unskilled workers.

Because of the relatively low degree of skill needed in many jobs, and because many jobs are transferable between employers, the amount of training is minimal. Consequently the industry is able to accept a rate of labour turnover which, in other industries, such as manufacturing, would probably be insupportable.*

The turnover of staff is one barometer of the success or otherwise of an employer's personnel management policies. Generally speaking, the higher the rate of turnover the poorer are his relationships with his employees and the lower the turnover, the better the relationships. High labour turnover often results in low levels of efficiency. It incurs high costs in recruitment and training and results in customer dissatisfaction. In most cases, therefore, when an employee leaves an employer, the employer should examine the circumstances very carefully to see whether he is in some way responsible for what is, after all, some degree of failure on his part. He may have failed the employee for a variety of reasons including wrong selection or placement in the

*See Angus Fisher of Reading University in *Catering Times*, October 1980.

first place, inadequate training, unsatisfactory conditions of employment or just poor management.

Further reading

Hornsey, T., and Dann, D., *Manpower Management in the Hotel and Catering Industry*, London: Batsford, 1984

Hotel and Catering Economic Development Committee, *Staff Turnover*, London: HMSO, 1969, pp. 26–43

Johnson, K., Labour turnover in hotels – Revisited, *The Service Industries Journal*, London: 1985

Johnson, K., Labour turnover in hotels — Revisited, *The Service Industries*

Mars G., *et al.*, *Manpower Problems in the Hotel and Catering Industry*, Farnborough: Saxon House, 1979

Riley, M., Recruitment, labour turnover and occupational rigidity: An essential relationship, *Hospitality*, **15**, 1981

Wasmuth, W. J., and Davis, S. W., Managing employee turnover, *Cornell Hotel and Restaurant Administration Quarterly*, **23**, No. 4, 1983

Wasmuth, W. J., and Davis, S. W., Why employees leave, *Cornell Hotel and Restaurant Administration Quarterly*, **24**, No. 1, 1983

Wasmuth, W. J., and Davis, S. W., Strategies for managing employee turnover, *Cornell Hotel and Restaurant Administration Quarterly*, **24**, No. 2, 1983

Hotel and Catering Industry Training Board publications
Manpower Changes in the Hotel and Catering Industry, London: 1983
Manpower Flows in the Hotel and Catering Industry, London: 1984

chapter 15

Industrial relations

The term 'industrial relations' has many different definitions. At one extreme are those who see industrial relations as being concerned with purely economic issues, that is the 'pay for work' relationship. At another extreme are those who see industrial relations as being concerned with politics and as an extension of party politics.

A useful definition of industrial relations, however, is that ' "industrial relations" describes the systems, formal and informal, public and private, for allocating rewards to employees for their services and regulating the conditions under which these services are provided' (Alton W. Craig, International Industrial Relations Association, Third World Congress, London 1973).

More simply the term industrial relations is generally used to describe the relationship that exists between the management of an undertaking and its work people, organized and represented often, but not always, within a trade union framework. In the hotel and catering industry the degree of organization of employees within trade unions varies considerably. At one end of the scale, industrial and institutional catering, more than sixty per cent of all employees' conditions of employment are determined by collective bargaining; yet at the other end of the scale, hotels and restaurants, the number of trade union members, although rising, is still comparatively low.

The attitude of management in the industry towards trade unions varies considerably too. Generally speaking, those managers with experience of trade unions accept their existence and believe that they have a useful role to play. On the other hand, most vociferous opponents of trade unions are to be found among those hotel and restaurant proprietors and managers who, by and large, have no experience of trade unions and who may never have knowingly spoken to union officials or shop stewards in their lives.

As stated earlier the degree of union involvement varies considerably from sector to sector but, if examined carefully, it appears that, generally speaking, there are certain factors which either contribute towards, or militate against, strong union involvement. These are shown in Figure 15.1.

If one looks more carefully at restaurants and hotels one may conclude that union membership is low for the following reasons:

1   The large numbers of small establishments that make it difficult for trade
     union officials to contact potential members and to organize meetings.
     (The average hotel has only about 25 bedrooms.)

Figure 15.1 *Factors contributing to low or high union involvement*

Low union membership	High union membership
Small units — small workforces Many part-timers and casuals 'Entrepreneurial' opportunities, e.g. tipping Ownership and management combined or closely related 'Secret' contracts Hostile ownership No other union involvement No tradition of union involvement	Large units — large workforces Few part-timers and casuals No 'entrepreneurial' opportunities Management distinct from ownership No 'secret' contracts Other unions involved in the enterprise Traditions of union involvement
Some examples: Restaurants, fast food, hotels, public house staff	*Some examples:* Hospital catering, university and college catering, school meals, Civil Service catering, public house managers

2 The highly dispersed and departmentalized labour force, even in the largest establishments, resulting in the absence of cohesive groups of workers with common interests.
3 The large number of part-time employees who are not so interested in belonging to a trade union as full-time employees.
4 A large number of foreign employees who are in the United Kingdom for short periods of time.
5 Shift working which makes it difficult to contact and organize employees.
6 Tipping which introduces an 'entrepreneurial' element into work, which many employees fear a trade union would try to eliminate.
7 Individual and secret contracts made between the employer and the employee.
8 No tradition of trade union membership within some sectors of the industry.
9 Employers' resistance, because employers fear that they have more to lose than to gain from the trade union movement.

Development of the trade union movement

In order to see the hotel and catering industry's relations in perspective it is important to look at industrial relations generally and, in particular, to examine the development of organizations of work people and of employers.

The organization of employers and workers came about from the eighteenth century onwards with the emergence of modern industry. Before this time most conditions of employment had been regulated by the State, often through the local magistrate, and it was an offence in common law to do anything (even with the intention of improving one's own conditions of work) which might have been in restraint of trade. A combination of workers, therefore, to strike or to do anything else to improve conditions that adversely affected the employer's business, was a criminal act of conspiracy. But at the same time it was illegal for employers to form such combinations. As industry became more complex, the State regulation of wages fell into disuse and employers themselves were able to fix the conditions of employment. Legislation followed banning combinations in one trade after another until the situation was made quite clear when the Combination Acts 1799–1800 provided for a general prohibition in all trades of combinations of employees or employers.

However, following the Napoleonic Wars there was an economic depression together with a movement to improve conditions which resulted in the repeal, in 1824, of the Combination Laws. The effect of this was to allow workers to enter into combinations for the purpose of regulating wages and other conditions without their committing the crime of conspiracy. This Act (the Combination Laws Repeal Act 1824) was followed shortly by another which somewhat circumscribed workers' rights, but it still preserved the right to withhold labour by collective action and this right has never been withdrawn.

Subsequent acts, including the Trade Union Act 1871 and the Conspiracy and Protection of Property Act 1875, gave trade unions legal status and also permitted peaceful picketing. Then the Trade Disputes Act 1906 protected a trade union from being sued for alleged wrongful acts committed by it or on its behalf. Thus trade unions were freed of any risk of a *civil* liability arising from their actions. A variety of other legislation followed which repealed certain preceding legislation, covered the amalgamation of trade unions, and tied up some other aspects that were not satisfactory.

However, the most notable legislation to date was the Industrial Relations Act of 1971, which replaced most preceding legislation regarding trade unions and followed both the main political parties' examination of the increasingly complex and potentially disruptive industrial relations scene. This Act granted to an individual the right to belong or not to belong to a trade union. This was subsequently repealed with many other provisions by the Trade Unions and Labour Relations Act 1974. However, certain provisions particularly relating to 'unfair dismissal' remained to protect the individual, but have since been altered by subsequent employment legislation.

Present position

The trade union movement, along with other sectors of our society, is undergoing a period of mergers and rationalizations, and although at the end of 1972 there were about 480 trade unions whose members totalled about eleven million, in 1987 there are now only 373 unions with 10.7 million members.

In some cases there is strong competition among unions for membership, and one notable case was in fact the hotel and catering industry where the Transport and General Workers' Union and the National Union of General and Municipal Workers came into conflict over recruiting hotel workers in Torquay.

The strength of the trade union movement obviously stems from its ability to present a united front, and therefore many individual unions join federations to further strengthen their movement. These federations are, however, in most cases rather loose, and the responsibility for action rests with the individual unions.

The trade union movement comes together within the Trades Union Congress (TUC), the aims of which are:

To promote the interests of all its affiliated organizations and generally to improve the economic and social conditions of workers.

The TUC, as with the federations of unions, has little authority over individual unions, but it does oblige affiliated unions to keep its General Council informed of any trade disputes that may involve large numbers of work people.

The role of trade unions

Trade unions are primarily concerned with representing their members in order to obtain what is considered by their members to be reasonable conditions of employment. Reasonable is, of course, relative; it may mean maintaining one's position in an 'earnings league' or it may mean merely preserving one's purchasing power.

Although unions are concerned with obtaining increased earnings they also strive to improve their members' other conditions of employment such as time off, holidays, safety and status. They do, in addition, show particular concern over job security and, very often, important political issues.

Their roles can be evaluated from a number of different perspectives.

Economic–Political

On the one hand unions may be concerned only with improving their members' conditions and, at the other extreme, unions may be an extension of a political movement. The Labour Party grew out of the British trade union movement. Some union leaders may use their unions in order to further their own political ends which may have little relationship with the wishes of the rank and file membership.

Economic–Political

Another view is concerned with the relative rights of those who provide labour and capital. There are those who believe that ownership bestows certain inalienable rights, whereas others believe that those who provide their labour have equal rights to those of the providers of capital.

Democracy–Autocracy (Pluralist–Unitarist)

Related to the former is the argument about the degree of participation in decision making. There are those who believe that managers, because of training and experience, should be responsible for taking decisions, whereas there are others who hold the view that decisions should be shared by all who are affected by them.

Rank and file versus union leadership

An important discussion is the extent to which union leadership is really representative of the membership. It is argued that the very process of moving up the union hierarchy separates leaders from their members.

Individual rights versus group rights

An important discussion, particularly where 'closed shops' may be involved, relates to the rights of individuals to choose whether to belong to a trade union. On the one hand it is argued that the rights of individuals must be upheld; on the other hand it is argued that the majority has greater rights. Certainly this would appear to be what democracy is about.

In essence however, whichever perspective or perspectives are adopted, industrial relations is concerned, explicitly or implicitly, with the power of the participants to influence the distribution of the wealth they generate or the resources they have made available. Unions themselves claim to be democratic organizations, that the organization represents the wishes of the majority of its members. To what extent union leaders do represent their members', or their own, aspirations varies from union to union. However, Figure 15.2 shows how one large union, the parent union of the Hotel and Catering Workers' Union, is structured.

Types of union

Over the years unions have evolved into four main types.

Craft unions

These usually consist of members with specific trade skills.

General unions

These unions consist mainly of members with little or no specific trade skills and they have no skill or training requirements. The general unions constitute the largest unions in Britain today (e.g. Transport and General Workers Union).

Figure 15.2   *Structure of a union*

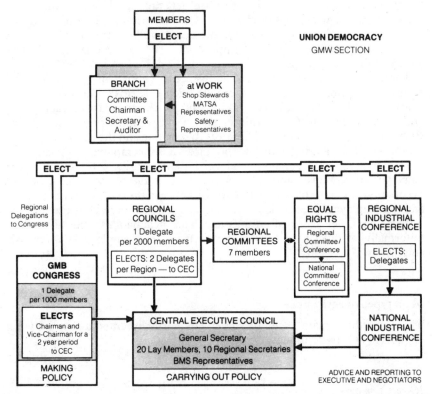

Industrial unions

These unions consist of most workers in one industry (e.g. the National Union of Railwaymen).

White collar unions

These unions consist of administrative, clerical and managerial employees (e.g. MATSA, a subsidiary of GMBTU).

Employers' associations

The first employers' associations of any importance were probably the merchant guilds and livery companies which existed throughout Europe from the early Middle Ages. They dealt with a variety of matters that affected trade and labour.

With the repeal of the combination laws and because of pressure from the growing trade union movement, employers' organizations grew rapidly during the nineteenth century. Nowadays they are, generally speaking, organized on a trade or industry-wide basis and because of this they deal with matters of trade, such as encouraging government to take defensive measures against foreign competition, and with matters of employment, such as negotiating industry-wide conditions of employment.

These employers' or trade associations come together in various national bodies, the main one being the Confederation of British Industries (CBI), which has individual employers, trade associations, employers' organizations, and nationalized industries within its membership. In the private sector, the British Hotels, Restaurants and Caterers Association and the Brewers' Society are the hotel and catering industry's principal trade or employers' associations.

The conduct of negotiation and consultation varies considerably from employer to employer and from industry to industry. In some cases all negotiations will take place at national level between the trade union concerned and the employers' association. This is sometimes referred to as the 'formal' system. In other cases all discussions and negotiations will take place 'informally' at plant level, that is, between the local employer and his own employees.

Main types of agreement

There are three main types of agreement normally entered into between employers and trade unions.

Recognition agreements

These are usually the first type of agreement entered into. Under such agreements the employer normally agrees to recognize the union in certain instances, such as representing members in grievance and disciplinary matters.

Negotiating agreements

Under a negotiating agreement, an employer agrees to recognize a union's right to negotiate on behalf of its members and employees doing the same work as the union's members. As an example, one major hotel company has such an agreement with the Hotel and Catering Workers' Union. Although less than 20 per cent of the company's employees are members of the HCWU the negotiating agreement actually sets rates for virtually all the company's staff.

Substantive agreements

These contain the 'substance' of an agreement and include elements such as pay, hours and overtime rates.

Procedural agreements

These lay down the various procedures to be followed, such as dates for agreements to be made, procedures to be followed in the absence of agreements.

Industrial relations in the hotel and catering industry

Trade union membership within the hotel and catering industry, excluding local authorities, is, generally speaking, very low (see Figure 15.3). Estimates for 1986 were that, including industrial and institutional catering, there were about 100,000 members including the members of the National Association of Licensed House Managers. This means that probably approaching 6 per cent of the total labour force are union members. This shows hardly any increase on the estimated 5 per cent in 1978. Membership is relatively strong in the industrial and institutional catering sector (about 20 per cent of all employees) because the catering staff are frequently part of a large totally unionized workforce of another industry. Membership is also high in local authority and hospital catering.

In the public sector the major bodies concerned with industrial relations are:

Hospitals — Whitley Council.
Education (e.g. polytechnics and colleges) — National Joint Council for Local Authority Services (Manual Workers).
School meals — officers — Soulbury Committee
　　　　　　　　manual staff — National Joint Council for Local Authority Services (Manual Workers).

These bodies are negotiating bodies consisting of representatives of employers and trade union representatives.

Individual contracts

A major feature of the industrial relationship in the hotels sector of the industry is the secret and individual nature of contracts (Mars and Mitchell, 1976). Because the vast majority of employers are small with only a few staff, contracts are made between the employee and the employer, who offers terms that will solve his immediate staff problem. These terms may be better than those currently enjoyed by other similarly graded staff. Consequently, an element of secrecy is expected. This system of individual contracts is made easier because a considerable proportion of recruitment is informal, on a person to person basis and may involve undeclared cash payments. While managers believe that this individual and secret contract works to their advantage, it is suggested that the ambiguity and confusion causes grievances which, while contributing to high labour turnover at the moment, will lead to increased union involvement in the longer term.

Figure 15.3   *The principal unions involved in the hotel, catering and associated industries*

Sector of the hotel and catering industry	Approximate number of employees*	Principal unions involved	Approximate number of members**				
			1973	1978	1980	1982	1986
Hotels and restaurants	497,000	GMWU*	20,000	25,000	30,000	31,000	33,000
	(10,500)	TGWU	3,000	9,000	9,000	7,750	6,000
		NUR	3,000	9,500	10,000	8,500	4,500
		TSSA					750
		USDAW	4,000			2,000	***
Industrial and institutional	670,000	GMWU		2,600	30,000	25,500	20,000
		TGWU		30,000	10,000	11,000	
		USDAW		8,000			***
Public house managers	18,500	NALHM†	10,000	15,000	17,500	18,000	15,500
		ACTSS	500	1,000		750	600
Motorway services		USDAW			2,500	2,500	—
		TGWU			1,500	2,500	
Club stewards		USDAW		3,000	3,000		***
Bar staff	200,000	GMWU		6,000	6,000	4,750	7,000
		TGWU				1,000	***
		USDAW					
		NUCS					2,760
Local authority and NHS catering	428,000	NUPE	250,000	250,000	250,000		250,000
		NALGO				700	
supervisors		NUPE					2,000

*The numbers quoted are taken from *Manpower in the Hotel and Catering Industry* (HCITB, 1978). They are likely to be slightly inflated due to double counting.

**These numbers are estimates provided by the unions themselves in 1980.

†The National Secretary of NALHM wishes to make it clear that his union's figures are always available for independent audit.

‡The GMWU membership is now largely organized within their specialist union; the Hotel and Catering Workers' Union.

§ At national level.

***USDAW did not provide a breakdown of membership in 1986; however in 1984 their total membership in the industry was reported to be 6,500.

Wages Councils

In 1945 with the enactment of the Wages Councils Act and the creation of wages boards it was recognized that where employees were not organized there was insufficient pressure on employers to ensure that wage levels and other conditions kept up with those offered to other sections of the community. In this industry this had been recognized earlier and resulted in the Catering Wages Act of 1943 which created the Catering Wages Board. This board laid down minimum conditions of employment. However, this Act and others have since been superseded by the Wages Council Act 1959 which regulates wages and other conditions for employees in the industry through Wages Councils which include employer and employee representatives. Councils exist for the following sectors of the industry:

Licensed residential establishments and restaurants.
Licensed non-residential establishments and restaurants.
Unlicensed places of refreshment.

The rates laid down by the various councils, however, are considered by most employers and employees to be absolute minima and market forces generally oblige employers to pay above these rates. The value of Wages Councils nowadays is therefore questionable and it is hoped by many that these will be phased out. In fact the CIR report on Industrial Catering (in 1973) recommended the abolition of the Wages Council for Industrial and Staff Canteens. The Wages Act 1986 reduced the scope of Wages Councils to merely specifying a minimum wage for all employment within an industry.

'Manpower Policy in the Hotels and Restaurant Industry' — EDC report

Probably the most important publication to date on industrial relations in the industry is *Manpower Policy in the Hotels and Restaurant Industry* (NEDO, 1975).

The main findings of this report are summarized here and are discussed at greater length in appropriate chapters.

Social trends

Four main areas affect employment within the industry:

1 Increased employment legislation.
2 Increased demand for leisure, higher standards of living and social status.
3 More democratic forms of social control.
4 Increasing trade union membership. (In 1986 trade union membership was declining.)

If, therefore, the industry is to attract an adequate supply of the emerging workforce, it must gear its management style and personnel policies accordingly. In fact, the EDC's research showed that the industry is more attractive to younger people than older people because of their needs (listed above in 1–4). Only those employers able to meet these needs will be able to retain the younger working people.

Fewer but larger companies

Over the last few years, the number of larger companies has reduced (for example, Trusthouse Forte's acquisition of Lyons' Strand Hotels). While this may provide opportunities for better work prospects and higher earnings (due to economies of scale), other problems, associated with administration and management of complex organizations, present themselves.

Labour costs

The difference between earnings of hotel staff and those in other industries has increased, with the consequence that the industry is not viewed very favourably as an employer. As in so many cases, such comparisons can be misleading, however. Many of the staff receive board and lodging or board at least, so they are insulated somewhat from rapid inflation on such items as fares, fuel, food and rates.

Employment Services' Agency and youth employment services

The industry now has over twenty-two specialist employment offices servicing its own needs. This service is unique to the hotel and catering industry. In spite of this, during the course of the EDC research, it was found that the relationship between the industry and the various official agencies connected with employment could be improved; for example, many managers seem to expect these agencies to act as 'staff selectors' as well as assisting in recruitment processes.

Employment policies

The EDC pointed to the need to improve staff retention so that pressure is taken off staff recruitment. Staff retention will only improve if employment policies are geared to the hotel employment market. Such policies will have to cover hours, pay, shifts, use of labour, management style and co-operation with the official agencies.

Senior management of companies

While the EDC research showed that deficiencies will not be corrected without new attitudes and approaches of unit managers, it is the responsibility of senior managers of companies to ensure that such changes occur through manpower planning which is integrated with the general company policy.

The trade associations

The image of the industry as an employer should be improved by co-operative effort of employers channelled through the trade associations.

These were the major findings of the EDC research and various detailed aspects of the report are referred to in other chapters of this book. The key to improvement probably lies in developing effective consultative machinery in the first place. Several other reports on manpower within the industry have also been produced, such as the BHRCA's *Manpower Problems in the Hotel and Catering Industry*, and these largely confirmed the findings of the EDC report.

These criticisms were made some time ago, and certain developments could indicate that there will be changes in company manpower policies in hotels and restaurants in the long term. Certainly the larger employers claim that they are making considerable improvements to the industry's conditions and reputation and they claim their lead will be bound to set the pace for smaller employers. Such changes will take many years, however, because an industry employing about 2 million people has considerable inertia and change will not be easy. It is likely that its employees will remain, in 'take home pay' terms, amongst the lowest paid for a long time into the future.

Another development worth noting in 1980 was the establishment of the Hotel and Catering Workers' Union, a section of the GMWU. This union has put considerable effort into recruiting new members. To date however it is difficult to assess progress, with conflicting reports from the union and the employers concerned. At the same time the TGWU, the main rival union, appointed a national hotel and catering officer.

Consultation

If good industrial relations are to be achieved, discussion must take place between management and staff on all matters related to conditions and methods of work. The size of the organization does not affect this principle; the only variation to it is one of degree, as the actual size and nature of the organization determines the type and degree of formality of discussions.

Within this industry there are probably three main types of consultative or negotiating procedure. The first and probably the least formal will be found in the individually owned hotel or restaurant, managed by the proprietor who works in the establishment with his staff numbering up to about twenty. In this case any formal joint consultation or negotiation should be unnecessary as the employer is close to his employees and should be aware of their problems and views. It is his job to keep himself informed of their opinions and feelings and he may well hold informal meetings at regular intervals with all staff. Such meetings may already be held to discuss menus, special functions, etc., and

Figure 15.4   *Industrial relations institutions*

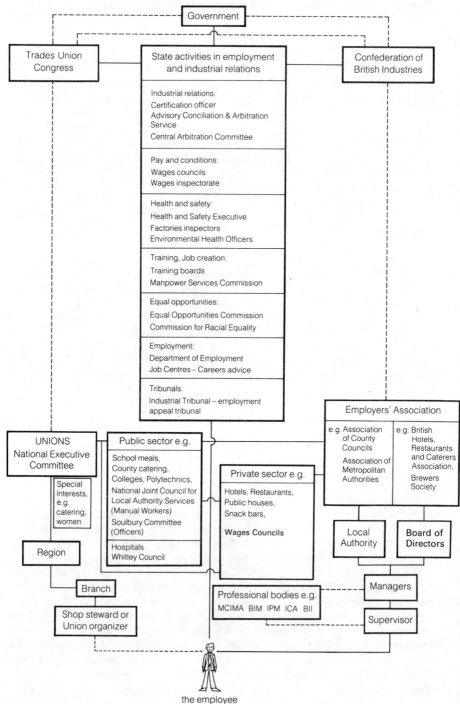

from time to time they should be enlarged to cover methods of work and conditions of employment.

The next level may be found in a hotel or restaurant probably having groups of employees in several departments. Typically this would be a hotel or restaurant complex with from twenty to several hundred employees. In this case there may be small groups of people working together — each group with its own aims — often not the same as those of the organization as a whole. One only needs to think of the conflict between cooks and waiters in many hotels or restaurants to accept that this conflict exists. In this case each department should nominate a representative to meet management's representatives on a regular basis — probably between four and eight times a year. Some formality would be needed and agendas would have to be circulated beforehand and minutes produced afterwards.

The level after this would be in a company or organization with several large units. Each establishment would have its own joint consultative committee, and in addition it may find it worth organizing a company-based joint consultative committee with representatives from each establishment meeting head office management. This system would be most appropriate where a company is heavily represented in an area — London, for example — and because management would wish to discourage unnecessary movements between units caused by varying supervisory or personnel practices within the company's establishments. On the other hand it may not be necessary where an employer's establishments are located far apart in areas where conditions are different.

These are the three main degrees or levels of consultation (and possibly negotiation), but whether all three should be conducted with trade union representatives or not is generally for management and the employees to decide. The second and third levels, involving the larger employers, certainly could, and do, involve trade union representatives. Whether employers will wish to enter into closed shop agreements also will depend on the particular circumstances, but employers must remember that a ballot by employees can make such an agreement compulsory for an employer.

Benefits of consultation

Managers may rightly ask what benefits can result from their taking the initiative in establishing joint consultation and even bargaining or negotiating procedures with their employees. First, and most important of all, it must be recognized that although employees may have no negotiating machinery they still push up rates of pay and win other concessions by 'voting with their feet'. They move from employer to employer continually looking for higher earnings and employers in turn have continually to increase their rates to attract replacement staff. Seasonal resorts will confirm that this practice is rife. The fear of 'runaway' wage increases consequently is generally exaggerated. Instead, because of continuous collective pressure from the employees their conditions would steadily improve, job security would become greater with the result that the staff turnover rate would almost certainly drop to reasonable proportions. There are many cases in those sections of the industry where trade unions are strong, where the annual staff turnover is not above 10 per cent per annum. As a result the economies to be made through not having to recruit and train a steady flow of replacement staff are considerable, apart from the benefits of being able to maintain consistent standards.

A second benefit of consultation is a more willing acceptance of change. By nature most people oppose change, but if they have been involved in discussing changes that affect them and they understand the underlying reasons, they will almost certainly be more prepared to make the changes work. A further benefit is that many work people have ideas that can improve working methods, and by consultation management can provide the opportunities for these to be expressed. A third view, however, is that whether these are measurable benefits or not, participation in decisions affecting working people is a right — not a privilege granted by management for instrumental reasons.

Disadvantages

On the other side of the coin there are disadvantages to be faced when entering into consultation with employees. First, management action will be open to question and discussion, with the consequence that management's decisions and practices will have to be so much better. Furthermore, even confidential information must be made available for discussion. Apart from this, it must be remembered that if trade unions are involved the possibility of industrial action such as working to rule, blacking, banning overtime and even striking must not be ruled out when agreement on such things as pay, working conditions, methods or procedures cannot be reached.

The industry's image

Of less immediate consequence to the individual employer, but of great importance to the industry as a whole, is the need to improve its image. The supply of continental staff is running down owing to increased standards of living in the traditional suppliers of catering staff and also because of our own government's action to reduce unemployment at home. The industry, therefore, has to attract an ever growing share of the domestic workforce.

To improve its image the hotel and catering industry needs to offer conditions that satisfy the average working man's expectations, and this will only be achieved through regular, frank consultation and negotiation between both sides, as happens in many other industries. Without this dialogue and the consequent improvement in conditions the industry will not attract the number of competent work people that are going to be needed in the future.

Establishing consultation

Once the decision has been taken to establish consultation within an organization, the scope of any discussions must not be limited, but should cover *all matters* of interest to both sides, including rates of pay, hours of work, fringe benefits, working methods, and company plans. It should be clear, however, that the purpose of these committees is consultation and not negotiation.

Setting up a staff consultative committee sometimes presents problems, because it is essential that the employees' representatives are chosen, and seen to be chosen by their colleagues and not by management. The following steps may be taken to achieve this.

1 Employees, known to be respected by their colleagues, should be called from each department to attend a meeting with representatives of management. At this meeting the intention of establishing a staff consultative committee should be explained by a senior member of management.
2 If the idea is accepted the representatives should be asked to discuss this with their departmental colleagues, and if the reaction of the majority of employees appears to be in favour of the consultative committee a ballot

Figure 15.5 *Example of a constitution and rules for a staff consultative committee*

Aim

The purpose of the Staff Consultative Committee is to establish and maintain an effective system of communication between the company's management and its employees so that by consultation the well-being of both sides may be promoted.

Constitution

1 The Committee shall consist of one staff representative from each department
2 Management shall be represented by the general manager,* the assistant manager (personnel) and one other member of line management
3 The chairman will be a member of management
4 The secretary will be nominated by management

Rules

1 Meetings shall take place not less than once every six weeks. Either side may call a meeting as necessary by notifying the secretary. In this case the meeting must take place within three weeks
2 The quorum shall be one management representative and more than half of the elected staff representatives or their substitutes
3 Elected representatives unable to attend a meeting may nominate a substitute, who must come from the representative's department
4 Subjects of mutual interest regarding methods of work and conditions of employment may be discussed by the SCC with the exception that no individual employee's case may be discussed
5 Rules may be altered or otherwise amended by mutual agreement

*Some companies avoid having the general manager involved. However, the effect of this can be to down-grade the importance of the committee from the employees' point of view.

should then be organized in each department to elect the departmental representative. The elected representatives should then be given the opportunity to hold a meeting at which they would elect their own officers.
3   A further meeting would then be held between the *elected* representatives and the representatives of management where procedures would be agreed for the future.

The outline of a constitution and rules for a staff consultative committee is illustrated in Figure 15.5.

Responsibility for good industrial relations

The responsibility for good industrial relations depends, within each undertaking, upon its management, and this can only result from frank discussion between management and staff. The Industrial Relations Code of Practice places the responsibility for stimulating this dialogue squarely on management. In the section on communication and consultation it says:

Management in co-operation with employee representatives should:
 i)   provide opportunities for employees to discuss matters affecting their jobs with those to whom they are responsible:
ii)   ensure that managers are kept informed of the views of employees and of the problems which they may face in meeting management's objectives.

Further reading

Anthony, P., *The Conduct of Industrial Relations*, London: Institute of Personnel Management, 1977
Employee Relations, London: HCITB, 1982
Farnham, D., and Pimlott, J., *Understanding Industrial Relations*, 2nd ed., Eastbourne: Cassell, 1983
Mars, G., Mitchell, P., and Bryant, D., *Manpower Problems in the Hotel and Catering Industry*, Farnborough: Saxon House, 1976
Reilly, P., *Participation, Democracy and Control: Forms of Employee Involvement*, London: British Institute of Management Report, 1979
Room for Reform, Industrial Relations Course Case Study, Milton Keynes: Open University, 1976

chapter 16

Law of employment

The evolution and development of our complex industrial society has been accompanied by the need to regulate many of the activities of various groups of people. Without this regulation society would not be what it is today. In the case of industrial relations law, the activities of employees were long regulated by legal institutions such as magistrates who had, amongst a number of powers, the power to set rates of pay. More recently, the activities of employers became subject to increasing regulation in order to provide employees with greater protection in economic and physical terms. Factories legislation is just one example. Most recently the increasing power of trade unions, as distinct from individual work people, caused concern particularly to Conservative governments, with the result that the power of unions has been circumscribed by legislation. As stated above, until fairly recent times in our history responsibility for regulating conditions of employment rested largely on parliament and on local magistrates. This was relatively easy while the number of categories of workers was small. Gradually, however, as society became more industrialized it became increasingly difficult to exercise this control. The pendulum swung the other way. As was seen in the last chapter various laws were passed that made it possible for both workers and owners to combine into trade unions and associations in order to bargain, until the stage was reached where the State appeared to avoid any direct involvement in the relationships between employers and employees. The whole system of bargaining and negotiation then rested on voluntary understandings between the workers and their employers. However, as our industrial society developed even further the power of trade unions grew and the concentration of certain vital resources and services into what became vulnerable positions made it possible for many groups of people to disrupt supplies to the whole community.

The government therefore felt obliged to re-enter the field of relations between employers and employees by creating a legal framework for the conduct of what is now called industrial relations.

The government's responsibility rests with a senior cabinet minister, the Secretary of State for Employment. In addition, several other ministers have responsibilities that are related to employment and these include the Secretary of State for Social Services who is concerned with such matters as national insurance and pensions, and the Secretary for Trade and Industry who is responsible for such matters as regional development policy.

The law relating to employment is considerable now and it is only possible in this book to cover a small part of it. The major areas of legislation have been selected and summarized below.

Contracts of employment

A contract of employment is the basis of the working relationship between employer and employee and is subject to the general principles covered by the law of contract. Consequently a contract of employment may be oral, written, or the terms may be merely implied. It consists of an offer by one of the parties and an acceptance by the other. A *consideration*, that is, an exchange of promises to perform certain duties and to pay certain wages and provide certain conditions, is necessary to create the contract. The *consideration*, as with all contracts, must have an economic value. The offer is usually (but not necessarily) made by the employer and should contain details of remuneration, hours, location and holidays. The offer may refer to other documents such as Wages Council publications. Not all conditions have to be included as some may be implied by custom and practice. The contract comes into existence when the offerer receives acceptance from the offeree.

Although, in common law, contracts need not be in writing, it is advisable that all offers and acceptances are in writing in order to avoid misunderstanding and possible problems. Furthermore, because most employees are entitled to a written statement of the main conditions of employment (see below) there is no real reason today for not preparing a proper, written contract of employment.

Employment Protection (Consolidation) Act 1978 — amended by the Employment Act 1980 and 1982

This Act provides the rights of employees, who work over a certain number of hours, to minimum periods of notice dependent on their length of service, and the Act also requires that employees are given written details of certain conditions of employment.

Where a contract provides for longer periods of notice the terms of the contract will apply, whereas contracts containing shorter periods are overridden by the periods laid down by the Employment Protection Act. Payment in lieu of notice may be made by the employer or the employee.

Written particulars

These must be given to people working for sixteen hours or more per week within thirteen weeks of employment commencing, or eight hours per week if employed for five years or more.

Written statements need not take any particular form but the contents are prescribed and they can refer employees to other documents such as manuals and booklets which must be reasonably available to them. There is no requirement in law for the employee or the employer to sign the statement. But it is advisable to issue all employees with a statement and to retain signed copies in the personal dossiers. The ideal way administratively is to design letters of offer so that they satisfy the Employment Protection Act requirements. An example is shown in Figure 6.2 (page 90).

Restraint on employees

In the case of some employees, such as chefs or managers, employers feel it necessary to include a clause in a contract restraining an employee from divulging trade secrets, entering into direct competition by operating his own business, working for another person in the same line of business or using lists of customers prepared in the course of employment in order to entice customers away.

In order to obtain protection against such eventualities any terms in a contract need to be clearly stated and not implied. It is important, however, to make such a term reasonable in the circumstances otherwise the right to any protection could be forfeited. At the same time such restraint clauses must be shown to be in the public interest and it is most unlikely that such a restraint clause will be upheld.

Searching employees

It is always advisable to obtain an employee's permission before attempting to search his or her person or property. To search a person without permission, and without finding evidence of theft, can result in the employer being sued for assault and battery. In those cases where the employer's right to search is considered to be vital, such as in hotels and industrial catering organizations, a clause to this effect should be written into every person's contract of employment. Even so an employee cannot be forcibly searched if he or she refuses. Such a refusal instead becomes the subject of disciplinary or dismissal proceedings.

Dismissals

Unfair dismissal

Under the Employment Protection (Consolidation) Act 1978 as amended by the Employment Act 1980 and 1982 there is protection for employees against unfair dismissal.

In the past, so long as an employer gave the agreed period of notice or money in lieu an employee had no recourse against the employer. The situation has

174 Human Resource Management in the Hotel and Catering Industry

changed and it is now necessary to show that reasons for dismissal were fair. Valid reasons include:

1 Lack of capability or qualification for the job for which an employee was employed.
2 Misconduct.
3 Redundancy, within the definition of the Redundancy legislation.
4 Unsuitability due to legal restrictions (e.g. loss of Justice's licence).
5 Some other substantial reasons (e.g. chronic sickness).

It should be noted that no complaint of unfair dismissal or of a worker's rights relating to trade unions will be heard by an industrial tribunal until a Department of Employment conciliation officer has looked into the circumstances to see if a settlement can be reached without a tribunal hearing.

Instant or summary dismissal

In certain instances an employer may be justified in dismissing an employee without giving the required period of notice or money in lieu. Although this may be permitted in such cases as an employee's permanent incapacity to perform his duties, in most cases it occurs where employees are guilty of serious misconduct. To dismiss a person instantly can have serious consequences for the employer, if a dismissed employee sues him successfully for damages, so it is not a step to be taken lightly. Reasons for instant dismissal include:

1 Serious or repeated disobedience or other misconduct.
2 Serious or repeated negligence.
3 Drunkenness while on duty.
4 Theft.
5 Accepting bribes or commissions.

The argument underlying instant dismissal is that the employee, through serious misconduct, has repudiated the contract, and the employer chooses not to renew it.

An employer can normally only dismiss an employee for misconduct committed outside working hours and away from the place of work if other employees were involved, which could have an effect on the employer's business, or if the employee is in domestic service.

Where an employer dismisses a person instantly it should be done at the time of the misdemeanour or when it first comes to the attention of the employer. To delay will imply that the employer has waived his right to dismiss. The reason for dismissal should be given at the time of the dismissal.

An employer may, in some cases, withhold money earned by an employee who has been instantly dismissed for good reasons, unless a contract states otherwise. However, legal advice should always be sought before taking such action.

Payment of wages

The Wages Act

Generally speaking the arrangements for the payment of wages are regulated by the contract of employment. The Wages Act 1986, however, provides specific rules on deductions. These specify that an employer must not make deductions or receive payment (e.g. as a fine) unless:

the deduction is authorized by statute
the deduction is authorized in the contract of employment
the worker has agreed in writing to the deduction

Certain deductions are exempted from the above conditions, such as the recovery of an over-payment.

In the case of the retail trade, including catering, employees can be required as a condition of the contract, to make good stock or cash shortages. However, such a deduction or payment must not exceed 10% of the gross pay due for the period. On termination of employment, however, such deductions may exceed 10%. They cannot be made retrospective for more than 12 months. Notice of intention to make such deductions has to be made in advance, and a written demand also has to be issued.

Payment of wages may be in a form agreed in the contract. This may be in the form of cash, cheque or credit transfer. It may also include food, and

Most wages in the Hotel and Catering Industry are regulated by the Wages Council orders (page 163).

Attachment of Earnings Act 1971

This Act enables a court to order an employer to make periodic deductions from an employee's earnings and to pay the sum deducted to the collecting officer of the court. The court specifies the amount and can make *priority orders* for payment of fines or maintenance of dependants, or *non-priority* orders for the clearance of civil debts. The court will also specify the *protected earnings* which is the level of income below which a person's earnings should not be reduced by these deductions. Any consequent shortfalls in payments will be carried forward.

Suspensions

In some circumstances, particularly involving alleged misconduct, an employer may wish to suspend an employee until the circumstances have been looked into and a decision has been taken regarding the employee's future. It is quite in order to do this so long as pay is not withheld — unless a contract specifically permitting the withholding of pay is in existence.

PAYE

Employers are obliged to deduct tax payable on money paid to any of their employees earning money falling under Schedule E (that is, emoluments from any office or employment). Some items are not subject to deductions: business expenses, and rent-free accommodation or temporary accommodation allowances which are provided because of the nature of the employer's business.

This responsibility covers service charge earnings and 'tronc' earnings where the employer is involved in the distribution. It is the duty of staff to declare tips where the manager is not involved in their distribution.

Employer's liability

There are two separate categories of liability that employers bear in relation to injuries suffered by their employees while in their employment. These are common law and statutory liabilities.

The common law responsibilities extend also to employees of other employers, such as contractors, while working on the employer's premises, and also to the employer's employees carrying out work for him on another person's premises, for example, an outdoor caterer's staff.

In common law employers are expected to provide protection that is reasonable in the circumstances. An employee will be compensated for injury if the employer was at fault in exposing the employee to unnecessary risk in the circumstances.

Unfortunately the common law is not able to provide for all developments in industry and therefore several statutes exist to specify the nature of protection to be provided and to lay down certain other regulations covering the working environment.

Health and Safety at Work Act 1974

In 1975 the Health and Safety at Work Act 1974 came into force, which provides very flexible legislation protecting all employees at work (excepting those in domestic service). The Act in principle provides that employers are to ensure the safety of their employees (and also the general public) at the employer's premises, by maintaining safe plant, safe systems of work and safe premises, and also by ensuring adequate instruction, training and supervision. Other people, too, such as designers, manufacturers, installers, importers and suppliers of goods for use at work, are to ensure, in so far as they are responsible, that any health and safety risks are eliminated. Employees also are made responsible for the safety of others.

Office, Shops and Railway Premises Act

The Health and Safety at Work Act also re-enacted the Offices, Shops and Railway Premises Act 1963 which includes most catering establishments within its scope. This Act covers such aspects as cleanliness, overcrowding, lighting, temperature, ventilation and sanitary arrangements for work people.

Young persons and women

Many statutes have been enacted in the past, which have been intended to protect groups of people from exploitation, including their being obliged to work excessive hours. The main groups protected in this way are young persons and women.

Children and young persons

Children are defined as being under the minimum school-leaving age, and 'young persons' refers to persons over school-leaving age, but under the age of 18. The regulations vary for the different groups and for the type of undertaking in which young persons are employed. The principal Acts are concerned primarily with protecting the physical well-being of children and young persons and with specifying the hours which they are permitted to work. Children, for example, are not permitted to work during school hours.

The regulations are quite detailed but can vary in detail from one part of the country to another as they are administered mainly by local authorities. Regulations cover the following points:

Hours of work
Hours on the employer's premises
Hours off duty
Frequency and duration of rest and meal breaks
Permitted overtime
Holidays
Medical examinations

For details of the regulations as they apply to a particular area it is advisable to contact the local office of the Department of Employment.

The Equal Pay Act 1970

The purpose of this Act is to remove differences in terms and conditions of employment between men and women employed on the same or very similar work. The onus of proof that any differences in pay result from reasons other than sex rests with the employer. Industrial tribunals deal with any complaints and are able to award arrears of pay and damages. Job evaluation plays a part in determining pay differentials between jobs.

Sex Discrimination Act 1975

The Sex Discrimination Act 1975 was introduced in order to grant equal opportunities to both sexes in the fields of employment, education and training and to make it an offence to discriminate against a man or a woman on the grounds of sex alone. The main provision of this Act is that if a job can be performed equally well by a man or a woman it is an offence to discriminate against a man or a woman on the grounds of sex alone. This applies to recruitment of new staff and also to promotion.

There are certain exceptions, of particular relevance to the hotel and catering industry, such as cloakroom attendants or where limited staff accommodation has to be shared.

The Employment Protection (Consolidation) Act 1978 grants women with at least two years' service the right to maternity pay, maternity leave and to reinstatement in the same or similar work when they return.

Social security

The Social Security Scheme provides a wide variety of benefits and welfare services such as benefits for unemployment, sickness, industrial injuries and also retirement. Most people over school-leaving age and under pensionable age are insurable. Persons who are insurable must register and obtain a National Insurance number.

Trade union legislation

The main legislation, covering trade unions currently, is contained in a number of Acts, including:

Trade Union and Labour Relations Act 1974 (as amended by the Employment Acts 1980 and 1982)
Trade Union Act 1984
Employment Acts 1980 and 1982

These Acts contain legislation concerned with 'collective' employment issues and cover a range of issues such as:

Trade disputes and immunities   trade disputes only attract immunity from actions for damages if they are disputes between employees and their employer and are concerned with matters central to their employment relationship. In addition, any dispute must have been approved in a ballot by a majority of those voting.

Picketing   picketing is only lawful if carried out as part of a trade dispute and should be at or near the place of work.

Employee involvement   all employers of more than 250 employees have to produce in the annual report a statement covering actions concerned with involving employees in the enterprise and keeping them informed.

Further reading

Boella, M. J., (ed.) *Catering-Croner's Loose Leaf Reference Book*, with regular up dating service, London: Croner Publications

Pannett, A., *Principles of Hotel and Catering Law*, Eastbourne: Holt, Rinehart and Winston, 1984

Sweeney, S., (ed.) *Reference Book for Employers*, with regular up dating service, London: Croner Publications

Sweeney, S., (ed.) *Croner's Employment Law*, with regular up dating service, London: Croner Publications

chapter 17

Manpower planning, records and statistics

In recent years the importance of an undertaking's human resources has become much more apparent owing to the considerable costs of labour and the growing staff shortages in some sectors of the hotel and catering industry. In many other industries and organizations these problems have led to much attention being paid to most aspects of human resource management. It has led, in particular, to accurate manpower planning so that an employer has the right resources available when required and also so that labour costs are not unnecessarily high. Because of this, well-conceived personnel policies are now playing an increasingly important part in furthering many undertakings' business objectives. They translate the overall business plan, normally concerned in the private sector with competitiveness and profitability, into a detailed manpower plan. Sound personnel policies can only be achieved through a thorough understanding of the organization, its objectives, its management, its operating style, and its social and political environment.

Personnel policies must play a positive and creative role in the plans, developments and day-to-day activities of an undertaking. They must be designed to provide competent human resources when required. The need to plan on a sound basis of reliable information has been emphasized and much of a manager's work revolves around certain basic and fundamental information; for example, the need for precise job descriptions has been shown to be vital not only to recruitment, but also to training, performance appraisal, job evaluation and salary administration.

Manpower planning is divided into two separate and distinct parts: strategic and operational. The strategic part of manpower planning is concerned with ensuring that the right manpower will be available in the longer term, for example for hotels that are not even built.

Strategic manpower planning for larger organizations requires a good understanding of that organization and its environment. Figure 17.1 shows a 'systems thinking' diagram — how an organization's manpower plan can be affected by its environment.

At the operational level management needs to know precisely what manning ratios are necessary. Each organization and each establishment will have its own, such as one waiter for ten covers and one chambermaid for fourteen rooms (see Figure 17.2).

Figure 17.1 *A 'systems thinking' diagram*

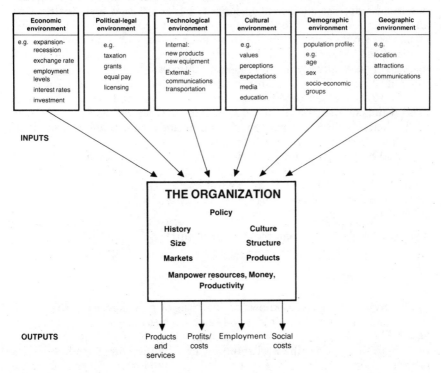

Figure 17.2 *Manpower planning — matching labour supply to demand*

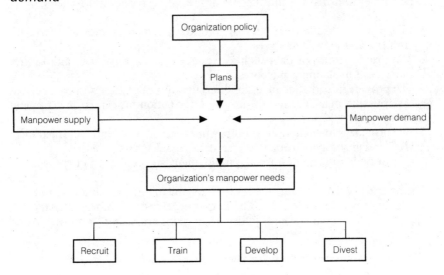

At the strategic level management needs accurate manpower statistics in order to develop the undertaking's long-term plans. This is best illustrated by an example. If, for instance, a brewery company wanted to expand its number of managed public houses by 100 it would need to recruit at least 100 new husband and wife teams to run these public houses. In addition, if it had 100 managed houses already it would have to anticipate finding replacements for some of these existing 100 managers. If wastage rates are unknown, it is not possible to calculate accurately what numbers to recruit and train. On the other hand if the company has kept records, these may show that wastage among established managers is 20 per cent per annum and among trainees 30 per cent. It is then simple to determine how many to recruit in a year.

As 100 couples are required for new houses and 20 couples are required for existing houses, this indicates that a total of 120 couples are needed to complete training. However, as wastage during training is 30 per cent, the number to be recruited will have to be increased to compensate for this loss.

Thus: $120 \times \dfrac{100}{70} = 172$ couples (rounded up).

This then is the number needed for training.

The brewery, therefore, knows on the basis of past experience that it will need to recruit about 172 couples to fill 120 vacancies likely to occur in the next year.[*] The actual phasing of this recruitment depends on other factors such as the length of training, the availability of new public houses, the policy for retiring or replacing tenants, etc. This illustrates that plans for the future are difficult to implement effectively without adequate records and statistics. However, as was said much earlier, the individual's needs, as well as the employer's, have to be recognized — consequently any records and statistical data must serve the individual as well as the employer.

Personnel information and records are required for several reasons:

1   To provide detailed operational information such as monthly strength returns and payroll analyses.
2   To provide ratios or data such as wastage rates, age analyses and service analyses for planning purposes.
3   To provide information on individuals for administration purposes such as salaries and pensions and to provide information for career development purposes.
4   To provide information for statutory purposes such as National Insurance, Redundancy Payment or Registered Disabled Persons Act.
5   To provide information for re-employment and reference purposes.

The nature of records and statistics that may be maintained and produced by employers varies considerably. The largest organizations in this country will require highly sophisticated information possibly using computer-based systems, whereas smaller organizations will need only minimal information. However, the following are probably basic to most organizations employing more than a few people.

Personal record

This is the backbone of a good records system. If both the contents and the layout are designed carefully, it can provide valuable information quickly and easily. Whether this record is a simple index card, a visible edge card, a punch card or on a computer file, depends on the number of employees and the amount of detail required.

The record should contain concise information which will be common to most employees such as age, education, qualifications, training, marital status. It is used primarily for statistical exercises or for the speedy retrieval of information; for example, the record may be used to produce an age distribution of all management employees in order to assist with management development plans, or, alternatively, the cards may be used to discover French speakers or all those with 'instructor' training. The personal record does not replace the need for a personal dossier for each employee.

A typical personal record card will look like the one shown in Figure 17.3.

Personal dossier

This should contain all documents relating to an individual employee. These may include:

Copies of letters of offer and acceptance
Application form
Copy of engagement form
Various reports and correspondence
Performance appraisals
Changes of conditions, e.g. salary increases
Records of company property issued to the employee

The dossier is usually kept for a period of time (a year or two) after an employee has left, in case of queries.

Employment requisition

This is a document produced by the heads of departments (in larger organizations) requesting authority to recruit a replacement or an addition to staff. The nature of this form will vary considerably and will depend on the degree of authority of individual heads of departments. In some cases, for example, heads of departments will need no special authority so long as the person to be recruited will be within the laid down staff establishment or within authorized budget levels. On the other hand, there are chief executives even in some large organizations who insist on personally authorizing the

Figure 17.3 *A personal record card. Source: Croner's Personnel Records 1/86, with kind permission of Croner Publications*

INDIVIDUAL HISTORY RECORD I

Personal

Surname	Forenames		Clock/Staff no.
Home address			

1st change of address — Telephone no.

2nd change of address — Telephone no.

Telephone no.

Sex	Date of birth	Nationality	Ethnic origin
Marital status	No. of children		

Emergency contact (name, address, tel. no.) — Relationship

Employment

Work address — Telephone no.

1st change of address — Telephone no.

2nd change of address — Telephone no.

Start date	Work permit	Expiry date

Job History

Date	Dept.	Job title	Reason for change	Date	Dept.	Job title	Reason for change

Terms and Conditions

PT/FT	Temp./Perm.	Working hours	Shift pattern	Hours pw
Holiday entitlement	Co. sick pay entitlement	SSP qualifying days	Pension	

Other

Pay History

Date	Current salary	Increase	Remarks	Date	Current salary	Increase	Remarks

Payroll

Payroll no.	NI no.	Tax code
Bank (name and address)		Bank sort code
		Account no.

Figure 17.3 *cont.*

Health

RDP	Disability	RDP no.
Medical restrictions		

Pension Scheme/Insurance, etc.

Date	Comments	Date	Comments

Skills and Qualifications

Educational achievements

Work qualifications

Languages and proficiency   Test scores

Other skills   Management experience

Miscellaneous

Professional bodies

Public offices   Territorial army

Union membership   Union or safety representative

First aid certificate   Check off   Driving licence

Previous Employment

Dates	Company	Position	Reason for leaving	Dates	Company	Position	Reason for leaving

Termination

Due retirement date	Termination date	Termination code

recruitment of all new staff whether they are replacing leavers or exceeding the staff establishment.

In most of the larger well-organized undertakings, the personnel department will also have to authorize the salary or wage to be paid in order to ensure that anomalies are not allowed to creep in.

A typical form is shown in Figure 17.4.

Figure 17.4   *Example of an employment requisition*

PERSONNEL REQUISITION II

Job title: _____   Grade: _____

Comp/div: _____   Dept: _____   Location: _____

Date required: _____   Refer questions/applicants to: _____
or: _____

---

1. Salary range: from _____   to _____   year ☐   month ☐   week ☐   hour ☐

   Permanent F/T ☐   Day shift ☐
   Permanent P/T ☐   Night shift ☐   If temporary, how long? _____
   Temporary F/T ☐   Two-shift ☐   If part-time, days and hours _____
   Temporary P/T ☐   Three-shift ☐   Shift hours _____

                                           Position budgeted?   Yes ☐   No ☐   (explain in box 4)

---

2. Is this an increase in staffing levels?   Yes ☐   (Give reasons in box 4 below)   No ☐

   Replacement for position held by _____ (name)   Job title _____

   Grade _____   Salary _____   Leaving date _____

   Reason position vacant: Promoted ☐   Transferred ☐   Terminated ☐   Retired ☐

                              Other (explain) _____

---

3. Brief description of duties

   Special experience or qualifications

   Education level required

---

4. Comments: Send confirmation to:

                                                 Name _____

                                                 Location _____

                                                 Approved to recruit

---

Office use only

Source: CRONER'S PERSONNEL RECORDS 1/86, with kind permission of Croner Publications

Engagement form

This form should be completed when a new employee joins an employer. The purpose is to inform all the relevant departments so that appropriate action is initiated. These departments may include:

Wages
Training
Pensions
Insurance
Personnel records

The information contained on the form will vary according to the system being used; for example, some employers may be able to use one engagement form for all departments and all levels of staff whereas other employers may need to use different forms for each. It is of prime importance, however, to ensure that the employee is paid and insured. Consequently information will have to include name, staff number, address, department, date of starting, rate of pay, bank address. Figure 17.5 shows one typical example.

Termination form

This form is necessary in order to fulfil several purposes:

1 To initiate documentation and administration procedures such as the preparation of the P45 and the final wages payment.
2 To provide statistical information regarding labour turnover.
3 To provide information for reference or re-employment purposes.

Other forms

There is a variety of other information that may have to be kept for statutory or other purposes. This can include:

Accident reports
Medical reports
Training reports
Absentee reports
Change of status, e.g. salary increases, promotions, transfers
Warnings

From these various documents the majority of statistical information required for the satisfactory planning and control of most undertakings can be produced. This information may include the following items.

Strength returns

This will show numbers employed by departments and should show changes in numbers. It may also incorporate 'establishment' numbers, that is the agreed

Figure 17.5   *Example of an engagement form*

Surname	Staff no.	
Other names	Job	
Address	RDP Number	**Splendide Hotel**
	Department	Newtown, Newtownshire
		Telephone: Newtown (0021) 12345
Telephone	Branch	

National Insurance No.

Next of kin *to be notified in case of accident*

Name   Telephone No.

Address

Date commenced

Hours and day of duty

Rate of pay

Service charge percentage

Method and frequency of payment

Bank address

P45 received   YES/NO

Special comments *such as holiday arrangements to be honoured*

Copies sent to:	Wages	Pensions/Insurance
	Personnel	Head of department

Completed by   Position   Date

numbers to be employed in each department. Any variation from 'establishment' will be shown.

Payroll analysis

This information (a development of the strength return) may be produced by a variety of departments including the wages department, and the cost or management accountant's department, or the personnel manager's department. It will include a breakdown, by departments, of labour costs. These may be shown in a large variety of ways including various ratios and percentages.

The figures should always include a comparison of the actual and budget figures.

Both the strength return and the payroll analysis should be produced on a regular, periodic basis. Where there is strict control over wage and salary levels the 'strength return' will be sufficient for most day-to-day management purposes, since cost variances will only arise where there are variances from the laid down 'establishment'. In any case the labour costs should show up elsewhere — in particular on periodic operating statements.

Staff/labour turnover analysis

This has already been discussed in Chapter 14. However, it must be stressed that the regular production of this information can assist considerably in staff recruitment and retention by identifying the problem areas.

The turnover rate for each department and for the undertaking as a whole will make up part of this report. This can be arrived at roughly by the following formula:

$$\frac{Number\ of\ employees\ who\ left\ during\ period \times 100}{Average\ number\ employed\ during\ period}$$

Such data must be prepared and considered carefully, however. One company, for example, found that all in-company transfers had been included, thus distorting the turnover rate.

In itself the turnover rate may be of little value as it gives no indication, for example, of turnover among long-serving employees. It may, therefore, be necessary to supplement labour turnover figures with further breakdowns. This may be done in a variety of ways including showing numbers of leavers by length of service as shown in Figure 17.6

Figure 17.6 *An analysis of leavers by length of service*

Analysis of leavers for 12 months ending 31 December 1987

Length of service	Number of leavers	Percentage
Years		
more than 5	4	5.0
more than 2 less than 5	8	10.0
more than 1 less than 2	10	12.5
up to 1	58	72.5
Total	80	100.0

Age and service analyses

For manpower planning and management development purposes it is important in the medium and larger-sized organizations from time to time to look at the make-up of the labour force and in particular at the age profile of the management team. If this is not done, an unanticipated spate of retirements and resignations can leave an undertaking without the necessary trained personnel. It is useful, therefore, to produce an annual age profile of management, headed by those due to retire. In some cases it may be desirable to link this with service and this can be done easily in this way (see Figure 17.7).

In examining the type of chart shown in Figure 17.7 one would hope to see the bulk of managers distributed fairly evenly through the chart, preferably with a slightly greater weight at the younger end. Where this is not the case the management team may not have the necessary combination of age, experience and inbuilt continuity. Consequently senior management may wish to take steps to put this right by promotion, transfers, recruitment and appropriate training.

Figure 17.7   *An age and service analysis*

					Service					
Age	*Under 1 year*	*1–5*	*6–10*	*11–15*	*16–20*	*21–5*	*26–30*	*31–5*	*36–40*	*41+*
61–5			1		2		2			
56–60						1				
50–5		6	3	3		1				
46–50	3		2							
41–5	1									
36–40			1	1	2					
31–5	2	8	1							
26–30	8	7								
21–5	2	3								
under 21	1	2								

Manpower audit

Some of the largest employers conduct detailed studies periodically which provide a complete breakdown of the labour force divided into various sections including job grades, age and service. They may also report on the quality of staff, their qualifications, performance and potential. The training plan, management development programme and manpower plan may be part of, or may be linked with, this audit.

Apart from the records and data discussed here, there are many more that may be necessary for effective planning and control. However, it is important to bear in mind that although the production of information and statistics, in itself, can be an attractive occupation, only those data that serve a useful purpose must be produced. They should clearly be aids to line management in providing an effective service. If they do not satisfy this requirement, the information being produced is almost certainly unwanted and consequently it is a waste of resources that could be employed more fruitfully elsewhere.

Computers in personnel work

One of the most common uses of computers within organizations has been for the preparation of the payroll. This is because the payroll system was ideally suited to the earlier magnetic tape storage system. Personnel records can now be kept easily and relatively cheaply on computer because of the random access facility provided by disk-based systems. Such facilities lead onto the ability to produce a range of systems; for example, a spread sheet enables a manager to input a number of variables, such as revenue, labour costs, predicted increases, and to manipulate data so as to predict what labour costs, average wage rate, number on the payroll, etc., should be for the future. See Figure 17.8 for an example.

Figure 17.8 *Example of a spread sheet applied to manpower budgeting*

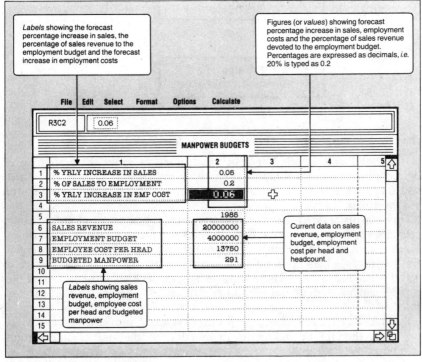

Source: *Personnel Management*, May 1986

Another system, 'Microprospect' (Institute of Manpower Studies, Brighton), is a model which examines the effects on groups of people within an organization. It deals with questions such as:

Number of trainees needed
Is the organization developing sufficient staff to meet its needs?
What are the promotion opportunities?

Effects of maintaining current promotion prospects
Effects of early retirement policy

Microprospect looks at an organization using a manpower system illustrated simply in Figure 17.9.

Figure 17.9   *Example of a human resource system in an organization*

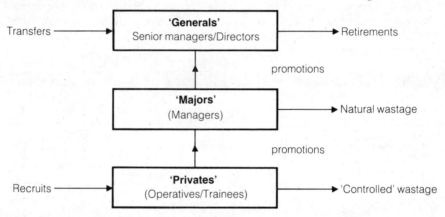

The effect of computers on employment levels

As the hotel and catering industry continues to grow there should be corresponding increases in levels of employment. In the whole of the tourist industry, this is estimated to be at the rate of about 50,000 new jobs per annum into the 1990s.

This expansion may be partially facilitated by the use of information technology where it enables organizations to provide new or improved services, such as faster counter service and check out, and to use the potential wealth of management information to maximize opportunities. This is referred to as the 'product effect.' There will also be some technological impact on the employment of clerical and administrative staff — known as the 'process effect'.

Table A8.1, page 271, shows the results of research into potential job losses and gains directly or indirectly attributable to the use of information technology.

Further reading

Armstrong, M., *A Handbook of Personnel Management Practice*, 2nd ed., London: Kogan Page, 1984
BIM Checklist no. 6, *Manpower Planning*, London: British Institute of Management, 1976
BIM Checklist no. 20, *Labour Turnover*, London: British Institute of Management, 1978

Bramham, J., *Practical Manpower Planning*, 2nd ed., London: Institute of Personnel Management, 1978

Canon, J., *Cost Effective Personnel Decisions*, London: Institute of Personnel Management, 1979

Croner's Personnel Records, London: Croner Publications, 1986

Evans, A., *A Guide to Manpower Information*, London: Institute of Personnel Management, 1980

Pratt, K. J., and Bennett, S. C., *Elements of Personnel Management*, 2nd ed., Wokingham: GEE, 1985

Wille, E., and Hammond, V., *The Computer in Personnel Work*, London: Institute of Personnel Management, 1980

chapter 18
Organizing human resources

The preceding chapters have concentrated largely on the various management techniques which are concerned with obtaining, training, motivating and administering staff. In addition to these different steps, however, managers also have to organize staff, that is, to create groups of people who will meet the organization's objectives. This is normally one of the major responsibilities of line management who organize their work people into groups in the manner they think best, basing their organization usually on what they have observed or experienced elsewhere. Nowadays, however, there is a growing recognition that organizing people into the most appropriate work groups is a highly skilled and complex task often referred to as 'organization development', which is concerned with 'improving an organization's ability to achieve its goals by using people more effectively'.* A major aspect of the work of many management consultants now is concerned with examining organizations and recommending the most appropriate structures. A related development is the increasing involvement, albeit slowly, of personnel managers in the actual design of organization structures.

Organization development as a process can have a number of different goals. The most common are:

Improvement in organizational performance, e.g. profits or service levels.
Improvement in decision-making processes.
Improvement in group or team work.
Responding to change.
Changing value systems, attitudes

A whole range of factors influence organization structures, each factor having some effect on the final type of structure, which may be either the result of careful design, the result of evolutionary development or merely expediency.

The main options open to organizations are:

Functional: where different individuals attend to the main management functions, i.e. finance, marketing, personnel, operations, research.

*D. French and H. Saward, *Dictionary of Management* (Pan 1977).

Product: where different managers manage different products, e.g. hotels or public houses or popular catering.

Geographical: where management attend to everything within a geographic region.

Project: where groups are set up for specific projects and disperse upon completion, usually relying upon existing hierarchical roles.

Matrix: a loose form of the above where individuals may be members of a number of different groups with leadership roles depending more on expertise than on hierarchical roles.

Power and the decision-making process

Underlying the process of organization will be the overall philosophy of senior management towards their workforce (see Chapter 2) and the principles of job design (see Chapter 3). Unitarist (or autocratic) style managers will tend towards concentrating decision making upon themselves, whereas a pluralist (or democratic) style manager will be prepared to share decision making. Public sector organizations tend to require committee-type decisions, made within a legislative or bureaucratic framework, whereas private sector

Figure 18.1   *Organization structure and factors influencing it (see also Figure 17.1)*

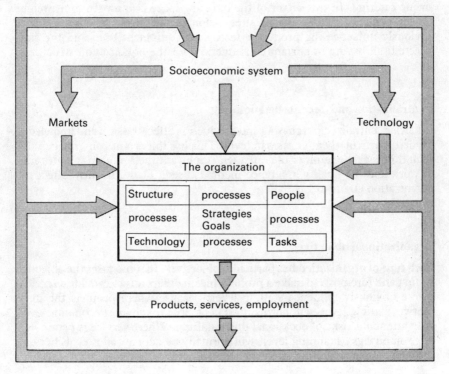

organizations have far fewer legislative or bureaucratic restraints and decision making can be a simpler process, requiring fewer participants. Such differences in types of organization can influence quite considerably the formal and informal approaches to organizations.

The market

The single most important factor is probably the type of market being catered for. Obviously consumer demands determine the type of staff required but also the degree of seasonal fluctuation influences organization structure. A hospital with predictable and stable levels of demand, where the catering service is ancillary to other services, will have manpower needs very different from those required by a highly seasonal resort hotel or holiday camp where the accommodation and catering services themselves are the end product. The hospital will have a relatively stable and permanent labour force, whereas the seasonal hotel will probably have a small nucleus of permanent, key staff which is boosted by seasonal and casual labour as demand increases.

Technology

The technology of a particular sector is also important. One simple example is airline catering. In this sector of the industry space is at a premium, weight carries penalties, and constant supervision is not possible. These factors obviously influence the product offered, the equipment used and the staff selected; all having important consequences for the organization structure.

Centralization and decentralization

Likewise centralized purchasing and production affect the skill and knowledge needed, particularly at craftsman level. This has important consequences for such things as the number of craftsmen employed, their morale and attitudes to work and the quality assurance methods used. These, in turn, affect the organization structure.

Organizational objectives

Each type of organization has particular objectives. In some cases the objective is, first and foremost, to make a profit, while in others it is to provide a service. These obviously influence staffing levels because where profit is the main motive, staffing levels will normally be kept close to the most economic level, with attendant risks of occasional understaffing. Where service is paramount (e.g. on oil rigs), manning levels will normally be kept at safer levels because the costs of short staffing could be tremendous.

Size and diversity

Two other major influences on the structure are the size of the organization and its diversity. However, there does seem to be some agreement among the largest organizations that they need to devolve responsibility to smaller, readily accountable units. This may be done on a geographic basis. An example is the way in which breweries organize their public house districts. Their management may be responsible for all activities in an area, such as managed houses, tenanted houses, catering and entertainment. Alternatively, an organization may prefer to make its management responsible for particular types of products or services. An example is how some companies may concentrate their steak houses into one division, their licensed houses into another and leisure into yet another. For the largest companies both 'regional' and 'product' organization structures will be necessary.

At the individual unit level the degree of specialization is an important question and of particular importance is the degree to which certain specialists such as sales executives and financial controllers may be responsible to the unit manager and to the head office specialist manager. This is a constant problem in hotels in particular, where sales executives may see themselves as part of a sales team rather than part of the unit management. A consequence is that the sales staff often sell 'products' the unit has difficulty providing.

Span of control

Something else discussed in the organizational context is the question of 'span of control' (i.e. how many subordinates can each supervisor successfully supervise). While most will agree that 'one over one' is rarely, if ever, justified, beyond this all the factors listed above play their part in resolving the question of how many subordinates one person can control. There are situations where one supervisor can quite successfully control a hundred or more subordinates. Likewise, however, there are many other situations where one person can successfully supervise, at most, a handful of subordinates. Generally speaking the more repetitious the work, and the more stringent the quality assurance methods, the more people supervisors can control successfully.

The products and services

Obviously shaping all these factors is the product being provided. At one extreme there is the *haute cuisine* meal experience involving an extensive range of technical, social and organizational skills which have taken many years of experience and training to acquire. At the other extreme nowadays we have fast foods and airline meals which involve very little craft skill but call upon management organization skills of a high order. In between these two extremes are numerous types and styles of product and service which make differing demands on capital, craft skill, social skill, training and organization ability. Each combination creates a particular set of organizational needs and constraints which should be reflected in the consequent organization structure.

Figure 18.2   *Organization chart of a large hotel*

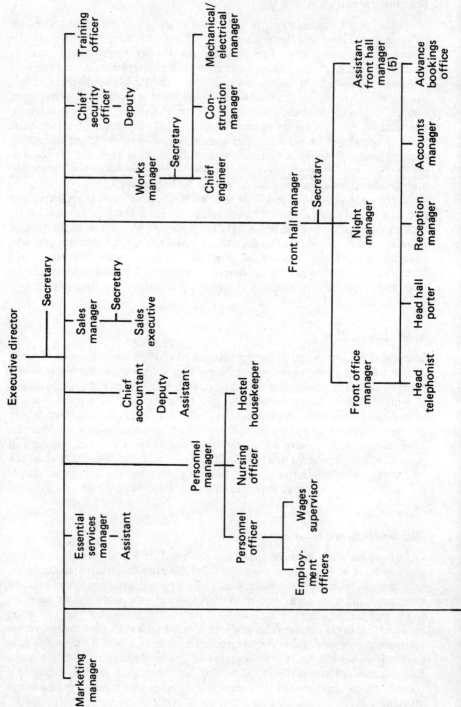

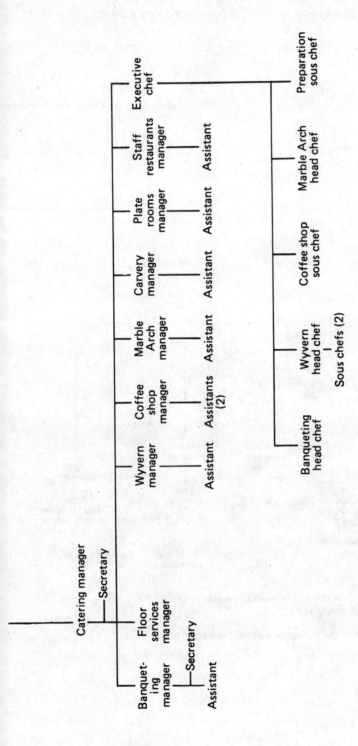

Organization chart of the Cumberland Hotel, Marble Arch, London W1. Number of rooms 910.

This organization chart shows the main management and supervisory positions.

It does not show operative staff who number in the region of 500.

Reproduced by permission of the Management of the Cumberland Hotel and Trusthouse Forte.

Figure 18.3   *Organization chart of a medium-sized hotel*

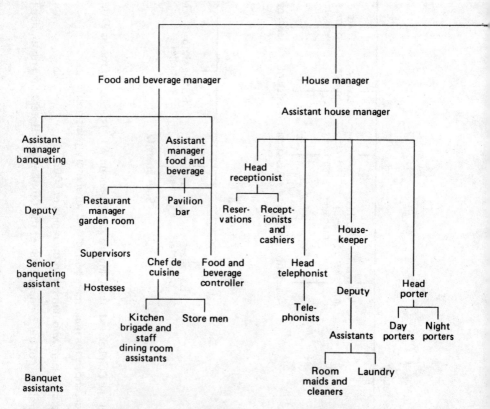

Organization chart of the Crest Hotel, Maidenhead.   Number of rooms 200.
Total staff numbers approximately 140.

Reproduced by permission of the Management of the Crest Hotel Maidenhead
and Crest Hotels Europe.

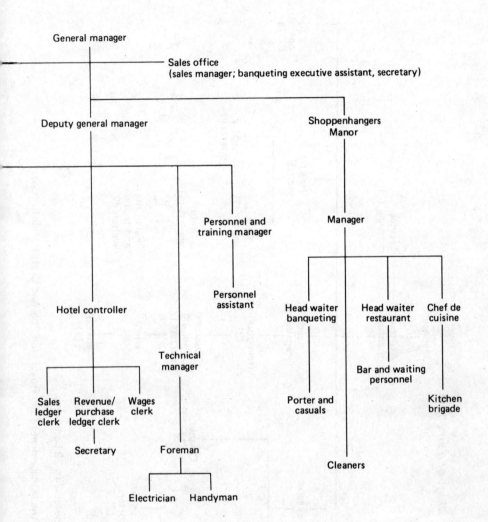

Figure 18.4 *Organization chart of a small hotel*

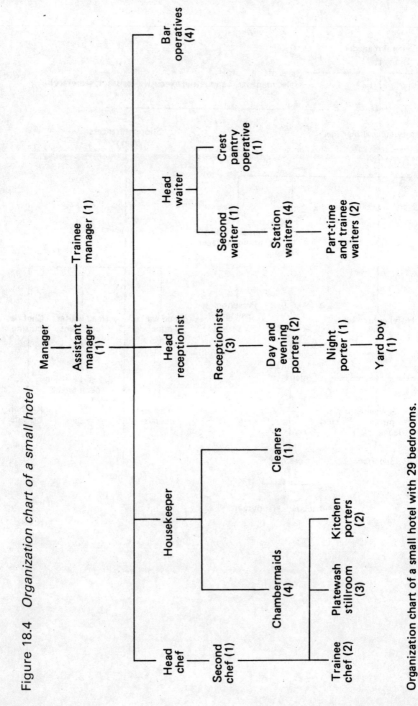

Organization chart of a small hotel with 29 bedrooms.

Reproduced by permission of the Management of the Royal Hop Pole and Crest Hotels Europe.

Figure 18.5 *Organization structure of a large hotel company with 30 hotels*

MANAGEMENT STRUCTURE FOR DE VERE & G W HOTELS

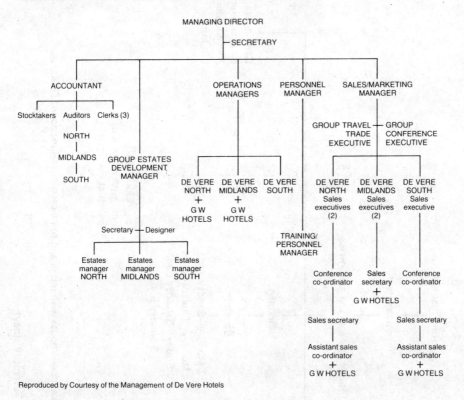

Reproduced by Courtesy of the Management of De Vere Hotels

Figure 18.6   *Organization chart of a public house*

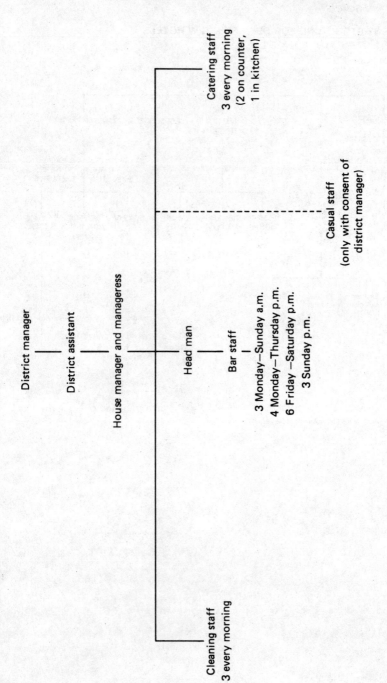

District manager

District assistant

House manager and manageress

Head man

Bar staff

3 Monday—Sunday a.m.
4 Monday—Thursday p.m.
6 Friday—Saturday p.m.
3 Sunday p.m.

Cleaning staff
3 every morning

Catering staff
3 every morning
(2 on counter,
1 in kitchen)

Casual staff
(only with consent of
district manager)

This is an organization chart of a typical public house with music and some catering, taking about £6000 per week (net of VAT).

Reproduced by permission of Albion Taverns (Watney).

Figure 18.7 *Organization chart of a university catering department*

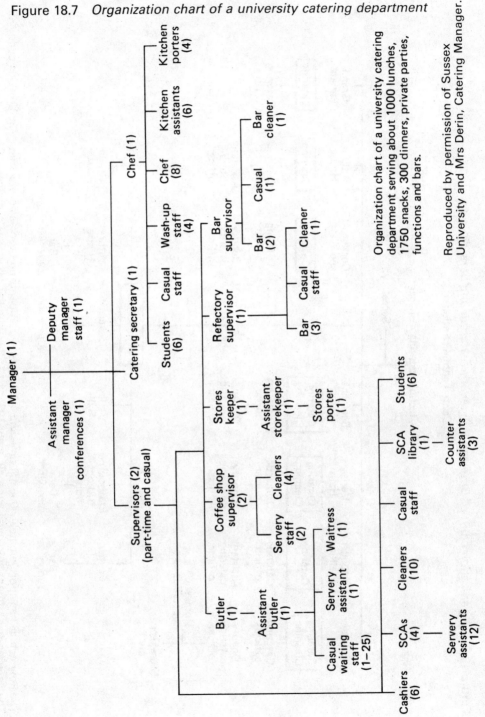

Organization chart of a university catering department serving about 1000 lunches, 1750 snacks, 300 dinners, private parties, functions and bars.

Reproduced by permission of Sussex University and Mrs Derin, Catering Manager.

Figure 18.8   *Organization chart of Brighton Polytechnic catering and bars division*

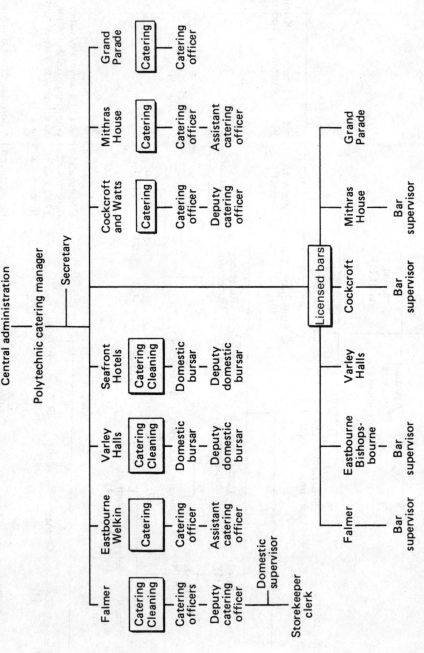

The Polytechnic has approximately 4000 full-time and 4000 part-time students and serves approximately 3800 meals per day. The catering department employed approximately 100 staff at the time this chart was produced.

Reproduced by kind permission of the Polytechnic, and with the help of Margaret Palmear.

Figure 18.9 *Organization chart of a fast food, take-away outlet*

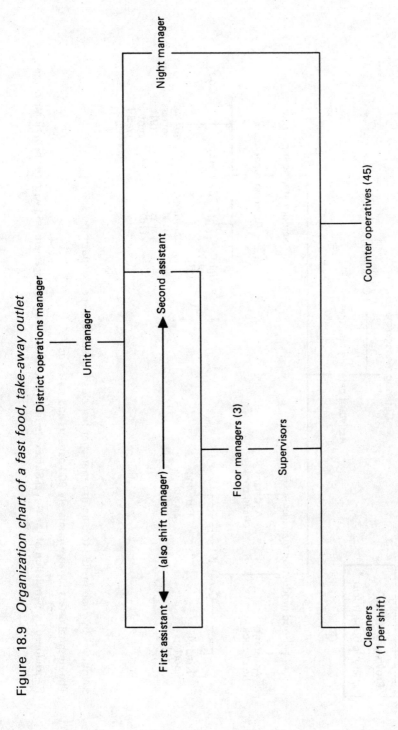

This organization chart of a fast food, take-away outlet consists of french fries area, preparation room, counter, grills section and lobby. Turnover is in the region of £25,000 per week.

Figure 18.10   Organization chart of the catering department of the Royal Sussex County Hospital

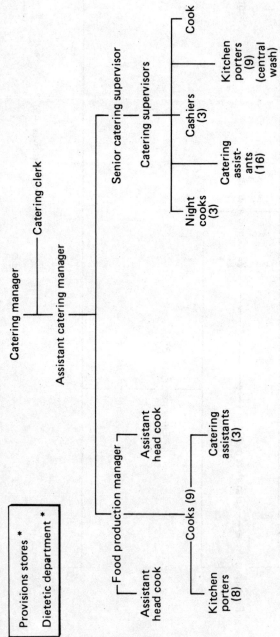

* Not directly responsible to catering manager but close liaison between departments.

The Hospital caters for approximately 900 patients and staff a day.

Reproduced by permission of the Royal Sussex County Hospital Catering Management and with the help of Mr Winter.

Figure 18.11 *Organization chart of the catering department of the East Sussex County Council*

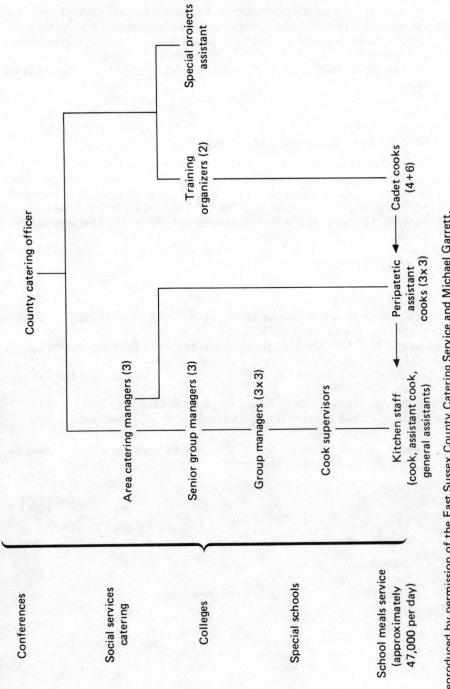

Reproduced by permission of the East Sussex County Catering Service and Michael Garrett.

Age and size

As successful organizations get older so they tend to become larger. Increasing size creates subdivisions and problems of co-ordination. Large size consequently creates conflicting effects. On the one hand size creates opportunities for economies of scale; on the other hand increasing problems of co-ordination and control can add to the administrative burden — the law of diminishing returns?

Objectives of organization development

In developing organizations a major consideration is the extent to which technical efficiency is pursued at the cost of job satisfaction or, at the other extreme, to what extent can organization structures sacrifice technical efficiency for job satisfaction. The objective should be to strike the balance between the technical and human demands so that an effective organization results.

Further reading

Armstrong, M., *A Handbook of Personnel Management Practice*, 2nd ed., London: Kogan Page, 1984

Corby, K., *Job Redesign in Practice*, London: Institute of Personnel Management, 1976

Margerison, C., *Influencing Organizational Change*, London: Institute of Personnel Management, 1978

Medlik, S., *The Business of Hotels*, London: Heinemann, 1977

Pratt, K. J., and Bennett, S. C., *Elements of Personnel Management*, 2nd ed., Wokingham: GEE, 1985

Thakur, M., Bristow, J., and Corby, K., *Personnel in Charge*, London: Institute of Personnel Management, 1978

chapter 19

Labour costs and productivity

In some industries it is reasonably simple to state with some degree of confidence what labour costs should be as a percentage of total costs, of revenue or of some other clear standard. However, because the hotel and catering industry often consists of a service to other industries, apart from creating an end-product in its own right, no such simple yardstick exists; for example, labour costs in a modern efficiently designed and well-managed public house may be as low as 10 per cent, whereas in many sectors of institutional and industrial catering labour may cost 60 per cent or 70 per cent of revenue. In some clubs labour costs can approach 90 per cent of trade done. In this case the apparently high labour cost is often caused by the very high level of subscription income not accounted for in the 'trade' revenue, and the low level of price charged for goods and services.

Employer's policy

The factors which influence labour costs are numerous but probably what determines labour cost more than anything else is the precise nature of the enterprise, and the employer's particular policy; for example, if it is to provide a subsidized service, with low selling prices to employees then labour costs as a percentage of revenue will be high. If, at the other extreme, it is to maximize profit in the short term, by providing a product involving minimum service from capital-intensive plant, using unskilled staff, as in many fast food operations, then the labour costs will be low.

Another major factor will be the efficiency of the design. Modern, carefully designed hotels can now expect room-maids to service around seventeen bedrooms per section, compared with older hotels where sections often have to be much smaller.

Equally important of course is the level of service provided. A fast food take-away operation or a wine bar may operate with a labour percentage of around 15 per cent, whereas a high class restaurant offering skilled personal attention may need to operate at around 35 per cent labour cost. Likewise a

Figure 19.1　*Some factors influencing payroll costs*

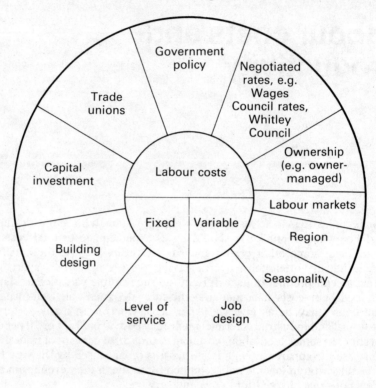

modern three star hotel with minimal personal service can operate around the 18–20 per cent labour cost with the five star hotel needing to spend around 40 per cent on labour.

Trade unions

Trade unions influence rates and labour costs in a number of ways. In the public sector they negotiate on behalf of catering workers, along with many other workers. In the private sector they represent employees on the industry's Wages Councils and hence they influence the Wages Council rates which are either the actual rates paid by many employers or the rates are those used by other employers as bench-marks or guidelines in setting their own rates.

Second, more rates are now being negotiated directly between employers and unions. Third, many catering employees' rates are determined along with those rates which unions have negotiated for another industry's primary workers such as motor manufacturers' or warehouse staff.

Owner managers

In establishments at the smaller end of the scale a vital factor influencing labour costs is whether an establishment is run by the owner or by an employed manager. Owners managing an establishment can influence labour costs in a number of ways. First, some owners 'pay themselves' unrealistic wages for a variety of reasons, not least to minimize tax liability. Second, owners generally are much firmer in controlling costs and, third, they avoid employing excess labour as 'cover' for themselves and for other employees.

The labour percentages in Figure 19.2 are intended to indicate the approximate level of labour cost (as a percentage of revenue) likely to be encountered in viable establishments. This does not mean that there are not successful establishments operating outside of these ranges. Likewise, it must be recognized that labour costs are partly fixed and partly variable so if trade drops dramatically there is a point beyond which labour costs can no longer be reduced to maintain them within the 'normal' percentages — a problem all too familiar to the management of seasonal establishments.

Figure 19.2 *Labour costs as a percentage of revenue*

Type of outlet	Percentage range (as a percentage of revenue) per annum	Factors which can affect labour percentage	
		low	high
Hotels		efficient design,	inefficient design,
2–3 star	18–32%	limited menu,	extensive menus,
4–5 star	25–35%	living-in staff,	high level of
rooms division	12–20%	limited services	service, e.g.
food & beverage	30–45%		room service
Restaurants — waiter/waitress service	25–35%	as above	as above
Popular catering — waitress service	22–35%		
Self-service	15–25%	as above	as above
Wine bars	15–22%	as above	as above
Fast food take-away	11–18%	as above	as above
Department stores	20–25%	as above	as above
Kiosks, mainly confectionery and tobacco	around 6%	very high tobacco element	
Public houses	10–20%	efficient design, e.g. one bar, mainly liquor sales	high catering ratio, several bars/ restaurants

This table is intended to be a guide only, and it must be recognized that businesses may still operate successfully outside of these. These should be viewed as the range within which most viable businesses operate on a long-term (e.g. annual) basis. There can be considerable fluctuation on a short-term basis as labour costs are not a completely variable cost.

Figure 19.3 *Employees' work schedule*

Unit number   15

Date   6:7:81

Projected volume

Projected labour

	6=7	=8	=9	=10	=11	=12	=1	=2	=3	=4	=5	=6	=7	=8	=9	=10	=11	=12	=1	=2
Projected volume		2	45	240	240	240	150	120	115	135	150	150	150	120	100			1955		
Projected labour		2	9½	16	16	16	13	8½	8	12	14	14	14	14	13	8		180		

Day — Station / Hours worked

Night — Station / Hours worked

Crew black line this side

Crew dotted line this side

F R I D A Y

Crew black line this side:
David, Robert, Edward, Rupert, Sally, Steven, Michael, Paul, Selina, George, Barbara, Thomas, Dennis, Hammond, Charles, Andrew, William

Crew dotted line this side:
Peter, Martin, Alice, Natasha, David, John, Sarah, Ashley

In some cases the wage percentage may well be reviewed on an annual basis. Most organizations however will monitor labour costs on a shorter-term basis, monthly or maybe even weekly, with many of the fast food outlets now planning labour on an hourly basis.

Figure 19.3 illustrates a format used by some fast food operators. The consequence of this precise hour-by-hour planning is that labour costs are planned and controlled accurately to precise percentages. One of the international fast food chains operates branches at an 11.5 per cent labour cost, with management costs ranging from 2 per cent for the most efficient and busy branches up to 6 per cent for others.

Productivity measurement

In many organizations, such as the school meals service, the hospital service and employee meal services, labour costs cannot be expressed as a proportion of revenue because there may be little or no revenue, or because subsidies distort the picture. Other measures, therefore, become necessary. Such measures vary amongst the different sectors and also within departments. These may be based on some constant (i.e. a factor unaffected by inflation) such as time. Some examples are shown in Figure 19.4. It should be borne in

Figure 19.4 *Some examples of productivity measures*

Department	Description of productivity measure	Some examples
Catering		
Employee meal service	(1) Number of meals served for each member of staff (full-time equivalent)	30 meals
	(2) Covers served per paid hour	4.5 covers
	(3) Paid minutes for each meal served	
	plate wash	7 minutes
	waiters	24 minutes
	cooks	15 minutes
	Coffe Shop	15 minutes
Hospitals	(4) Labour as a percentage of direct costs $\frac{\text{Labour} + \text{Materials}}{\text{Labour}} \times 100$	e.g. 52%
School meals	(5) Labour to materials ratio	£3 labour to £2 material
Hotels	(1) Employees per room	e.g. 0.8 per room
	(2) Number of sleeper nights for each member of staff (full-time equivalent)	21 sleeper nights for each member of staff
	(3) Number of rooms served for each member of staff on duty	17 rooms to 1 member of staff
	(4) Number of paid minutes for each sleeper night	
	room-maids	27 minutes per room (maids on duty only)
	reception	33 minutes per sleeper night
Public houses/bars	(1) Revenue per hour paid	Liquor; £16 per hour Food; £7 per hour Combined; £14 per hour
	(2) Barrels and barrels equivalent per full-time equivalent	3.7 barrels per week

mind, however, that straight comparisons can be dangerous; for example, in one industrial catering situation a 'main meal' may offer each customer a wide choice, while in another situation there may be no choice. Other factors such as shift work and night work also play an important part, as do national and international work patterns; for example, in Britain an Industrial Society survey (*Catering, Prices, Costs and Subsidies*) shows that for every individual catering worker employed, about 22 main meals were served. The author's own consultancy work shows that in some other European countries the number of meals served is frequently between 50 and 60 for each industrial catering worker employed.

The principal approaches to measuring productivity are described here.

Number of units sold per employee

A commonly used crude measure of productivity is that of the number of units produced/sold for each employee. This measure is frequently used, for example, to compare car manufacturing productivity between nations. In hotels and restaurants one very simple measure is to relate the number of employees to the number of units of service, e.g. rooms, guests, meals served. These are usually extremely crude measures as comparisons are rarely like with like. Some rooms may be larger than others, some meals more complex than others, some guests may stay for longer periods than others.

Sales to payroll index

This is another way of expressing the labour cost as a proportion of revenue. It indicates the amount of revenue in pounds generated by each pound spent on labour. For hotels in Europe, for example, the index for *rooms* was $5.4 for every dollar spent on labour, while for *food and beverage* the index was £2.5 (source Worldwide Lodging Industry, Horwarth and Horwarth London; Medlik, 1977).

Sales and payroll cost per employee

Another way is to look at the sales per employee and after deducting the employee cost, the net sales per employee.

Added Value

This method assesses the value added by each pound spent on labour. It is calculated by representing the gross profit (sales less material costs) as a proportion of the labour cost. The Worldwide Lodging Industry survey showed the added value for rooms division in Europe was $5.4 for every dollar spent on labour, and for food and beverage the added value was $1.7 for every dollar spent on labour.

Materials to labour ratio

In many catering operations where there may be little or no revenue, or where there is a subsidy element (e.g. hospitals, schools, employee meal services, clubs) expressing labour costs as a proportion of sales is either not possible or it is meaningless for comparative purposes. Other measures are, therefore, necessary — these can include the materials to labour ratio, i.e. how much labour is needed to process the materials required. In hospitals this can be around a 1:1 ratio, whereas in some school meals operations it can range from around 0.4:1.0 labour to materials in centralized production operations to as high as 2.6:1.0 in some labour-intensive, localized production systems. See Figure 19.5 showing comparisons of different forms of production in school meals.

Figure 19.5 *School meals data*

Productivity — School meals actual data referred to eight English local authorites

These figures were correct in April 1985

County	School meals produced per day 1000s	Staff required to produce 1,000 meals per day	Paid minutes per meal produced	Labour cost per meal £
Leicestershire	76.8	24.2	6	0.26
Kent	10.6	25.4	6	0.29
Lincolnshire	17.4	27.4	6	0.30
Staffordshire	82.3	27.3	6	0.29
Essex	81.5	28.0	7	0.31
Warwickshire	28.6	29.3	7	0.32
Cornwall	30.5	34.3	8	0.38
Bedfordshire	26.8	54.1	13	0.58
Average of group	56.6	26.7	6	0.29

Production methods — simple comparison

Production method	Labour costs	Materials	Transport	Total
Centralized production				
Individual meals	0.18	0.37	0.05	0.60
Bulk	0.15	0.37	0.05	0.57
Other forms of production				
Mainly local	0.26 – 0.58	0.22		0.48 – 0.90

Production Method	Labour to materials ratio in pence
Centralized production	
Individual meals	$\dfrac{\text{labour}}{\text{supplies}}\ \dfrac{18}{37} = 0.48 / 1.0$
Bulk	$\dfrac{\text{labour}}{\text{supplies}}\ \dfrac{0.15}{0.37} = 0.40 / 1.0$
Local production	
Division A	$\dfrac{\text{labour}}{\text{materials}}\ \dfrac{26}{22} = 1.18 / 1$
Division B	$\dfrac{\text{labour}}{\text{materials}}\ \dfrac{18}{22} = 0.82 / 1$

Good productivity measurement enables comparisons to be made between units or groups of workers on the same operations, or the same unit or groups of workers at different times and in spite of the many problems encountered in attempting to make comparisons, productivity measurement is a vital tool for management, helping with budgeting, forecasting, manpower planning, incentive schemes and diagnosis of poor performance. Productivity measurement has the advantage over straight labour percentages of providing constant measurement which is unaffected by inflation and changes in wage rates.

Further reading

Catering Prices, Costs and Subsidies, London: The Industrial Society, Annually
Medlik, S., *The Business of Hotels*, London: Heinemann, 1977

appendix 1

A review of personnel management in the private sector of the British hospitality industry

This article, written by the author of this book, is reproduced from the *International Journal of Hospitality Management*, 5, No. 1, pp. 29–36, 1986 with the permission of Pergamon Press Ltd.

In setting out to present a review of the literature of a particular subject area or discipline it is essential that the objectives are absolutely clear because, even within a relatively immature subject area such as personnel management in the hotel and catering industry, there is, potentially, a considerable amount of work to review. The objective of this paper has been to select material which is considered to be of value to the understanding of the development of personnel management in the private sector of the hotel and catering industry in Britain. It is confined exclusively to texts published in Britian, leaving colleagues elsewhere the task of reviewing their own literature. Also works which (in the author's opinion) are of general sociological (or similar) concern and which merely had their locus in the hotel and catering industry, with two exceptions, have been avoided.

Most people, in reviewing the management literature of the hotel and catering industry, tend to start with the work of W. F. Whyte (1948), which was based on Whyte's research into human relations in a number of hotels and restaurants in the United States. The other work which tends to be regularly cited is that of George Orwell (1969) which gave valuable insights into the nature of menial work in hotels. It was based on Orwell's experience of working in hotels in Paris in the 1930s.

The purpose of this paper, however, is to review the British texts which have contributed to the development of the personnel management function in British hotels and restaurants, and the relevant starting point appears to be later than Whyte's and Orwell's work.

In fact it appears that it was legislative change in the 1960s, which radically altered the practice of personnel management, particularly where unions were not strong. Until the early 1960s the employment relationship was governed mainly by the law of contract. Employers could dismiss any employee including long-serving staff merely by giving notice which was the same as the pay period (weekly-paid staff received 1 week's notice) even after years of service. No written terms and conditions were required and employers could modify their expectations of their employees arbitrarily, given that they had the 'divine right of dismissal'. Obviously employment practices in a fragmented, small unit, industry like hotel and catering differed vastly from the concentrated industries (such as manufacturing) where unions had already been responsible for creating the need for a professional personnel management function.

In the industry — outside the public sector — the number of managers concerned entirely with personnel work in the whole of the United Kingdom was probably in the region of 20. Most of these devoted their time to recruitment, with some companies beginning to show interest in the training activity. These included J. Lyons who had trained staff very effectively for many years, Trust Houses who ran a training centre at the Berystede Hotel in Ascot, and Forte's, who with a considerable nationwide expansion programme, employed a small team of recruiters and trainers. However, changes were imminent because in 1963 the Contracts of Employment Act created the right of employees to receive a written description of their main terms of employment. So started the need to create written contracts and records, in addition to pay records, and with it the need for staff to attend to these 'personnel' issues. In 1964 the Industrial Training Act became law, an event which probably had more impact upon manpower management, in large sections of the hotel and catering industry, than any other single influence.

It was at this time also that the first personnel management courses for the hotel and catering industry were organized by Philip Nailon and some of his colleagues at the Battersea College of Advanced Technology — soon afterward to become the University of Surrey. Also the first college graduates who had studied in Britain specifically for management started to make an impact on the industry. The formation of the Graduate and Student Management Society in the early 1960s brought together a number of young, aspiring managers, who started to question the industry's practices, running meetings on such topics as the need for a Code of Ethics. Interestingly, there were no texts of direct interest to managers, and particularly to the aspiring personnel and training specialists, about the industry's manpower or manpower practices.

It was at this point, largely as a result of the Industrial Training Act, that the Hotel and Catering Institute (one of two bodies subsequently to merge, creating the Hotel, Catering and Institutional Management Association) formed its own Hotel and Catering Industry Committee and pressed for the formation of a training board for the hotel and catering industry. The efforts of the Institute were successful. The Hotel and Catering Industry Training Board was formed in 1966 and the Institute's Secretary was seconded to the newly-formed Board.

The first Industrial Training Act was responsible for long-term changes in employment. For the first time many companies examined carefully what their employees did and, in order to provide comprehensive training programmes, companies needed to develop job descriptions, training manuals, standards of performance, etc. They also needed to develop scores of supervisors and senior staff as on-job trainers — in other words, to develop their communication skills. This was done by many employers initially in order to recover grants rather than because of any intrinsic belief that it was the right thing to do.

Towards the end of the sixties growing awareness began to develop of the crucial importance to Britain of the hotel and catering industry (as a major ingredient of the tourist product). As a consequence the government-sponsored National Economic Development Office created the Economic Development Committee for the Hotel and Catering Industry. Interestingly, at its first meeting it set up a manpower working party. Its task was to 'identify the manpower problems of the industry . . . not only how to recruit more, but also, . . . how to do with less' (NEDO, 1967), p. iii). The book, one of the earliest concerned with the industry's personnel, was devoted almost entirely to presenting data derived from the 1961 census. One interesting conclusion, a reflection on the personnel management of the time, was that 'The industry has nothing approaching the information about labour turnover [found] in manufacturing industries.' (NEDO, 1967, p. 40). As a result the EDC commissioned a report on the industry's labour turnover 'to identify the causes, the cost of high labour turnover and the action that can be taken to reduce it' (NEDO, 1967, p. 40).

Two years later in 1969 the results of the study into labour turnover were published. The research had been carried out by the Tavistock Institute on behalf of the EDC for Hotel and Catering. The study, as anticipated, discovered that the industry's turnover was generally high compared with most other industries, canteens having the lowest rate and hotels the highest. The importance of this study, however, was that it went beyond a quantitative analysis of labour turnover. Approximately half the report (about 24 pages) was devoted to conclusions and recommendations. Probably most important (but missed by many in the industry?) was the statement, 'The study findings support the view that there is a *management style* that tends to attract and retain entrants.' (NEDO, 1969, p. 44). The recommendations were made with the full knowledge of the tremendous difficulties likely to be encountered and 'that the changes recommended in the study will not be universally welcomed . . . . Some managers will find their acceptance psychologically difficult while others will be inclined to shrug the problem off as being of little practical significance.' (NEDO, 1969, p. 47).

In 1972 the Industrial Relations Act 1971 came into force which provided, for the first time, the right of protection from unfair dismissal. This granted the individual a permanent right to his or her job — so long as the contract was fulfilled and there was a need for the job. No longer could a boss dismiss an employee arbitrarily. The consequence of this removal of 'the divine right of dismissal', linked with the Contracts of Employment Act's requirement for a properly recorded contract, started the process of putting employees in a protected position — which only those protected by powerful unions had previously enjoyed.

The obvious development was that many employers, particularly the larger ones, now removed hire and fire decisions from junior managers and adopted at the least the 'grandfather principle', that is, any dismissal had to be authorized by the dismissing manager's own superior.

The beginning of the 1970s also saw the publication of two reports by the Manpower Research Unit of the Department of Employment; Manpower Studies No. 10, *Hotels* (Department of Employment, 1971) and Manpower Studies No. 11, *Catering* (Department of Employment, 1972). The objectives 'were to analyse current manpower . . . to forecast requirements in five years time . . . both in terms of numbers of employees and in the nature of their work' (Department of Employment, 1971, p. 5).

The manpower problems of the industry were now becoming very pressing as a consequence, largely, of a growth in demand encouraged by the Development of Tourism Act which stimulated the building of no fewer than 250 new hotels between 1970 and 1973. The report concluded that 'little attention was being given to forward manpower planning even by companies committed to opening new hotels' (Department of Employment, 1971, p. 41).

Concurrent with these reports were two reports published by the Commission on Industrial Relations. The Secretary of State for Employment and Productivity recognized the lack of formal negotiating machinery in the hotel and catering industry and referred the industry to the Commission in order to 'report the functioning and the development of voluntary collective bargaining in the hotel and catering industry with particular reference to the securing of any improvements in industrial relations that appear necessary and desirable' (Commission on Industrial Relations (CIR), 1971, p. iv). The two reports concerned themselves with the hotel and catering industry (Report No. 23; Commission on Industrial Relations, 1971) and with industrial catering (Report No. 27; Commission on Industrial Relations, 1972).

The first report identified clearly the lack of formal negotiating machinery (i.e. involving trade unions) and recommended 'that the hotel and restaurants industry should acknowledge the contributions which it can make to better industrial relations . . .' (CIR, 1971, p. 57). The report also formally recorded the formation in April 1970 of the Hotel and Catering Personnel Managers' Association. The objectives of this new association were to carry out research in areas such as 'recruitment, management development, staff structuring, training attitudes, improving job image . . ., a five day working week and the reduction of labour turnover' (CIR, 1971).

Here, therefore, was probably an important milestone in the industry's personnel activities. For the first time, managers responsible for personnel matters were to get together to share knowledge on matters of mutual concern.

Interestingly, the other report, on industrial catering, concluded that collective bargaining and the determination of conditions of employment were so well organized that the Commission of Industrial Relations recommended the abolition of the sector's Wages Council.

In addition, these reports gave considerable insight into the workings of the industry and the nature of those working in the industry, referring for example to 'This individualistic, competitive outlook of the hotel employee . . . supported and extended by the degree of isolation of many employees and the independent nature of a number of work tasks' (CIR, 1971, p. 36).

So was the industry beginning to come of age from a personnel management point of view? Certainly there was the emergence of a group of personnel specialists in hotels and restaurants. In another major sector the determination of conditions was such that the Wages Council could be abolished.

It was shortly after this that the first book devoted entirely to personnel management in the hotel and catering industry (Boella, 1974) was published. It was not an evaluation of the industry's personnel management. However, in looking at the contents, and bearing in mind that at the time of writing the author had had recent experience with two of the industry's leading employers and was a member of the Hotel and Catering Industry's Personnel Management Association, it evidences much of the industry's attitude to its workforce. In all, about 98% of the book was concerned with personnel techniques: how to recruit, how to train, etc. Less than 2% was concerned with underlying research findings or theory — for example, why people work.

The mid-seventies, however, appeared to be an important turning point. Whilst the Department of Employment studies of 1971 and 1972 into the Manpower of Hotels and Catering were quantitative in nature, in that they set out to produce manpower forecasts, the NEDO report, Manpower Policy in the Hotels and Restaurant Industry (NEDO, 1975) produced the first detailed qualitative report designed 'to assist the industry to recruit the labour it requires, to improve staff retention, and to make the fullest and most efficient use of its available manpower' (NEDO, 1975, p. xi). The report drew many critical conclusions on the industry's style of managing its workforce.

In essence it was really saying that the best recruitment and training techniques were worth nothing unless managers adopted new attitudes and new approaches. A range of detailed recommendations was made which was directed at developing a professional approach to managing the industry's personnel.

In the mid- to late-seventies the HCITB levy exemption scheme provided an important impetus to improving the management of manpower resources. Previously many companies had set out to maximize their grants, irrespective of their real training needs. Under the new levy exemption scheme however, companies could avoid paying the statutory training levy (around 1% of the payroll) by demonstrating that they were meeting their real needs. The consequence was that many companies, including some of the country's largest, who had still done little in the way of realistic (needs-driven) training, now faced a financial penalty unless they set about training adequately. For many companies this meant professionalizing the training function and, because of the interdependence between training and the other personnel activities, the whole personnel function. A number of personnel professionals were recruited from outside the industry, and this had the effect of importing effective personnel practices into the industry, at least into some of the larger companies.

In 1977, Magurn's book, *A Manual of Staff Management in the Hotel and Catering Industry* (Magurn, 1977), was published. This was concerned, as the title implies and the author intended, with personnel techniques. Nothing of significance appears on underlying theory, the peculiar nature of the industry or personnel policy.

The industry's first two specialist textbooks appeared, therefore, to suggest that the personnel manager's task was to find staff for the operators, evidenced possibly by the statement — 'they [personnel managers] assist management to find the best possible candidates and to provide training for the successful candidates' (Boella, 1974).

Neither book tackled the issues of 'attitudes and approaches' identified by the NEDO report. They reflected the industry's own management perspective of the role of personnel management — which could be encapsulated as 'get us the staff but don't expect us to change anything'.

Throughout this time the HCITB was publishing booklets, research papers, etc., which in the main were of a quantitative nature. Little important work concerned with the industry's underlying issues, apart from the NEDO and CIR reports, was made public until Mars (1973) wrote on hotel pilferage, Mars and Mitchell (1976) published their study *Room for Reform*, their report on low pay in the industry (Mars and Mitchell, 1977) and Mars *et al.* (1979) published 'Manpower Problems in the Hotel and Catering Industry'. They too recognized that 'the vast majority of the industry was really asking for . . . a short practical guide to managing human relations at the level of the individual' (Mars *et al.*, 1979, p. vii). Certainly the industry has received plenty of guidance on techniques from the HCITB, Boella and Magurn. Mars and his colleagues, instead, using a variety of different sources, examined the underlying issues by looking at causes, not merely the symptoms. They looked at, amongst other things, the work of the American W. F. Whyte, which included the examination of 'labour turnover, factional strife, interdepartmental friction, autocratic supervision, unclear lines of authority, and union grievances' (quoted from Mars *et al.*, 1979, p. 21). As a result of their examination of seven case studies Mars *et al.* drew conclusions and made recommendations concerning the changes in the use of manpower. In essence they found that:

(i)   'The style of management in the industry . . . can be best characterised as "fire fighting" '.
(ii) 'The money earnings of hotel and catering workers are universally low'.
(iii) 'Such earnings are nonetheless *supplemented* in a wide variety of ways, some recorded, many illegitimate, and most involving a high degree of local management collusion' (Mars *et al.*, 1979).

Nineteen seventy-six saw the publication of Angela Bowey's book *The Sociology of Organization*. The aim of the book was 'to present a model of behaviour in organizations . . . for the practising manager it will be an aid in the search for relevant management policies for influencing human behaviour in organizations' (Bowey, 1976, p. 15).

Essentially the book, whilst based upon the study of behaviour in a number of Manchester restaurants, is of more interest to organization theorists than practising personnel managers. However, for students of management in the restaurant industry it provides valuable insights into the socio-technical culture of restaurants.

It was during the seventies that the trade union movement became more active in the industry. In the public houses sector, because of the threat by the Transport and General Workers Union to organize public house managers, the brewers had fostered the formation of the National Association of Licensed House Managers which quickly moved to a position of virtual monopoly of public house managers. The General and Municipal Workers Union formed the Hotel and Catering Workers' Union and, as a consequence, a spate of industrial relations training was started and a small number of industrial relations experts were employed by major companies. Another consequence was that middle and senior line managers were now needing to use, and rely on, specialized personnel techniques concerned with job evaluation and salary administration.

In 1980 the second edition of Boella's work *Personnel Management in the Hotel and Catering Industry* was published. It reflected in a small way the underlying concern of many that personnel techniques, however well practised, were not enough. What was needed was an understanding of people's behaviour at work. This was evidenced by the inclusion of a chapter on personnel policy and an attempt to enlarge the understanding of the employment relationships by including a page on Etzioni's work in addition to continuing with the, by now, 'old hat' and well tried, Maslow and McGregor.

In the introduction to this paper it was stated that only those works which could materially assist in a greater understanding of the practice of personnel management in the industry would be considered. One such work, whilst not a 'mainstream' personnel text, is that by Conrad Saunders, *Social Stigma of Occupations* (Saunders, 1981). Its contribution is that, in the same vein as Mars *et al.*, he gives insights into the very nature of the work of many of the industry's labour force, with recommendations for reducing some of the industry's manning problems. For example, about kitchen porters he writes, 'We found little evidence of . . . use of mechanical or technological aids that could take the drudgery out of this work . . . but established that no fewer than 85% of the sample highly value proper tools . . . and that these would be conditions to do this work more permanently' (Saunders, 1981, p. 148).

By 1983 Boella's book *Personnel Management in the Hotel and Catering Industry* came to its third edition and the two additional chapters are of interest because they reflect the growing expectations of personnel management. The first of the new chapters, 'Organizing Manpower', without being explicit introduces the concept of organization development from a contingency theory viewpoint and its inclusion demonstrates that senior managers in the industry were now beginning to look to personnel managers to be their 'organization' specialists.

The other chapter emphasized that personnel managers should be in the front line of organizational effectiveness by concerning themselves with labour costs — something their colleagues have done for many years in other industries.

The two chapters taken together, therefore, indicate that the personnel specialist could find himself in the crucial decision-making locus of the company — no longer just the 'hirer and firer' or the 'do gooder'.

In 1984 two further books specifically concerned with manpower matters were published. One was *Manpower Management in the Hotel and Catering Industry* by Hornsey and Dann; the other was *People and the Hotel and Catering Industry* by Lockwood and Jones. Both books were certainly important additions to the literature because, for the first time, textbooks were available which set out to relate theory and practice. The books by Boella and Magurn were largely concerned with personnel techniques, leaving aside the underlying theory. They described the 'what and how' of personnel management but largely omitted the 'why'. The books by Mars *et al.*, Bowey and Conrad based on their own research gave interesting insights into the idiosyncratic nature of the industry, whilst Hornsey and Dann, and Lockwood and Jones set out to relate academic theory about people and work to the practice of manpower management in the hotel and catering industry.

So what can be said of the current state of personnel management in the hospitality industry? There is no simple answer. All industries and many sectors of individual industries are, to a greater or lesser extent, idiosyncratic. To suggest that one industry has good personnel management practices when compared with those of other industries, in the final analysis, is a value judgement. If, however, an attempt is to be made to evaluate the personnel practices of an industry one approach is to compare its practices against what are considered to be the expected practices generally. Where does one find a résumé of such expected practices? The answer probably lies, if anywhere, in the personnel practitioner's professional body, as indicated by what the professional body considers to be its current corpus of knowledge and professional ethics. The professional body for personnel management in the United Kingdom is the Institute of Personnel Management which has a corpus of knowledge as contained in its examination syllabus. In addition, the Institute publishes a range of texts, the most important of which, because it sets out to look at the full scope of personnel management, is Thomason's *Textbook of Personnel Management* which sets out 'to produce a coherent summary of the position we have now reached in "personnel management" ' (Thomason, 1981, p. xi). In this a clear definition of personnel management emerges. He writes, 'the personnel function has come to be regarded as distinct from the technical and financial functions . . . and as having its own "technology" . . . and its own "ideologies" (generally bifurcated between the welfare of the individual employee and the welfare of the undertaking as a whole)' (Thomason, 1981, p. 49). So here we see that personnel management should be concerned with the welfare of the employer and the individual employee. Thomason then details the scope of personnel management demonstrating the major activities and how each relates to the employer and the employee.

Torrington and Chapman (1984), in their book *Personnel Management*, assert that personnel work has three elements:

(i)   Determining the expectations that employees have of their organisations and the expectations that organisations have of their employees.
(ii) Setting up a series of contracts or agreements between organisation and employee that describe the mutual expectations.
(iii) Servicing the contracts to ensure that the expectations are fulfilled (Torrington and Chapman, 1984, p. 4).

They justify their assertion by drawing on work of a number of authorities, including Mumford, Dubin, McCarthy and Ellis.

They point out that, whilst there is still a great deal of 'unilateral decision-making' as opposed to 'management by agreement', there is a clear trend away from unilateral decision-making' in *all* aspects of the employment of people' (Torrington and Chapman, 1984, p. 6). They summarize this position: 'Personnel management is a series of activities enabling working man and his employing organization to reach agreement about the nature and objectives of the employment relationship between them, and then to fulfil those agreements' (Torrington and Chapman, 1984, p. 12).

Armstrong defines personnel management as:

- obtaining, developing and motivating the human resources required by the organisation to achieve its objectives;
- developing an organisation structure and climate and evolving a management style which will promote co-operation and commitment throughout the organisation;
- making the best use of the skills and capacities of all those employed in the organisation;
- ensuring that the organisation meets its social and legal responsibilities towards its employees, with particular regard to the conditions of employment and quality of working life provided for them (Armstrong, 1984, p. 13).

Armstrong's book is divided into the five main areas, as laid down by the Institute of Personnel Management.

Taken together, these three texts, together with the examination syllabus, may be considered to present a current over-view of the scope, but not necessarily a common perspective, of the personnel management function. Table 1 shows the coverage of personnel management topics by the main British textbooks devoted entirely to personnel issues in the hotel and catering industry. The topics listed by chapter numbers in the top of the table (Part A) are those identified by Thomason (1981) in his review of the general personnel texts. The lower part of the table (Part B) identifies topics which have been covered specifically in the textbooks written for the hotel and catering industry and which do not appear to fit easily with Thomason's list. The texts show that the nature of interest in personnel management in the industry has changed considerably in the eighties. Many of the areas formerly considered either unnecessary to the health of an organization, such as organization development, labour costs and productivity now feature as subjects of concern in the literature.

In the mid-1970s Boella and Magurn were concerned almost entirely with personnel techniques. The NEDO publication 1975, followed by Mars and Mitchell (1976, 1977, 1979), consisted of more thorough examinations of management practice as it affected the industry's workforce. By the 1980s, however, Boella (1983) had added organization development and labour costs to the scope of personnel management, whilst Lockwood and Jones (1984) and Hornsey and Dann (1984) had selected a considerable range of material from the behavioural sciences and showed its application to the industry's manpower.

The 1980s has been a period of consolidation and possibly of maturation. There are now hundreds of managers with major or total responsibility for personnel matters. Their responsibilities now go well beyond those of the few personnel managers of twenty years ago. Many more are now recruited from outside the industry, as senior managers recognize the value of employing professional personnel managers rather than making one of the new junior managers responsible for personnel. The fear of the middle and late seventies

Table 1. Coverage of personnel management topics†

	Boella (1974)	Magurn (1977)	Mars & Mitchell (1979)	Boella (1980)	Boella (1983)	Hornsey & Dann (1984)	Lockwood Jones (1984)
Part A							
Objectives							
Policy				2	2	2	
Organization							
Function							
*Manpower							
Planning	16			17	17	2	
Employment							
Recruitment	3, 4, 5	1, 2		4, 5, 6	4, 5, 6	3	
Wage							
Determination	9, 10	9	1	10, 11	10, 11		
Termination	13	16, 17	7	14	14		
Employee records	16	5, 6		17	17	2	
Promotion							
*Employee services							
Welfare		13					
Health/safety		12, 14					
Employee development	7, 8			8, 9	8, 9		
Interviewing/counselling	4, 6	2, 10, 15		7	7		
*Resource control							
Standard setting	2			3	3		
Appraisal	6	10		7	7		
Training	7, 8	4, 11		6, 8, 9	6, 8, 9	5	
Discipline/rules		15, 16					
Motivation/incentives	11, 12	9		12, 13	12, 13		4
Wage and salary administration	9, 10			10, 11	10, 11	9	
Supervision							
*Industrial relations	14	18		15	15	8	
Negotiations	14	18, 20		15	15	8	
Joint consultation	14	18		15	15	8	
Procedures	14	19		15	15	8	
Organizational development			5				
Job analysis	2						
Work groups							
Organizational analysis							
Communication							
Organization development					18		
Environment							
Part B							
Social science issues							
The individual		7				4	2
Groups, interpersonal relationships			4			4	6, 7
Perceptions							3
Communication		8					5
Leaderships		7	6				8
Organizations			5				10
Managing change			8, 9			7	
Productivity			9				
Law	16	3	16	16			
Structure of the industry		1		1	1		
Labour costs				19			10

*Chapter headings as identified by Thomason (1981).
† Numbers indicate chapter numbers.

that trade unions would ride rough-shod through the industry did not materialize as the unions attempted to confront a highly-fragmented, individualistic and entrepreneurial workforce.

If, however, questions are to be asked about the present and the future of personnel management in the industry they could well concern themselves with the decision-making process. Torrington and Chapman suggest that there are trends towards a more pluralistic approach. They write 'that there is a clear trend away from unilateral decision making in *all* aspects of the employment of people' (Torrington and Chapman, 1984, p. 6). If their contention is correct then this could prove to be a fruitful area for exploration.

References

Armstrong, M. (1984) *A Handbook of Personnel Management Practice*, 2nd edn. Kogan Page, London.

Boella, M. (1974) *Personnel Management in the Hotel and Catering Industry*, Barrie & Jenkins, London.

Boella, M. (1980) *Personnel Management in the Hotel and Catering Industry*, 2nd edn. Hutchinson, London.

Boella, M. (1983) *Personnel Management in the Hotel and Catering Industry*, 3rd edn. Hutchinson, London.

Bowey, A. M. (1976) *The Sociology of Organisations*, Hodder & Stoughton, London.

British Hotel, Restaurant and Caterers Association (1975) Manpower Problems in the Hotel and Catering Industry, BHRCA, London

Commission on Industrial Relations, U.K. (1971) *Hotel and Catering Industry*. Part 1. *Hotels and Restaurants*. Report No. 23, Cmnd. 4789. H.M.S.O., London.

Commission on Industrial Relations, U.K. (1972) *Hotel and Catering Industry*. Part II. *Industrial Catering*. Report No. 27, H.M.S.O., London.

Department of Employment, U.K. (1971) *Hotels*, Manpower Studies No. 10. H.M.S.O., London.

Department of Employment, U.K. (1972) *Catering*. Manpower Studies No. 11. H.M.S.O. London.

Hornsey, T. and Dann, D. (1984) *Manpower Management in the Hotel and Catering Industry*, Batsford Academic and Educational, London.

Lockwood, A. and Jones, P. (1984) *People and the Hotel and Catering Industry*, Holt-Saunders, Eastbourne.

Magurn, J. P. (1977) *A Manual of Staff Management in the Hotel and Catering Industry*, Heinemann, London.

Mars, G. (1973) Hotel pilferage: a case study in occupational theft. *The Sociology of the Workplace*, Warner, M. (ed.). Allen & Unwin, London.

Mars, G. and Mitchell, P. (1976) *Room for Reform? A Case Study of Industrial Relations in the Hotel Industry*. Unit 6, Industrial Relations Course, P881. Open University Press, Milton Keynes.

Mars, G. and Mitchell, P. (1977) Catering for the Low Paid: Invisible Earnings. Low Pay Unit Bulletin No. 15, June.

Mars G., *et al.* (1979) *Manpower Problems in the Hotel and Catering Industry*. Saxon House, Farnborough.

National Economic Development Office (1967) Economic Development Committee for Hotels and Catering. *Your Manpower: a Practical Guide to the Manpower Statistics of the Hotel and Catering Industry*. H.M.S.O., London.

National Economic Development Office (1969) *Hotel and Catering EDC: Staff Turnover*. H.M.S.O., London.

National Economic Development Office (1975) Economic Development for Hotels and Catering. *Manpower Policy in the Hotels and Restaurant Industry — Summary and Recommendations*. NEDO, London.

National Economic Development Office (1975) Economic Development Committee for Hotels and Catering. *Manpower Policy in the Hotels and Restaurant Industry — Research Findings*. NEDO, London.

Orwell, G. (1969) *Down and Out in Paris and London*. Penguin Books, Harmondsworth.

Saunders, C. (1981) *Social Stigma of Occupations*. Gower, Farnborough, Hants.

Thomason, G. (1981) *A Textbook of Personnel Management*, 4th edn. Institute of Personnel Management, London.

Torrington, D. and Chapman, J. (1984) *Personnel Management*, 2nd edn. Prentice-Hall, London.

Whyte, W. F. (1948) *Human Relations in the Restaurant Industry*, McGraw-Hill, New York.

appendix 2

The IPM Code of Professional Practice in Personnel Management

Introduction to the Code

Personnel management is that part of management concerned with people at work and with their relationships within an organization. Its aim is to bring together and develop into an effective organization the men and women who make up an enterprise, enabling them to make their best contribution to its success.

This Code is a guide to those engaged in personnel management on the essential principles and practices appropriate to the profession. The object of the Code is to establish high standards of practice and publicly declare them. While the Code is directed primarily to members of the Institute of Personnel Management, it is commended to all those working in this field.

The Institute of Personnel Management

The IPM exists to promote and develop the professionalism of personnel management and in particular the development and application of policies governing:

Industrial relations.
Manpower planning, recruitment, selection, placement and termination of employment.
Education, training and development.
Organization development and the effect of change in organization and methods of working.
Terms of employment, methods and standards of remuneration and employee benefits.
Working conditions, health and safety.
Formal and informal communication and consultation between representatives of employers and employees and with employees at all levels in the organization.

The Institute adopts a positive and initiating role, seeking to influence the occupational and social environments, legislation and management thinking — locally, nationally and internationally. It aims to be a leading authority in the field of the management of human resources and the guardian of high standards in the practice of personnel management.

A member of the Institute commits himself to its aims and objects. He is interested in the establishment of good practice within the profession as a whole and in the development of younger members. He is mindful of his responsibilities to his employer and the special nature of his relationship with the employees. At the same time he is concerned that those engaged in personnel management who are not members of the Institute should adopt its standards and understand its objects. In his relationships he should conduct himself with due regard to the high standards of integrity and behaviour demanded by the particular responsibilities of the profession, and will not knowingly take any action which may be liable to bring the good name of the Institute or its members into disrepute.

The personnel manager

While the management of people forms part of every manager's job, the personnel manager provides specialist knowledge, advice and services for other members of the management team so that they may be assisted to make the most effective use of the human resources of the organization. He should have a clear understanding of the economic factors affecting the success of the organization, particularly the cost-effectiveness of manpower and associated expenditure.

A personnel manager is concerned with the long-term success of the organization both as an industrial, commercial or public enterprise, and as a social entity. He has, however, a special involvement in the livelihood of people, their working conditions, security of employment, reward and development, and is also a privileged recipient and guardian of personal information and confidences.

Responsibility to the employer

A personnel manager's primary responsibility is to his employer. He should conduct himself as a responsible member of the management team committed to the achievement of the organization's objectives with the optimum use of resources. He will:

1   Advise on good personnel practice concerning: terms and conditions of employment, staffing and the labour market, the organization of work, training and development, employee benefits, welfare facilities and the working environment.

2 Seek to establish and maintain good working relationships with trade unions and employee representatives.
3 Encourage the development of effective consultation and communication at all levels in the organization.
4 Respect the employer's requirements for the confidentiality of information entrusted to him during the performance of his duties, including the safeguarding of information about individual employees.
5 Promote non-discriminatory employment practices, and common standards of justice in the treatment of individuals by the corporate employer.
6 Constantly update his professional skill and knowledge in respect of new learning and legislation in the personnel field and the impact of technological, economic and social change on people at work.

Responsibility to employees and potential employees

By his conduct and good practice a personnel manager will establish confidence in himself and understanding of his role and thus resolve the conflict which must sometimes exist between his position as a member of the management team and his special relationship with the workforce in general and with individual employees. In particular, he will:

1 Be available to act in a counselling role to individual employees and to advise them about their personal development and career opportunities.
2 Seek to achieve the fullest possible development of the capability of individual employees commensurate with the opportunities available and the needs of the organization.
3 Ensure the privacy and confidentiality of personal information to which he has access or for which he is responsible, subject to any legal requirements and the best interests of the employee.
4 Ensure that existing and potential employees are given full and accurate information concerning employment with his organization.
5 Observe the Institute's Codes of Practice and use his best endeavours to ensure they are applied throughout his organization.
6 Be concerned with the welfare of pensioners and the dependants of deceased employees.

Relationships with other organizations

In his relationships with other professional bodies, government departments, institutions, employer and trade associations, trade unions and other employee associations, a personnel manager will use his best endeavours to enhance the standing and good name of his profession. He should not disclose information about an employee to external bodies without the agreement of the individual concerned, except where this would conflict with his public duty, or when responding to legitimate requests for references.

Notes

1 The use of masculine throughout this Code is deemed to include the feminine.
2 The term personnel manager is used to include all those working at an executive level in the personnel function whether specialized or not.
3 The terms 'enterprise' or 'organization' are used to include the industrial, commercial or public service sectors.

appendix 3
The IPM Recruitment Code

Introduction

In the spring of 1977, Michael Dixon's Job Column in the *Financial Times* highlighted the resentment felt by many job applicants against recruiters. It made no difference, it seemed, whether the recruiter was a company personnel manager, a small company managing director or a selection consultant. All were guilty of meting out callous injustices to the innocent and defenceless applicant. What was needed, said Michael Dixon, was a *candidates' charter* so that the much-abused applicants were protected with a minimum standard of behaviour by the recruiters. This must have caused many readers with experiences of recruitment and selection to shake their heads with a tired sigh. It is, after all, well-known that a satisfied, rejected applicant is almost as rare as a man who believes his dismissal was justified. Fortunately some recruiters decided to take issue with the *Financial Times* and Michael Dixon's column echoed with demands for a *recruiters' charter* to protect them against the thoughtless, the unreliable, the rude and the downright dishonest who surface in any large batch of job applicants. In an inspired compromise Michael Dixon suggested a 'two-way agreement' giving simple, basic guidelines which, if followed by recruiters and applicants, would eliminate the causes of the complaints. The Institute of Personnel Management was suggested as an appropriate national sponsoring body.

The IPM's National Committee for Pay and Employment Conditions (under the then Vice-President and Chairman, Robert Fleeman) took up the challenge and meetings with Michael Dixon and other interested parties followed. Ideas were aired and a draft code published in the *Financial Times* and the IPM *Digest*. The response revealed an unexpectedly high level of support for the venture and brought many ideas for embellishments and additions. All of these were carefully examined and some found their way into the final document, *The IPM Recruitment Code*. The Code is above all simple and brief. Those who have had experience of such things will know how much easier a longer document would have been.

What it is

The Code aims to set down briefly and clearly guidance on those matters which most commonly cause resentment to recruiters and applicants. The faults are most often the result of inexperience or thoughtlessness, rarely the result of deliberate intent. Many well-run personnel departments will believe that they have nothing to learn from the 'recruiters' obligations', but experienced recruiters know how necessary it is to check regularly that good procedures are not being bypassed. Even in the best-run organization therefore, the Code might be a helpful prompter. Small companies, which want to do their occasional recruitment well — and which are conscious of their public image — will find that the Code provides a useful check list.

Considerable time was spent in refining the Code and making it as short as possible. A crisp, concise, compact Code has a better chance of acceptance and survival. Furthermore, if it is a short document, organizations might be tempted to issue it to applicants, thus reminding them of their obligations (which also are more often casualties of thoughtlessness than intent).

The IPM would like to see the Code mentioned in recruitment advertisements and literature and publicized by trade associations, professional institutions, employment agencies and other bodies. In other ways the IPM will be doing all it can to encourage the use of the Code. It will follow up apparent breaches and seek the co-operation of the 'offending party' in at least avoiding a repetition. Most lapses are unintentional and most companies are unaware of the damage being done to their public relations. For these reasons it is expected that most organizations will respond positively to a carefully phrased and polite approach. Perhaps we can then look forward to the day when the Code has to be revised — because some of yesterday's common faults are no longer common.

What it is not

No one associated with the development of the Code would lay claim to its being revolutionary or even highly original: it does not seek to repeat or replace the laws of the land. Those who support the Code are, in any case, unlikely to ignore the law deliberately on (say) sex or race discrimination, recruiting people under the age of 16, or charging employment agency fees to applicants. The absence of a list of illegalities does not mean that the IPM condones them; it means that the need for the Code did not arise from breaches of the law. Nobody complained to Michael Dixon or the IPM of illegalities; they did complain in volume of the common discourtesies, the inefficiencies and the simple lack of thought that bedevils so much of the recruitment process. Certainly the IPM wants people to act within the law and anyone in doubt about the legality of some matter connected with recruitment should seek professional advice or turn to one of the IPM's publications on the subject. For instance the IPM's Joint Standing Committee on Discrimination has made a special study of the problems of discrimination in recruitment and anyone experiencing difficulties of this type should study the Committee's Report *Towards Fair Selection: A Code for Non-Discrimination* which is obtainable from the IPM Publications.

The IPM Recruitment Code is not a mandatory document. How then will its aims be enforced? The answer is that if we tried to force it on people we would negate its effect. There are examples enough of this happening in the legislative field. Far better to encourage the adoption of the Code voluntarily and although there is no thought of coercion the IPM will take every opportunity of reminding people of the Code and will follow up any alleged breaches which are reported to it or which come to its notice.

The recruitment code — 4th edition

The aims of the code

The Code seeks to promote high standards of professional recruitment practice by encouraging recruiters and applicants to adhere to common guidelines.

The IPM hopes that employers will adopt the Code throughout their organizations on the grounds of common courtesy. The way in which candidates are treated also reflects on an employer's public relations image. Poor publicity can result from bad recruitment practices. Many organizations have excellent recruitment standards, but the Institute accepts that the current levels of unemployment result in large numbers of applications for most vacancies, and other organizations may be unable to meet these standards at all times. The Code, therefore, sets out the basic elements of a professional recruitment policy, which should be implemented in practice wherever possible.

Although some parts of the Code may apply more to white collar employment, the IPM believes that the spirit of this Code should apply to all recruitment. Common courtesy is the right of all applicants, whether for a shopfloor job or for the position of managing director.

The Code aims to provide guidance on those matters that most commonly cause difficulty to recruiters and applicants. Faults usually arise from inexperience or thoughtlessness, and rarely from deliberate intent. Many well-run personnel departments will have little to learn from the Code, but experienced recruiters know that it is necessary to check regularly that procedures are being followed. Even in the best run organizations, the Code should prove helpful as a basis for auditing and updating recruitment practices. Small companies should find that the Code provides a useful checklist and training device for line managers.

Unsolicited applications/Keeping interview appointments

A major concern of recruiters is that of unsolicited applications and how best to deal with them. Large employers can receive many thousands of such applications every year, and the IPM believes that it is unreasonable to expect them to bear the cost of reply. Where, however, the hopeful applicant has enclosed a stamped addressed envelope the recruiter should, at least, acknowledge receipt of the application.

Many recruiters also mention the problem of applicants who fail to keep interview appointments or who do not notify changes of circumstances, such as accepting a job elsewhere.

The Institute accepts that it is difficult to enforce adherence to the Code among applicants and can only remind them that they too have obligations, particularly to help the recruiter. A list of the courtesies that the IPM expects applicants to show appears at the end of this appendix.

Expenses

From the applicants' point of view a number of irritations still, unfortunately, seem to arise, of which the payment of expenses is a significant one. The IPM believes that recruiters should be prepared to pay reasonable and significant expenses incurred by applicants in attending interviews. However, it must be recognized that some recruiters have determined not to do so. In these cases it is reasonable to expect that the recruiter's policy concerning expenses is clearly explained to applicants when they are called to interview and not, as is often the case, at the interview or even afterwards.

Taking up references

The practice of taking up references before making a job offer is largely restricted to the public sector. **Employers should make it clear that they will not approach current or previous employers without the candidate's permission.** Employers should also bear in mind that the high level of company liquidations in recent years means that personnel records may be incomplete for some applicants and it may be impossible to obtain references from some of their previous employers.

Selection techniques

Many complaints are received that the selection techniques of some organizations fall short of professional standards. Employers are urged to bear in mind the damage done to their image in the eyes of both successful and unsuccessful applicants by poor recruitment and interview methods.

Similarly, psychological tests should preferably have been scientifically validated and should always be interpreted by qualified staff. Recruiters should beware of the results of non-scientifically validated tests. Personality tests, in particular, require sensitive handling and interpretation.

Employer: employer relationships

The institute has received complaints from employers about the practice of other employers approaching existing staff at their place of work. Potential and existing employers do have a responsibility towards each other, which is primarily one of trust (e.g. in respect of references). This relationship is considerably damaged by activities amounting to the recruitment of employees in their existing employer's time and at their existing employer's expense.

Discrimination

Sex and race

Unless employers have appropriate employment policies and procedures, discrimination on grounds of race and sex will continue to be practised. This point is particularly important with regard to indirect discrimination. Any requirement which excludes a high proportion of ethnic minorities or women, and is not a realistic requirement of the job, creates indirect discrimination and is unlawful.

Methods of recruitment exist other than advertising such as executive search, recruitment consultants, agency introductions and 'word of mouth'. Whichever is chosen, care must be taken to ensure that the method is fair to applicants and potential applicants and does not effectively screen out minorities or members of one sex. In particular, the 'word of mouth' approach can be unfair and discriminatory, since it will tend to perpetuate a workforce from the same sources as at present.

Keeping records of the sex and ethnic origin of job applicants is recommended by the EOC and CRE in their Codes of Practice. A record of the sex and racial origin of all candidates for employment, the jobs applied for, their qualifications and whether or not selected, would provide a means of analysing in detail the recruitment experience of different groups.

It is generally best to obtain these data from the application form, but it is also advisable when asking questions about ethnic origin to include an explanatory note that the information is needed for monitoring purposes and to explain why monitoring is necessary.

Recruiters are also advised to avoid the use of questions at interviews which might be construed as discriminatory, for example, a tendency to inquire into the marital and domestic circumstances of female applicants and not of males.

Disabled applicants
Another form of discrimination operates against disabled people. It is important to get disability into perspective. It does not necessarily affect a person's ability to do the work, although sometimes it may affect the manner or the place in which they perform it. When interviewing the rule should be to test the ability for the job first, discussing the disability only if adjustments need to be made to allow the applicant to do the job.

The MSC has produced a Code of Good Practice on the Employment of Disabled People which is supported by the IPM. Copies of the Code and further information and advice can be obtained from the MSC's Disablement Advisory Service through Jobcentres.

Rehabilitation of offenders
Naturally, employers will have regard to the provisions of the Rehabilitation of Offenders Act 1974 and not discriminate against or dismiss the applications of candidates with spent convictions. The Act has implications for the design of application forms and interview methods. Guides to the Act are available, published by HMSO.

Recruiters' obligations
1 **Job advertisements should state clearly the form of reply desired, in**

particular, whether this should be a formal application form or by curriculum vitae. Preferences should also be stated if hand-written replies are required. Many applicants complain of labouring to produce a detailed application letter, only to receive an application form asking for the same information. Stating the form of reply saves the time of both the recruiter and applicant. Closing dates should give a reasonable length of time for return of applications. Advertisements should reflect the job as truthfully as possible and preferably carry some indication of remuneration. A number of people complained of bogus advertisements by some employment agencies which were replenishing their files of available candidates. There were also instances of advertisements which appeared largely because of bureaucratic procedure and not because any outside applicant was really wanted. The Institute condemns both practices.

2   An acknowledgement or reply should be made promptly to each applicant by the employing organization or its agent. If it is likely to take some time before acknowledgements are made, this should be made clear in the advertisement.

Applicants should understand that unsolicited applications may not always be acknowledged without receipt of a stamped addressed envelope.

3   Applicants should be informed of the progress of the selection procedures, what these will be (e.g. group selection, aptitude tests), the steps and time involved and the policy regarding expenses.

Employers should bear in mind that attendance by the applicant of interviews will usually involve expenses and they should therefore have an explicit policy in respect of the reimbursement of expenses. The policy should be set out clearly when inviting applicants to interview.

Employers should also make every effort to keep to interview times. Applicants who put themselves forward for interviews are entitled to careful consideration whether or not they are ultimately successful. Unsuccessful applicants should be sent a courteous rejection letter.

Employers using confidential box numbers may have difficulty in meeting this obligation while remaining anonymous. This can be achieved by such means as using blank notepaper and either postal franking without an advertising slogan or ordinary stamps.

4   Detailed personal information (for example religion, medical history, place of birth, family background) should not be called for unless it is relevant to the selection process.

It is not intended that this should bar any request for personal details. There will be some jobs in which it will be necessary to know certain information at the initial application stage. With many others some personal details may never be required. It is not intended that interviewers should be hamstrung. It is the interviewer's job to get to know the applicant, and incidental reference to personal details is inevitable: this is unlikely to offend anyone. What candidates object to is answering an exhaustive list of personal questions on an application form at a very early stage of the selection. Few will, however, object to being asked for certain personal details if the reason is given (or is obvious); for instance, employment agencies should state when asking for nationality that they are statutorily required to do so.

Recruiters must take every care to keep within the guidelines of the codes of practice on sex and race discrimination and should be ready to explain why certain information is required.

5   Before applying for references, potential employers must secure the permission of the applicant.

It still happens that the applicant's current employer is approached for a reference without the applicant's knowledge. If a rule is made that *all* reference approaches must be approved by the candidate, this situation (and others which could be equally embarrassing) will be avoided. If the candidate raises any apparently unreasonable objections, the recruiter will need to know why and may properly take this into account in making the selection.

A further problem is the practice of some organizations of requiring reference names before the shortlisting stages which entails unnecessary approaches to potential referees.

6   Applications must be treated as confidential.

Complaints of breaches of confidence are usually connected with indiscriminate reference checks. It also still happens that an applicant's details are passed to another organization without the applicant's approval.

Applicant's obligations

Just as the code aims to reduce the irritations often felt by applicants, and to give them the right to certain courtesies, it also imposes certain obligations on them. Their main obligation is to show respect and courtesy to employers and to assist them in recruitment. As a minimum, therefore, the Institute believes it reasonable to expect applicants to show the following courtesies.

1   Advertisements should be answered in the way requested (for example telephone for application form, provide brief details, send curriculum vitae).

It is common to receive lengthy details in response to a request for brief initial replies or for people to turn up on the doorstep. Such actions are likely to be remembered to the applicant's disadvantage, and they do hinder a carefully arranged selection procedure.

2   Appointments and other arrangements must be kept, or the recruiter be informed promptly if the candidate discovers an agreed meeting cannot take place.

About one in every five candidates is late. One in ten never shows up.

3   The recruiter should be informed as soon as a candidate decides not to proceed with the application.

This decision presumably is the commonest reason for one in ten failing to attend an interview and the explanation for countless letters from recruiters which are not answered.

4   Only accurate information should be given in applications and in reply to recruiters' questions.

Deliberately supplying inaccurate information may be a cause for terminating any subsequent employment contract. A skilled interviewer will usually detect any inacurracy.

5 Information given by a prospective employer must be treated as confidential, if so requested.

Applicants need a lot of information to decide about a job. To encourage recruiters to give as much information as possible, it will be evident that confidences must be respected.

Staff recruitment organizations

The following organizations can be of assistance in recruiting staff.

Department of Employment

The Department of Employment now operates in the region of thirty branches which specialize in hotel and catering staff. The address and telephone number of the nearest such branch can be obtained from the local office of the Department of Employment.

In addition the Department runs a specialized hotel and catering staff service at:

Job Centre for the Hotel and Catering Trades
1–3 Denmark St
London WC2H 8LR
Telephone 01–836 6622

Employment agencies

The Federation of Recruitment and Employment Services of Great Britain is the principal association of employment agencies in Great Britain. The Federation lays down a code of conduct to which members agree to conform. The names, addresses and telephone numbers of member firms in any given area can be obtained by contacting the Federation. The address is:

The Federation of Recruitment and Employment Services
10 Belgrave Square
London SW1X 8PH
Telephone 01–235 6616

Management consultants

There are several management consultancy firms that can be of assistance in recruiting staff of middle and senior management positions. The names of such firms can be obtained from:

British Institute of Management
Management House
Parker St
London WC2B 5PT
Telephone 01–405 3456

Hotel Catering and Institutional Management Association
191 Trinity Rd
London SW17 7HN
Telephone 01–672 4251

Institute of Management Consultants
23 Cromwell Place
London SW7 2LG
Telephone 01–584 7285

Management Consultants Association
11 West Halkin St
London SW1X 8JL
Telephone 01–235 3897

Recruitment of overseas workers

Queries regarding the recruitment of foreign staff should be directed to the local office of the Department of Employment, or to:

The British Hotel, Restaurants and Caterers Association
40 Duke St
London W1M 6HR
Telephone 01–499 6641

Training organizations

The following organizations can be of assistance in providing advice, training materials or courses for the training of staff or management.

Trade/official bodies

British Association for Commercial and Industrial Education
16 Park Crescent
London w1N 4AP
Telephone 01–636 5351

British Institute of Management
Management House
Parker St
London wc2B 5PT
Telephone 01–405 3456

Hotel and Catering Training Board
International House
High Street
Ealing
London w5 5DB
Telephone 01–579 2400

The Industrial Society
3 Carlton House Terrace
London sw1y 5DG
Telephone 01–839 4300

Management consultants

The names of management consultants can be obtained from:

British Institute of Management
Management House
Parker St
London WC2B 5PT
Telephone 01–405 3456

Hotel Catering and Institutional Management Association
191 Trinity Rd
London SW17 7HN
Telephone 01–672 4251

Institute of Management Consultants
23 Cromwell Place
London SW7 2LG
Telephone 01–584 7285

Management Consultants Association
11 West Halkin Street
London SW1X 8JL
Telephone 01–235 3897

appendix 6

Salary administration, job evaluation and industrial relations

The following organizations can be of assistance in job evaluation and salary administration.

Professional bodies

British Institute of Management
Management House
Parker St
London WC2B 5PT
Telephone 01–405 3456

Hotel Catering and Institutional Management Association
191 Trinity Rd
London SW17 7HN
Telephone 01–672 4251

Institute of Personnel Management
IPM House
Camp Road
Wimbledon
London SW19 4UW
Telephone 01–946 9100

Management consultants

The names of firms can be obtained from:

British Institute of Management
Management House
Parker St
London WC2B 5PT
Telephone 01–405 3456

Institute of Management Consultants
23 Cromwell Place
London SW7 2LG
Telephone 01–584 7285

Management Consultants Association
11 West Halkin St
London SW1X 8JL
Telephone 01–235 3897

Other organizations

ACAS (Advisory, Conciliation & Arbitration Service)
Head Office
11–12 St James's Square
London SW1Y 4LA
Telephone 01–214 6000

Brewers' Society
42 Portman Square
London W1H 0BB
Telephone 01–486 4831

Hotel and Catering Training Board
International House
High Street
Ealing
London W5 5DB
Telephone 01–579 2400

appendix 7

Effective staff training

An abridged version of the publication *How to Get the Best from Your Staff: An Introduction to Staff Training Skills* by Michael J. Boella.

Author's note

This book sets out to cover the basics of staff training. It covers in a simple, step-by-step process, each of the main areas of knowledge and skills required by senior staff, supervisors and managers responsible for training. Because it is a partially programmed text it enables those who do not have the opportunity to attend a course to study and practise the basics. It also helps more senior managers to know just what is expected of their supervisors and staff trainers. Third, it can be used as a refresher for those who may have already attended a staff trainers' course. Finally, for those who themselves run staff training courses this makes a concise, easy-to-use guide and hand-out.

This book is not however to be seen as a substitute for attendance at a proper course.

Acknowledgements

My thanks are due to many people, known and unknown, who over the years have contributed the knowledge, experience and material which have made this short book possible. Regretfully, I cannot acknowledge everyone personally. However, I would like particularly to record my gratitude to the Tack Organisation and the Industrial Society whose courses I attended and to the HCITB with whom I have collaborated on many occasions.

Introduction

The success of every business depends upon its staff and it has been found that people work most satisfactorily when they have confidence in their employer, in their surroundings and particularly in their own performance of their job.

Obviously no single factor contributes to creating this sense of confidence. But possibly more than anything else, effective induction, that is, the introduction of everything surrounding a person's job, and thorough training in the knowledge and skills necessary to do the job, are responsible for creating the confidence which can lead to a person doing his job in a competent and satisfactory manner. Unfortunately however there are those who feel that systematic training is unnecessary, is too costly, and is beyond their capabilities – or they feel that the ability to train others is something that one is born with. Yet most managers know that a person such as a secretary or a chef, who is skilled in his or her job, is more efficient than an unskilled person. This principle applies equally to the *skill of training* which is distinct from, and additional to, the *job skills* to be passed on. The skilled trainer trains more effectively than the unskilled trainer and, in contrast to the myth that there is not enough time to train, the skilled trainer makes training opportunities throughout the normal working day and will help to create a well-trained employee in a shorter time than an unskilled trainer.

Training others is a skill which can be learned by many normal staff and it makes sound business sense to train key staff, particularly the heads of departments, in this essential skill.

Benefits of training

Training, as with all other activities of an organization, should benefit the organization in the short or long term. These include:

1 Increased customer satisfaction.
2 Increased customer demand.
3 Better use of time.
4 Safer working methods.
5 Reduced waste.
6 Reduced damage.
7 Reduced staff turnover.

Hence — more efficiency.

However, because the staff are the people being trained they should also benefit in some way. These include:

1 Increased efficiency.
2 Increased earnings.
3 Improved job security.
4 Improved job prospects.

Hence — increased job satisfaction and confidence in the job.

Planning training

If you are to train your staff efficiently it will need to be properly planned and in order to do this four main elements have to be considered:

Who is to do the training?
What is to be taught?
How is it to be taught?
How is it to be judged?

Who is to do the training?

We all know that some people can do a job very efficiently themselves but when it comes to teaching others they are no good at all. This is because to teach others requires certain characteristics which are additional to being able to do the job well.

Anyone who is selected to teach others consequently will need to have certain characteristics. These include:

1 Wish to help others.
2 Sympathetic and patient manner.
3 Competence in the job.
4 Understanding of trainees' needs and problems.
5 Systematic approach to work.
6 Knowledge and skill of teaching techniques.
7 Ability to be self-critical.

From this description it is apparent that most trainers will be more mature people, generally employed at some supervisory level. However, this is not always the case as many craftsmen and even more junior staff make excellent trainers; they enjoy the responsibility and often they are in the best position to train their colleagues, and the task of training others can be a valuable step in developing such people for promotion.

As a principle, however, everyone who has to give some form of instruction or coaching during the normal working day should have or should develop some training skills. This applies particularly to every manager and supervisor. A trainer once trained is going to be able to:

1   Know what performance is expected of the staff.
2   Recognize training opportunities and make use of them.
3   Make training opportunities.
4   Know which tasks and critical points need to be learned by trainees.
5   Recognize shortcomings in performance.
6   Analyse tasks.
7   Plan training.
8   Prepare and give instruction.
9   Produce training aids.
10 Keep records.
11 Review training.

What is to be taught?

Training in a business context is concerned with bridging the gap between an individual's capabilities and the employer's requirements. This gap is a *training need*. Put this way it sounds simple but in practice it can be quite difficult. This is because what a person needs to bring to a job is a mixture of:

General knowledge
Technical knowledge
Aptitudes
Attitudes
Skills

Training needs, apart from consisting of knowledge, skills and attitudes, occur at different times in the working life of employees and organizations. For example when:

A new employee starts
Changes take place
Things go wrong

When a new employee starts

Of course a whole range of things need to be known. You should include items from each of the following:

Relationships between staff and departments
Hours and other conditions
Safety and security practices
Rules and regulations
Methods of work

When changes take place

A person needs training when the following occur:

Changes in methods, products or standards of performance
Changes in equipment
Transfers and promotions

When things go wrong (remedial training)

A person may need training when any of the following occur:

Unsatisfactory trading results or standards
Customer complaints
Breakages, waste

What can be taught?

Some things, such as knowledge and skill, can be transferred to most reasonable trainees quite easily given adequate training expertise on the part of the trainer.

Attitudes, on the other hand, are very difficult and in many respects it is better to aim to select people with the attitudes you want rather than to attempt to 'instil' attitudes into unwilling employees. If, for example, a person resents serving others, it is unlikely that you will have the time and psychological expertise to change his attitudes. Much better to avoid recruiting him in the first place. It is apparent therefore that most training should be concerned with transferring knowledge and skills. To do this the trainer will need to examine his own knowledge and skill and break it down so that he is completely aware of what he has to put over.

This process — job analysis — can be vital, because most skilled people take for granted large parts of their own knowledge and skill.

The managers' responsibility

These different activities have to be set in motion and monitored constantly by management. And as with most other management processes it is a cyclical one starting and finishing with the planning stage.

Figure A7.1   *The manager's responsibilities*

The manager responsible for training must:

1 Set training objectives. To do this, job descriptions may be needed and these will, so far as possible, set standards of performance. For example, if a person is expected to attend to twenty people in an hour, then the trainer should use this standard as his training objective and set progressively more difficult targets during the programme.
2 Select trainers and, where appropriate, he will arrange for them to be trained in training skills. May be he should be the first to attend such a course.
3 Delegate training responsibilities.
4 Provide training facilities such as rooms, equipment and training aids.
5 Inform staff of any changes and any training to be given to cope with changes.
6 Show that he really believes in training by participating in it himself.
7 Review the effectiveness of training by checking upon the work of people who have finished their training and occasionally by interviewing some or all of them or having informal chats with them to obtain their views on the training they received.

What is to be taught?

What has to be taught?

The types of factors staff may have to learn have been listed. One of the problems, however, of teaching others is that the experienced person automatically (even subconsciously) does many things which the trainee is going to have to learn step-by-step. A good example is the difference between a novice driver, who consciously thinks about each element of driving, and the expert who integrates each element unconsciously into the total driving process. Consequently, to be sure that all points are taught the trainer needs to use a systematic process for listing everything that is going to be taught.

If this is not done, many points, sometimes essential or even vital, may be overlooked in training. The omission will then only be highlighted when the trainee (or ex-trainee) does something wrong — possibly with expensive consequences for the employer. Unfortunately in these circumstances the trainee and not the inadequate training is usually blamed.

Here is a simple job broken down into duties.

A room-maid's duties:

1 Collection of guest departure list, and early morning tea and breakfast lists and keys from head housekeeper's office.
2 Service of early morning tea and breakfasts in bedroom.
3 Preparation of trolley for servicing rooms.
4 Servicing of bedrooms.
5 Servicing of bathrooms.
6 Checking of all appliances.

7 Checking of all literature.
8 Final room check.
9 Reporting back to housekeeper.

Task analysis

After this the duties may be broken down into tasks. Some tasks may be very simple to learn and they may not need to be broken down further. Such tasks usually draw upon a person's knowledge and skills which have been acquired in every day life (the life skills).

Servicing a bathroom

1 Check quantity and take out dirty linen, leave outside bathroom on floor.
2 Check, empty and clean bin and ashtray, remove dirty soap.
3 Wash bath, tiles, clean all chrome fittings, mirrors and lights.
4 Wash toilet bowl, 'U' bend, seat and lid, wash tiles behind toilet and air vent.
5 Put toilet cleanser in bowl and leave.
6 Clean basin and top of vanitory unit then wash and dry drinking glasses after washing hands.
7 Replenish soap, towels, bathmat, disposal bags and toilet paper according to room quantities list.
8 Wash bathroom floor and door, wipe bath and wash basin pipes.
9 Replace bin also checking that shaver socket is off.
10 Quickly check around and take out dirty linen to maid's trolley.

More difficult tasks, however, will need to be analysed into the various steps in order to identify exactly what a person has to learn and what he has to avoid. This is called 'task analysis'.

Task analysis — the main elements

Task analysis consists of:

1 *Listing WHAT is done*	This should be one word or a brief phrase describing each distinct step: Greet guest Take glass
2 *Describing HOW the action is performed*	This should be a brief description of how each step is carried out starting with: by taking . . ., by saying . . .,

Table A7.1 *Task analysis sheet*

What	How	Critical point	Additional information
List each key step or stage, using short phrases starting with words such as:	Describe concisely the method to be used, start sentences with words such as:	Describe the critical signs which indicate that the operation is proceeding satisfactorily or otherwise. Use words which encourage a trainee to use his senses; look for, feel, taste. This column includes elements which involve using the senses in order to make judgements.	Add any additional information which may be necessary for the satisfactory performance of the task or to enhance a normal performance.
write, greet, cut, dispense	by writing by greeting by cutting by dispensing		This column is omitted in some task analyses.
For example, take a glass	For example, by taking a 6 oz Paris goblet by the stem	For example, check that the glass is clean and undamaged	——

Table A7.2 Task analysis work sheet preparing grapefruit segments

What is done?	How is it done?	Critical points (see/feel/smell/listen/taste)	Additional information
Select a grapefruit	By handling.	Feel for firmness — weight. Look for bruising.	
Cut off ends	By cutting downwards, on to a board with an 8 inch stainless steel knife across growing end, judging thickness of skin.	See the flesh is exposed. See and feel the fingers are bent away from knife.	Safety. Effect of acid on steel.
Cut off skin	By placing the fruit on end and cutting downwards, using all the blade of the knife, following the shape of the fruit. Turn after each cut.	See and feel the knife is cutting between the flesh and the pith.	Wastage.
Remove remaining pith	By lightly cutting downwards, using tip of knife.	See no pith remains on fruit. See any over-ripe patches are removed.	Bitter taste of pith.
Clear the waste	By scraping into bowl with hand.		Tidy work place. Safety
Segment grapefruit	By gently cutting between the membranes, with a stainless steel paring knife, using a 'V' cut for the first two large segments, then an in-out cut for the remainder and pulling the membrane out of the way with the thumb of the hand holding the fruit. Remove any pips while cutting to aid removal of unbroken segments.	Feel tough pith in centre. See all pips are removed.	
Remove excess juice	By hand squeezing what juice is left into bowl.	Feel 'skeleton' free from juice. See no pips fall into bowl.	

Reproduced by permission of the HCTB.

3 *Describing CRITICAL points*

This should describe signs which inform the person carrying out the task that it is going well or otherwise. Such points should consist of sentences or phrases such as:
Check that totals cross-cast
See that the sauce has not curdled

4 *Adding any additional points that should be taken into account,* such as security, safety, sales promotion.

NOTE: This is omitted in some task analyses.

Lesson plans

Once the job has been broken down into the key words or phrases which list all the tasks, and once complicated tasks have been broken down into analysed tasks — the next step is to put all this knowledge and skill into a planned training session.

Not only does the trainer have to analyse and then organize what he is to transfer, but also he has to consider how he is going to:

1 Motivate his trainees to learn.
2 Present the knowledge and skill so that it is assimilated.
3 Give his trainees the opportunity to 'cement in' or consolidate the new knowledge and skills.
4 Ensure that what he has been attempting to transfer has been transferred permanently.
5 Motivate his trainees to use what they have learned.

These processes are incorporated into what is generally called a lesson plan. A lesson plan consists of:

Introduction — motivate to learn
Development — transfer knowledge
Consolidation — make it permanent
Close — motivate to use it

The introduction

The introduction is concerned primarily with motivating the person to want to learn. It should be used to:

1 Establish a personal contact with trainees.
2 Reduce their nervousness.

3 Overcome any particular worries they may have, such as: when the training finishes, what it covers, what will be expected of them.

Unless the introduction is effective the trainee may not be receptive to what is to follow. To help in preparing the introductory phase a useful mnemonic or memory aid has been used by people for many years. It is:

I   interest
N   need
T   title
R   range
O   objective

Interest

The first thing anyone communicating with others has to do is to attract their attention. This can be done in one of many ways, including:

Making a personal connection between the trainee and the subject, for example, giving a taste or sample, and giving them useful information or news.
Telling a funny story.
Referring to something topical.
Referring to (or inventing) something relevant from one's own personal experience.
Stating something with an apparent contradiction, for example coffee is more important than caviar.
Asking questions.
Giving a demonstration or showing something relevant.

Whatever method is used, however, it should be relevant to the trainee and what is being taught.

Need

The need for the training session should be explained. This should be in two parts, from the employer's point of view and the employee's, but it is essential to emphasize why the trainee needs the training and what benefits he or she will receive.

Title

Obviously the trainee will need to know what is to be taught — usually this is incorporated early on and can be linked with one of the other elements of the INTRO.

Range

The trainee needs to know what is to be covered in the training session and sometimes it is equally important, in order to keep his attention or to reduce his anxiety, to tell him what is not to be covered. It is useful to link back to previous training sessions in order to check, to build confidence and to build on known material.

Objective

Finally the trainee needs to know what he will know or what he should be able to do as a result of the session.

While these five separate elements should be in an introduction, they may be combined skilfully into one or two sentences or, if the training is a long course, the introduction could take thirty minutes or more.

Development

The development stage is the main part of any training session and contains everything to be learned during the session. This should be organized so that:

1 Everything is in a logical sequence.
2 The trainer starts with a quick review of what the trainee knows so that the trainee starts from the known — and therefore feels confident — moving on to the new, the unfamiliar, material.
3 Essential material is picked out ensuring that it is covered, and desirable material is identified — to be covered if the time or opportunity presents itself.

The development stage is concerned with transferring the instructor's knowledge and skills to the trainee. It is, however, rather like serving a meal. The food has to be treated in certain ways to make it appetizing and digestible. In the same way any knowledge and skills to be transferred have to be presented so that they interest the trainee and are retained permanently by him.

There are a number of important rules which will help the trainer to prepare and present his material so that this happens, and these are covered in more depth on pages 261–266.

Consolidation and close

Throughout a training session the trainer must use various means of assisting his or her trainee to learn. One major technique is the correct use of questions and this is covered on pages 264–265. It is vital, however, that at the end of a session the trainer:

1 Tests that the training objectives have been achieved by questioning, testing or observing.

2 Reinforces the instruction by recapitulating and questioning so that key points will not be forgotten.

In addition to testing the effectiveness and reinforcing the instruction the instructor should also make quite clear what is now expected of the trainee in work terms and he will also arouse interest in the next session by explaining:

1 What it is about.
2 When it will be.
3 What the objective is.

A useful form for planning a lesson is shown in Table A7.3.

The learning 'sandwich'

Every piece of instruction should be a sandwich consisting of:

> a slice of motivation; motivating to want *to learn*; the filling; the main body of the instruction; a slice of motivation; motivating to want *to use* what has been learned.

How do we learn?

The ability of people to learn is dependent to a great extent upon their reasons for wanting to learn something. If someone is very keen to learn, he will apply himself. On the other hand, if he is not keen to learn, he will amost certainly bring little enthusiasm to the learning process.

Why do people learn?

Obviously there are many reasons for people wanting to learn and in a work setting these will be closely linked to why people work. If the trainer knows and understands why each individual wants to learn, he or she should be able to use this to motivate the person — and keep his or her interest. To attempt to treat all people in the same way is certainly not the way to being a successful trainer or supervisor. A key supervisory and training skill therefore is to discover what motivates each of his or her subordinates or trainees.

If a generalization is to be made, however, the main reasons are likely to be one or more of the following:

1 To obtain rewards such as pay, promotion, esteem.
2 To avoid punishment such as dismissal, reprimand, loss of esteem.
3 Interest.
4 Curiosity.

Table A7.3 *Lesson plan*

Subject:

Preparation and use of
a room-maid's trolley

Aim:

At the end of this session trainees will be able to:
1 Prepare their trolley for use
2 Recognize and know the use of all the contents of the trolley

Time:

30 minutes

Key point	Detail	Aids
Cleanliness of trolley	Emphasize that a clean trolley is necessary in order to ensure that clean linen is not made dirty	The actual items Questions
Linen	Show the different types of linen and how the number of each is arrived at, to include: towels sheets pillow cases	The actual items Questions
Cleaning	Show the different cleaning materials and explain what each is used for, to include: lavatory cleaner bath and basin cleaner floor polish	The actual items Questions

How do people learn?

Learning is the process of acquiring knowledge, skills and attitudes. It occurs when knowledge, skills and attitudes are transferred to the learner from other people or situations. The transfer is through five primary senses and is best when as many senses as possible are used — particularly in combination. For example, in teaching a person to cook it is possible merely to give him detailed recipes but the results are not likely to be edible! In addition to the recipes, however, the trainee could watch demonstrations and the results are likely to be an improvement. But to involve the trainee fully so that he sees, hears, smells, touches and tastes, is the best and only effective way of teaching cookery.

We learn: 1 per cent with our sense of TASTE
1.5 per cent with our sense of TOUCH
3.5 per cent with our sense of SMELL
11 per cent with our sense of HEARING
33 per cent with our sense of SIGHT

(SOURCE: Industrial Audiovisual Association, USA)

The transfer is made more effective by ensuring that:

1 The amount and type of material is suited to the person being trained. Frequent, short sessions are much more effective than infrequent long ones.
2 It is transferred in logical, progressive steps, building on the known.
3 The methods and choice of words used must suit the capabilities of the trainees.

How do we remember?

We remember: 10 per cent of what we READ
20 per cent of what we HEAR
50 per cent of what we SEE and HEAR
80 per cent of what we SAY
90 per cent of what we SAY and DO simultaneously

(SOURCE: Industrial Audiovisual Association, USA)

In addition, trainers must recognize that there are many factors which inhibit a person's ability or desire to learn and consequently a trainee will have difficulty learning if he is:

1 Nervous, tired or frightened.
2 Worried about his or her job, money, family.
3 Distracted by noise, interruptions.
4 Uncomfortable, too cold, too hot.

So far as the training session itself is concerned people will not get the most out of it if they are bored by:

1 The trainer's style, tone and language.
2 The length of the session.
3 The content.

The rate at which people learn varies from person to person but most people learn in steps — sometimes making rapid progress and sometimes appearing to make very little progress at all. This is quite natural and a good trainer will recognize this and he will know when a trainee is stuck and needs sympathy and help rather than badgering. A trainer's main duty is to build up confidence and this will only be achieved by sympathy and understanding. Criticism and lack of patience reduce confidence and only slow down the learning process.

Question technique

A trainer can make use of questions in three main ways. These are, to test a person's level of attainment (test question), to stimulate a person to 'learn for himself or herself' (a teaching or extension question), and thirdly to generate understanding and exchange of information and attitudes between members of a group by tossing questions and answers back and forth (bonding questions).

Questions may be used principally for:

1 Testing the level of attainment before a 'training' session.
2 Testing the effectiveness of training.
3 Helping people to work out answers for themselves, thus teaching themselves.
4 Encouraging an exchange of knowledge and information, in a group.
5 Obtaining or focusing interest.
6 Maintaining interest.
7 Creating understanding between the group, and between the group and the instructor.

Question structure

Questions generally are most effective when they are 'open-ended'. This encourages a person to think for the answer. Where questions give simple alternatives or anticipate yes or no, less thought is required by the trainee and the question consequently is less effective both in testing and in consolidating learning. Most questions should contain why, where, when, what, who or how.

Questions, particularly teaching questions, should be planned beforehand — and should relate particularly to the 'critical points' identified in the 'task analysis' stage.

Where questions are not answered satisfactorily by the trainee, the trainer must consider first if the question was properly framed and understood. If not the question should be rephrased and put again. If the question still remains unanswered the trainer must consider whether the training he has given is satisfactory or not.

Putting questions (the three Ps)

When questions are put to a group of people this should be done in a way which encourages everyone in the group to participate. This is achieved by:

1 Putting the question — *without naming* anyone to answer it.
2 Pausing so that everyone thinks about the question and answer.
3 Pointing out who is to answer the question.

Aids to training

Because people learn most easily by using a variety of their senses and their different faculties, trainers should always attempt to support their own instruction with training aids. These include visual aids such as blackboards and film slides and audio aids such as tape recorders. They should only be used to:

Support but not.substitute
Simplify complex instruction
Emphasize
Interest
Aid memory

Training aids ideally should be the real thing, but in some cases the equipment or procedures may be too complex for a clear explanation, so a diagram may help. The preparation of training aids should be carefully planned to support the instruction given.

Training aids include:

Actual equipment or equipment specially modified for training purposes
Drawings and diagrams
Films, slides, recordings
Graphs and charts

Recently, for various reasons, the need for job descriptions and similar documents has grown considerably with the result that many employers — even small ones — now use such documents as an essential tool of effective management. Unfortunately these documents are rarely used for training purposes although with a little forethought they can be designed to serve the purpose of:

1 Job descriptions.
2 Instructor's training programme and checklist.
3 Trainee's training programme and checklist.
4 Work manual.

Job aids

Many jobs can be made easier with descriptions of the methods or procedures to be employed. Such descriptions may be called job aids.

Job aids can be of value to the experienced worker as a reference, and to the trainee as a learning aid. As such, they can substitute for parts or all of certain training sessions because they enable trainees to teach themselves and they can relieve the trainees from having to attempt to memorize unnecessarily.

Job aids can be used:

1　Where supervision is minimal.
2　Where procedures are changed.
3　Where company standards need to be adhered to.
4　Where mistakes cannot be risked.
5　When memory needs assistance because of the complexity of a procedure, or the infrequency of its use.
6　Where staff may speak limited English but where a drawing or design will describe what is required.

Job aids include:

1　Diagrams.
2　Photographs.
3　Price lists, menus.
4　Procedural instructions, recipes.

Introducing staff to a new employer

How do people feel?

Most people approach a new job feeling nervous and worried. Sometimes this is quite apparent. In other cases, however, it is well-concealed. But whether it is obvious or not, until people have settled into an organization they will be nervous or worried and this will influence their ability to learn their job — to do it effectively and in particular to get on with their colleagues, supervisors and customers. They will not have the feeling of confidence which is essential to their being able to do a good job.

Success during the first few days in a new job is vital and while most managers admit this, less than 10 per cent of managers in some industries actually carry out a formal induction of new employees.

What a job consists of

Induction is not something that takes place on the first morning of a new job, it can be a relatively long process, with some people taking many weeks to settle in. This is because every job has two parts to it. First, there is the work itself and secondly, there are all the peripherals to the job including conditions and the social contacts.

Figure A7.2 *The main elements of a job*

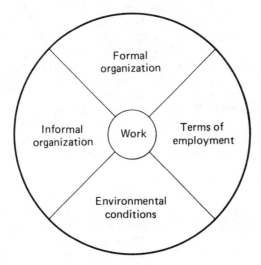

People will not be able to cope with the work part of their job unless they understand and are reasonably happy with the surrounding elements. These include:

1 Location and physical layout.
2 Conditions of employment and contracts.
3 Company and house rules.
4 Customers.
5 Management, supervision and formal relationships.
6 Colleagues and informal relationships.

The induction process is concerned with introducing an employee to all these elements as quickly as possible so that he or she need not worry about them any more. This enables the trainee to concentrate on the work which is the main purpose of the job rather than having to learn and worry about all the elements surrounding the work.

Benefits of induction

The employer benefits from effective induction by:

1 Reducing staff turnover.
2 Improving staff efficiency and work standards.
3 Improving staff morale.

The employees benefit by:

1 Fitting in and feeling a part of the team.

2 Being accepted as part of the team.
3 Becoming competent and hence confident in the shortest possible time.

Every organization will need to induct its employees in its own particular conditions, rules and methods, so no example can cover all circumstances. However, the checklist below shows the type of subjects that need to be covered. This, however, shows only the formal aspects of induction, and managers and supervisors should ensure that newcomers are inducted into the informal aspects as well. By definition, however, this can rarely be done by managers or supervisors. Instead, what they need to do is to put a newcomer under the wing of a 'sponsor', that is someone who 'knows the ropes'. This person may well be the newcomer's trainer also.

Checklist for induction programmes:

1 *Documentation*
Are the following points covered?

Name   Address   Tel. no.
Next of kin   Name   Address
Tel. no.   National Insurance no.
P45   Bank address

2 *Information*
Are the following departments informed?

Wages/Pensions/Insurance/
Personnel/Training/etc.

3 *Terms of employment*
Are the following explained and understood?

Hours of duty/Meal breaks/Days off/
Method of calculating pay/Holiday arrangements/Sick leave/Pension scheme. Grievance procedures.
Rights regarding trade unions and Staff Association.
Additional benefits such as Group Insurance rates or other discounts.

4 *History and organization*
Are the following explained and understood?

Origin and development of the organization. Present situation/objectives.

5 *Establishment organization*
Are the following explained and understood?

Layout of establishment including toilets, showers, etc.
Names of relevant supervisors and colleagues, introduction where necessary, to supervisor, shop steward, etc.

6 *Rules and regulations*
Are the following· explained and understood?

(a) Statutory; licensing laws and hours, food hygiene, Innkeepers Liability Act, etc.
(b) Company rules; punctuality, drinking, smoking, appearance, personal business, use of employer's property, etc.

7 *The job*
Are the following explained and understood?

Purpose/methods/training needs

When things go wrong, who can help?

Frequently, when things go wrong, management and supervisors jump to quick conclusions regarding the cause. Quick conclusions are often wrong conclusions which lead to wrong solutions. Wrong solutions obviously do not solve the problem and frequently they do the reverse by aggravating people who recognize what is the real cause and just how ineffective is the solution.

Correcting errors depends upon the correct diagnosis of what causes things to go wrong. The correct procedure for putting things right consists of:

1 Identifying a fault as a variation or departure from a standard of performance which may be either specified verbally, in writing or by custom and practice.
2 Identifying the cause or causes.
3 Identifying the person or persons responsible. The person committing the error may not be at fault, but rather the person who issued the order or trained the person responsible.
4 Deciding what action to take, how to communicate this action and how to motivate the person who may take the new instructions as a criticism.
5 Deciding how to prevent a repetition.

Heads of departments and other senior staff are responsible for the prevention and correction of faults. They should, therefore, pay particular attention during training to 'critical points', that is, the points at which things could go wrong.

This book* is designed to assist managers and heads of departments to understand more clearly the knowledge and skills they need to bring to their responsibility in training their staff. The book, however, cannot substitute for thorough practical and theoretical training in the techniques of training because, as the book itself says, effective training makes use of various methods to transfer and consolidate knowledge and skill. Consequently the best way to become an effective trainer and supervisor, having attended a proper course on the subject, is to practise and to be critical always of one's own performance.

'There are no bad staff, only bad managers'

*How to Get the Best from Your Staff.

appendix 8

Technology and employment in hotels and catering

by Marian Whitaker, Brighton Polytechnic

According to HCITB statistics, employment in the industry generally increased rapidly up to 1980 before falling back in 1981–82. Certain sectors, e.g. industrial catering, have slumped badly with the onset of recession, while others, most notably fast food, have continued to grow and provide more jobs. There is a marked tendency, however, for new job opportunities to be of the part-time variety, even in the more 'permanent' clerical occupations.

There are, of course, major problems in trying to separate the impact of technology on employment from the impact of the recession. It is particularly difficult when the use of technology appears to be recession driven.

If the predicted growth of the leisure and entertainment sector proves well founded, the hotel and catering industry should expand overall with a corresponding increase in employment levels as the demand for their services grows.

This expansion may be partially facilitated by the use of information technology where it enables companies to provide new services, e.g. video conferencing, fast counter services, and to use the new wealth of management information to plan and market existing services more effectively. This employment-generating aspect of the technology is known as the 'product effect'. The use of information technology may also be an important factor in maintaining competitiveness in international markets — particularly in the hotel conference business. However, there will be some technological impact on the employment of clerical and administrative staff; this will be referred to as the 'process effect'.

It would be useful to the industry's manpower planners to know which of these effects will dominate. Table A8.1 presents the results of research so far into potential job losses and gains which may be directly or indirectly attributed to the use of information technology.

Smaller firms clearly have fewer opportunities to reduce staff numbers, so job losses have been concentrated in larger firms and the public sector.

Much depends, however, on the firm's trading position and their attitude towards information technology. Firms who have suffered heavily in the

Table A8.1   *Potential job losses/gains by occupation*

Occupation	No significant change	Significant losses	Significant gains	Increase in part-time ratio
Senior managers	*			
Administrative staff				
Typists		*		*
Secretaries		*		*
Accounts clerks				*
Payroll clerks		* (1)		
Stock clerks				*
Junior managers		*		
Sales staff			*	
Operational staff				
Cashiers				*
Receptionists				* } (2)
Reservationists				*
Telephonists		*		
Supervisors		*		
Chefs	*			
Other kitchen staff	*			
Waiters				*
Bar staff				* } (3)
Housekeepers	*			
Cleaning staff	*			
Porters	*			
Storekeepers				*
Technical staff				
Systems managers			*	
Programmers			*	
Analysts			*	
Maintenance staff			*	
Technical trainers			*	

(1)   Very significant job loss. Payroll clerks are apparently an endangered species.
(2)   These front office functions frequently merged to form one full-time or several part-time jobs.
(3)   Traditionally part-time jobs anyway, computer provides trading information which allows hours of waiters and bar staff to be scheduled to reflect more accurately peaks and troughs in customer traffic.

recession may look towards information technology as a labour-saving device offering opportunities for direct cost reductions. Given the degree of labour turnover in the industry there have been very few notified redundancies, the reductions can usually be achieved by natural wastage.

There has been very little collective employee resistance to the introduction of computer systems. The only negotiated new technology agreements have been in the public sector, but they are rarely implemented. However, that does not mean that managers can or should introduce new equipment and methods without consulting their staff. The efficient use of a computer system can only be realistically achieved by involving employees in the decision to computerize and obtaining their commitment from the outset.

The use of information technology can lead to dramatic improvements in productivity, particularly in administrative/clerical areas. In expanding firms all or part of that increased capacity can be absorbed or redeployed in the provision of new and better services. In addition, a number of new jobs have been created for technical specialists and support staff.

Across the industry the number of jobs for information technology specialists is really quite small — they are expensive to recruit and difficult to retain. Hence there is now a trend towards recruitment of a few highly skilled specialists, supported by a layer of internally trained 'computer literate' administrators (often accounts staff). This trend has also been noted in other industries. Given the degree to which computer systems are now 'user-friendly', it is anticipated that the need for specialist workers will gradually diminish (MSC, 1985, p. 88).

The quality of employment: skills and job satisfaction

In the past, clerical workers were usually considered to be more skilled than shopfloor workers in terms of status, responsibility and the less repetitive nature of their work (Lockwood, 1958). But later Braverman argued that the use of technology would inevitably lead to the conversion of office work into a high speed industrial process. The effect would be to de-skill and reduce levels of autonomy and responsibility among white collar workers (Braverman, 1974).

More recently, Crompton and Reid (1982) have argued that substantial changes in the size and nature of the white collar labour force (including feminization) during the post-war years really meant that the majority of clerical workers were semi-skilled at the most and enjoyed very little autonomy and responsibility in their jobs even before the impact of new technology. They conclude that information technology may be one more factor in a long process of de-skilling that has taken place since the 1950s.

Research into the hotel and catering industry has indicated that the technology can have a de-skilling effect in the lower-grade, clerical occupations; however, in many cases there has been some compensating skill enhancement. It would be wrong therefore to take a deterministic stance on the potential impact of technology on skills.

Typists have clearly lost many of their layout skills to the word processor, so that it is now possible for anybody familiar with a keyboard to produce 'professional' documents. Some companies have eliminated the traditional typing pool altogether; managers and other administrators produce their own letters and documents using word processors.

Secretarial staff have also lost out to the word processor — shorthand skills in particular are less in demand. However, the removal of routine work such as typing and filing should mean that secretaries now have more time to attend to the more interesting and varied PA aspects of their work, and even to enter into decision-making roles. Very often the secretary is a great source of informal knowledge and takes on an important intermediary role which would be difficult to automate (Silverstone and Towler, 1982).

Accounts staff may find that the computer takes away most of the complex calculative routines that they were trained to carry out, and book-keeping now involves a lot of keyboard work. This leaves the field open for less skilled people familiar with keyboards to carry out this work. But again this should give accounts staff more time to spend on the production of summary reports, and the actual interpretation of results.

The roles of receptionists, cashiers and booking clerks are increasingly being merged into a single front office function. It is now important for hotel front office staff to have experience of computerized reservations systems. People without this experience may find themselves at a disadvantage in the job market. There is a noticeable decline in the use of numerical skills; all ledger work can be performed by the computer and/or shifted to back office. There is now a trend towards removing administrative duties from the reception area and increasing the personal service element, placing greater emphasis on communications and social skills.

Supervisors or junior managers in large organizations have occasionally been upgraded to the role of data processing manager. It is usually only supervisory staff that become totally competent with the computer system, hence their ability to move into these positions. At the same time, the need for direct supervision and checking of clerical work is reduced since the computer performs most of the calculation work. However, the importance of accuracy at point of data entry is now doubled, given that input errors can have far-reaching consequences.

On the catering side, use of EPOS equipment has virtually solved this problem in restaurants with pre-set keys and PLU facilities for each menu item. The cashier does not need to know the price of any item. However, the use of similar systems in bars has brought problems. Bar staff are generally very good at mental arithmetic and find the new systems slow and awkward to use. At peak times, the system can prove too restrictive and staff will take shortcuts (which of course throws the stock out).

The solution to this may be found in microprocessor controlled dispensing equipment, which coupled with EPOS equipment can, in theory, provide a total stock and cash control system. It would involve a certain amount of reorganization however. In a large bar, several terminals would be installed with bar staff restricted to serving in a particular area. This is said greatly to improve efficiency. The advertising literature for one company supplying these systems explains:

Our design staff provides each location with blueprints for a compact, five-foot work area built around the computer bar station. Work motion studies have confirmed a 20% or greater increase in the number of drinks a bartender can serve using the computer bar and this 'cockpit efficiency'.

However, this option is still very expensive and technically troublesome.

This is perhaps an example of technology that is ergonomically unsound! The solution favoured by one major firm has been to recruit all new, inexperienced staff when introducing EPOS equipment.

Storekeepers can suffer a major reduction in job satisfaction with the introduction of a computerized stock control system. Their work would normally involve constant checking, counting, recording and updating, and a great deal of book work. The computer can take on most of the book work leaving the storekeeper with little else to do other than physically count the stock. In one case a storekeeper argued that he had been reduced to the status of an unskilled manual worker, and spent most of his time loading and unloading pallets.

This de-skilling effect of computer technology can sometimes be extremely wasteful for the employer as well as the individual concerned. Why pay a semi-skilled man to do an unskilled job in the first place? It can only really be justified in cases of labour shortage where it is necessary to dilute the labour force allowing skilled labour to be redeployed more effectively in tasks that cannot be computerized. De-skilling also has a poor effect on staff morale, and it is then a difficult task for management to gain commitment of employees towards the use of new methods, machinery, and techniques.

The role of the manager

The most significant impact of the technology is likely to be on the role of the manager. Some junior managerial/supervisory posts have been cut by larger organizations, and there is more potential for job loss among regional/area managers where network systems are in use. The role of the manager as an information provider must soon give way to the more significant role of information user. Less managers are required but those that remain will need to be more highly skilled in the use of information and the management of innovation itself.

Initially it is the management who are responsible for choosing and implementing the computer system. Industry-wide lack of experience and knowledge in this area has led to slow rates of technological diffusion. To define information requirements and specify the size and scope of the system is something that most managers are unable to do unaided at present. If the use of information technology is to diffuse widely across the industry, managers will probably have to become involved in the process of design and development of computer systems. Clearly then the technically minded manager will be an important asset for hotel and catering organizations.

Given the degree of staff turnover in the industry, managers and supervisory staff will need to be fully competent with the computer system to ensure continuity in staff training.

The most important shift in emphasis will be away from routine processing work towards the application of interpretative skills. There is little point in having a computer system that will provide accurate, up-to-date information if people do not have the skills to use it. Information management is generally neglected as part of the hotel and catering manager's training. This must surely change if computer systems are to be used effectively as management tools instead of simple electronic clerks.

Conclusions

Given the slow rate of technological diffusion the impact of information technology on employment levels has so far been quite small. However, its use can be positively associated with job loss amongst clerical and administrative staff.

The use of computerized tills also permits precise monitoring of labour productivity in relation to sales and covers per hour. With this information management can arrange staff rotas to reflect more accurately peaks and troughs in customer traffic. The result has been an increase in numbers of part-time staff at the expense of full timers.

There have been some increases in employment associated with the use of new technology particularly among technical specialists, programmers and maintenance staff. However, across the industry their numbers are small and likely to decline.

Higher rates of productivity in clerical and administrative areas have allowed firms to expand without increasing employment. Overall the impact of technology on white collar employment in the industry will be negative, though far less significant than the general impact of recession.

As important as the impact on employment levels are the qualitative effects of information technology on skills, status and job satisfaction. The 'mechanization' of a number of clerical tasks now means less tedious paperwork, which can leave people free to spend more time on interpretative work. This is most likely to occur where companies are expanding. However, the use of information technology sometimes means the removal of some quite satisfying and hard-earned skills, e.g. secretarial shorthand and ledger work. New skills mainly involve the use of computer keyboards.

Most of the jobs affected in this way are traditionally performed by women and most of those likely to disappear have been traditionally performed by women. Most of the technical posts created have been filled by men. In short, the scope for women to obtain 'good jobs' in the hotel and catering industry is narrowing.

The disappearance of jobs and the erosion of some skills may be all the more rapid for the absence of formal industrial relations practices and procedures in the hotel and catering industry.

The service sector, as a whole, is expected to provide the focus for future employment growth in the United Kingdom. The research so far has shown that things are likely to be less straightforward than this suggests. The current pattern of employment changes clearly limits the scope for job creation. Those jobs likely to be created are restricted to certain occupational groups, namely cooking, cleaning and waitressing; jobs which are generally considered to be menial and certainly low paid. If we are relying on the hotel and catering sector to provide new jobs for the future, we need to look closely at the quality of employment in addition to the quantitative aspect.

However, it has been suggested that information technology could be used as an expansionary tool, particularly when closely linked to the marketing function. A significant change in emphasis in management training will be required before that potential is realized.

Bibliography

See also chapter reading lists.

Armstrong, M., *A Handbook of Personnel Management Practice*, 2nd ed., London: Kogan Page, 1984

Boella, M., *Personnel Management in the Hotel and Catering Industry*, London: Barrie & Jenkins, 1974

Boella, M., *Personnel Management in the Hotel and Catering Industry*, London: Barrie & Jenkins, 1975

Boella, M., *Personnel Management in the Hotel and Catering Industry*, 2nd ed., London: Hutchinson, 1980

Boella, M., *Personnel Management in the Hotel and Catering Industry*, 3rd ed., London: Hutchinson, 1983

Bowey, Angela M., *The Sociology of Organisations*, London: Hodder and Stoughton, 1976

British Hotel, Restaurant and Caterers Association, *Manpower Problems in the Hotel and Catering Industry*, London: BHRCA, 1975

Commission on Industrial Relations, U.K. *Hotel and Catering Industry. Part I. Hotels and Restaurants*, (Report No. 23) Cmnd. 4789, London: HMSO, 1971

Commission on Industrial Relations, U.K. *Hotel and Catering Industry. Part II. Industrial Catering*, (Report No. 27) London: HMSO, 1972

Department of Employment, U.K. *Hotels*. (Manpower Studies No. 10). London: HMSO, 1971

Department of Employment, U.K. *Catering*. (Manpower Studies No. 11) London: HMSO, 1972

Doswell, R., and Nailon, P., *Case Studies in Hotel Management*, London: Barrie & Rockliff, 1967

Doswell, R., and Nailon, P., *Case Studies in Hotel Management*, 2nd ed., London: Barrie and Jenkins, 1973

Hill, J. M. M., *Labour Turnover in the Hotel and Catering Industry*, TIHR Doc. No. CASR 123, London: Tavistock Institute of Human Relations, 1968 (Restricted document)

Hill, J. M. M., and Menzies, Isabel E. P., *Productivity Measurement in the Hotel and Catering Industry*, TIHR Doc. No. CASR 30, London: Tavistock Institute of Human Relations, 1967 (Restricted document)

Hornsey, T., and Dann, D., *Manpower Management in the Hotel and Catering Industry*, London: Batsford Academic and Educational, 1984

Knight, I. B., *Patterns of Labour Mobility in the Hotel and Catering Industry*, London: HCITB, 1971

Kotas, R., *Labour Costs in Restaurants: a Study of Labour Costs in Catering Establishments in the Greater London Area*. London: Intext, 1970

278   *Human Resource Management in the Hotel and Catering Industry*

Lockwood, A., and Jones, P., *People in the Hotel and Catering Industry*, Eastbourne: Holt Saunders, 1984

Magurn, J. P., *A Manual of Staff Management in the Hotel and Catering Industry*. London: Heinemann, 1977

Mars, G., Hotel pilferage: a case study in occupational theft. In: Warner, M. (ed.), *The Sociology of the Workplace*, London: Allen & Unwin, 1973, pp. 200–10

Mars, G., Some implications of 'fiddling' at work. In: *The Social Psychologist in Industry*. Proceedings of the British Psychological Society Conference at Loughborough University, March 1977. Department of Social Sciences, Loughborough University, Loughborough 1977

Mars, G., and Mitchell, P., *Room for Reform? A Case Study of Industrial Relations in the Hotel Industry*, Unit 6, Industrial Relations Course, p. 881, Milton Keynes: The Open University Press, 1976

Mars, G., and Mitchell, P., *Catering for the Low Paid: Invisible Earnings*, Low Pay Unit Bulletin No. 15, June 1977, London: HMSO

Medlik, S., *Profile of the Hotel and Catering Industry*, London: Heinemann, 1972

Nailon, P., *A Study of Management Activity in Units of an Hotel Group*, Department of Hotel and Catering Industry Research Unit, University of Surrey, London 1968

Nailon, P., *Organisation Climate and Communication. First report on the organisation improvement programme conducted at the Sonesta Tower*, London, 1970

Nailon, P., *Organisation Climate and Communication. Second report on the organisation improvement programme conducted at the Sonesta Tower*, London, 1970

National Economic Development Office, U.K., Hotel and Catering EDC: *Staff Turnover*, (Chairman: Sir W. Swallow), London: HMSO, 1969

National Economic Development Office, U.K. Economic Development Committee for Hotels and Catering, *Your Manpower: a Practical Guide to the Manpower Statistics of the Hotel and Catering Industry*, (Chairman: Sir W. Swallow), London: HMSO, 1967

National Economic Development Office, U.K. Hotel and Catering EDC. *Why Tipping?* London: NEDO, 1969

National Economic Development Office, U.K. Economic Development Committee for Hotels and Catering. *Manpower Policy in the Hotels and Restaurant Industry — Research Findings*, London: NEDO, 1975

National Economic Development Office, U.K. Economic Development Committee for Hotels and Catering, *Manpower Policy in the Hotels and Restaurant Industry — Summary and Recommendations*, London: NEDO, 1975

Orwell, G., *Down and Out in Paris and London*, Harmondsworth, Mdx: Penguin Books, 1969

Saunders, C., *Social Stigma of Occupations*, London: Gower, 1981

Shamir, B., *A Study of Managers' and Staff Attitudes to Living In and Other Aspects of Hotel Employment*, London: Cornwell Greene, 1975

Thomason, G., *A Textbook of Personnel Management*, 4th ed., London: Institute of Personnel Management, 1981

Torrington, D., and Chapman, J., *Personnel Management*, 2nd ed., London: Prentice-Hall, 1983

Whyte, W. F., *Human Relations in the Restaurant Industry*, New York: McGraw-Hill, 1948

Index

Italicized figures indicate pages on which figures appear.